DANGEROUS
LIAISONS

DANGEROUS LIAISONS

Organized Crime and Political Finance
in Latin America and Beyond

Kevin Casas-Zamora
Editor

BROOKINGS INSTITUTION PRESS
Washington, D.C.

Copyright © 2013
THE BROOKINGS INSTITUTION
1775 Massachusetts Avenue, N.W., Washington, DC 20036
www.brookings.edu

All rights reserved. No part of this publication may be reproduced or transmitted in any form or by any means without permission in writing from the Brookings Institution Press.

Library of Congress Cataloging-in-Publication data

Dangerous liaisons : organized crime and political finance in Latin America and beyond / Kevin Casas-Zamora, editor.
   pages   cm
Includes bibliographical references and index.
ISBN 978-0-8157-2529-9 (pbk. : alk. paper)
 1. Organized crime—Political aspects—Latin America. 2. Organized crime—Latin America. 3. Political corruption—Latin America. 4. Organized crime—Political aspects—Italy. I. Casas Zamora, Kevin, editor of compilation.
   HV6453.L29D36 2013
   364.1'323098—dc23   2013027294

9 8 7 6 5 4 3 2 1

Printed on acid-free paper

Typeset in Minion

Composition by Cynthia Stock
Silver Spring, Maryland

Contents

	Acknowledgments	vii
1	On Organized Crime and Political Finance: Why Does the Connection Matter? *Kevin Casas-Zamora*	1
2	Argentina: Two Cases *Delia M. Ferreira Rubio*	22
3	Brazil: Crime Meets Politics *Bruno Wilhelm Speck*	42
4	Colombia: Coexistence, Legal Confrontation, and War with Illegal Armed Groups *Mauricio Rubio*	76
5	Costa Rica: Four Decades of Campaign Finance Scandals *Kevin Casas-Zamora*	107
6	Mexico: Organized Crime and Elections *Leonardo Curzio*	136
7	Bulgaria: Perception and Reality *Daniel Smilov*	165
8	Italy: The Godfather's Party *Donatella della Porta and Alberto Vannucci*	195
	Contributors	247
	Index	249

Acknowledgments

As with all academic projects, this one has been a collaborative effort. I would like to express, above all, my deep gratitude to the authors of the chapters in this volume for their excellent articles and their infinite patience. I would also like to thank the other participants at the project's two workshops, held in Washington, D.C., in March and July of 2010, for their valuable contributions to our debates. This show of gratitude is particularly deserved in the cases of Michael Pinto-Duschinsky and Marcin Walecki, two world-class experts on comparative political finance from whose talent, advice, and friendship several of the authors in this book have long benefited. Indeed, this project stems from a casual conversation with Marcin in early 2009.

The administrative, research, and editorial support of Diana Padilla, Fernanda López, Consuelo Amat, and Marian Vidaurri was essential in ensuring the volume would see the light of day. I would also like to thank my former colleagues at the Brookings Institution, especially Ted Piccone, who kindly invested part of his holidays poring over an earlier version of the text and making suggestions to improve it. Janet Walker, of the Brookings Institution Press, deserves a thank you for shepherding this book through its final stages.

This research endeavor would have not been possible without the generous support of the Open Society Institute, which David Holiday and Sandra Dunsmore played a key and much appreciated role in securing. The same applies to the funders of the Latin America Initiative at Brookings Institution, particularly the Liberty Mutual Group and a kind donor who has asked to remain anonymous.

I initiated this project during a very enjoyable stint as a senior fellow at the Brookings Institution. I have since moved to the Organization of American States (OAS). Therefore, it is appropriate for me to stress that nothing I write here can be attributed to the OAS or its secretary general. Interpretations and conclusions herein are the responsibility of myself and the other contributors alone.

KEVIN CASAS-ZAMORA

1
On Organized Crime and Political Finance: Why Does the Connection Matter?

The relationship between criminal syndicates and politicians has been around for a long time and has been the subject of endless fascination. The presence of organized crime in the United States, for example, can be traced back to the Puritans. As early as the 1680s, records from the Massachusetts Bay Colony mention organized groups participating in prostitution and selling stolen goods.[1] These groups were as much a part of the landscape as local elections (which were common in some British colonies, such as Virginia, since the early seventeenth century). Peter Lupsha, a scholar of organized crime, writes that before the American Revolution, "well-financed and organized criminal enterprises, using corporate buffers, bribery, political payoffs and corruption, quite similar as a process to

Note: For the purposes of this book, the term *political finance* encompasses all aspects related to the funding and spending of resources by political parties and candidates in the context of election campaigns as well as in nonelectoral times. As such, it is a broader term than *campaign finance*, often used in the literature to cover the whole subject, particularly in the United States. For the sake of simplicity, both terms—*political finance* and *campaign finance*—are used interchangeably, except when otherwise indicated. The definition of the term *organized crime* is complex and contested (see, for instance, Maltz, 1994, and the more than 150 definitions collected by Klaus von Lampe, available at www.organized-crime.de/OCDEF1.htm). The authors of the chapters of this book, generally speaking, embrace a definition of organized crime as a collective and coordinated endeavor to perpetrate illegal activities aimed at obtaining material benefits. This follows the spirit of the UN Convention against Transnational Organized Crime (2000), which defines an organized criminal group as a "structured group of three or more persons, existing for a period of time and acting in concert with the aim of committing one or more serious crimes or offences established in accordance with this Convention, in order to obtain, directly or indirectly, a financial or other material benefit" (article 1). Criminal behaviors such as drug trafficking, human trafficking, human organs trafficking, arms trafficking, and trafficking in endangered species, as well as the laundering of proceeds from all those activities, are nearly always considered examples of organized crime activities.

1. Browning and Gerassi (1980, pp. 78–79, 89–90). I thank my former student at Georgetown University, Michelle Brown, for bringing the stories mentioned in this paragraph, and their sources, to my attention.

modern organized crime, operated in the major port cities of the colonies."[2] He describes an organization led by a father and a son who owned fleets of merchant ships and who controlled the waterfront in colonial Boston: "Under this commercial cover, they were among the premiere contraband smugglers in the colonies."

The family operation so described was that of Thomas Hancock and his son John Hancock, the same John Hancock who would go on to sign the Declaration of Independence. The Hancocks understood well the need to make powerful political connections that could help shield them from the consequences of their illegal activities. Indeed, in ways that resemble those of a modern-day drug lord in a Latin American slum, they made themselves popular in Boston "through the selective use of bribery and political and charitable contributions." Lupsha adds, "When the [British] crown finally indicted [them] . . . for smuggling over a ton of French wines valued at over 300,000 British pounds, the letters and testimonials of support from Boston's business, religious, and local political community were such that the British prosecutor was advised to drop the charges for fear of open riot and rebellion on the Hancocks' behalf." That's political protection of criminal activities at its best.

These are merely early episodes in a long history of political involvement by the underworld in the United States. These came to include the shenanigans of Tammany Hall's party machine, the political sheltering of alcohol smuggling and bootlegging during Prohibition, and the financial contributions by diverse crime syndicates to later campaigns, estimated by Alexander Heard to have been about 15 percent of total election expenditures at the state and local levels in 1960s America.[3]

Organized Crime and Latin American Politics

If the issue has become less prominent in the United States since then, the same cannot be said for Latin America. In the latter, the confluence of a vigorous, regionwide democratization process with the noticeable expansion of organized crime—especially drug trafficking—has attracted the attention of political reformers. Indeed, over the past two decades, Latin American countries have enacted myriad reforms to regulate the role of money in political campaigns.[4]

---

2. Lupsha (1986, pp. 40–41).

3. Heard (1962, p. 142). On the historical interaction between organized crime and politics in the United States see, among many, Lupsha (1986); Woodiwiss (2001); and the invaluable chapters in Kelly and others (1994).

4. For surveys of these regulatory efforts, see del Castillo and Zovatto (1998); Casas-Zamora (2005); Griner and Zovatto (2004); Posada-Carbó (2008); Casas-Zamora and Zovatto (2010); Zovatto and Gutierrez (2011).

While the traits and results of these reforms have been heterogeneous, the reasons put forward to justify the regulation of political finance activities have been remarkably homogeneous. The risk that money from organized crime, and drug trafficking in particular, poses to the integrity of political parties and electoral processes has been cited in country after country.

This is a collective response not to an abstract danger but to one repeatedly proven real. There is evidence that criminal syndicates began pouring money into campaign coffers in Latin America a long time ago. As this volume shows, even the highly regarded Costa Rican democracy exhibits very troubling examples of this perverse relationship, dating back to the arrival in the country in the early 1970s of U.S. financier Robert Lee Vesco, a master swindler and fugitive who, according to the U.S. Drug Enforcement Agency, was involved in heroin smuggling.[5]

By the 1980s the example of Costa Rican politicians cozying up to Vesco was hardly exceptional. The campaigns of the Bolivian president Jaime Paz Zamora in the 1980s was tainted by accusations of links to drug traffickers, as was the 1994 campaign of Panama's president Ernesto Pérez Balladares.[6] And then there were the more serious cases of Colombia and Mexico, where the role of drug barons in underwriting campaigns has been an open secret since the 1970s. In Colombia, in particular, the election of the drug lord Pablo Escobar as congressman in 1982 was a sobering as well as farcical moment.[7] The day of reckoning, however, would come later, with the emergence of tapes showing that the campaign of President Ernesto Samper had sought and received several million dollars from the drug cartels in the run-up to the 1994 election. This revelation, the mother of all drug-trafficking-cum-campaign-finance scandals in Latin America, not only doomed Samper's administration but also rattled Colombia's otherwise solid democracy.[8]

Since then, the problem has not subsided. In fact, there are many reasons to think that it has grown worse in some countries. The situation in Mexico, now in the middle of a drug-trafficking maelstrom, is an obvious concern. One example should suffice to convey the gravity of the situation. In early February 2010 the ruling Partido de Acción Nacional (PAN) decided to suspend all open primaries in the border state of Tamaulipas, due to the systematic risk of infiltration into the process by criminal rings. The PAN's national chairman at the time, César Nava, bluntly said, "In the case of Tamaulipas everybody knows the possible influence of crime in candidate selection. Hence we won't leave any

---

5. See chapter 5, this volume.
6. Mayorga (1998, p. 35); Casas-Zamora (2003); "Drugs Are Back" (1996); "Well I Never" (1996).
7. Bowden (2001, pp. 30–35).
8. See chapter 4, this volume. Also see Jordan (1999, pp. 158–62); Vargas, Lesmes, and Téllez (1996).

room for that to happen."[9] Open primaries are a luxury that Mexico's democracy seems unable to afford.

The case of Tamaulipas illustrates the very real dilemmas that beset democratic systems in Latin America in trying to coexist with a huge illicit industry that requires political protection as humans require oxygen. While not unique to Latin America, these challenges manifest themselves in the region with uncommon intensity. Notwithstanding considerable efforts to eradicate illicit crops and to interdict drugs, Latin America continues to be the world's largest cocaine producer and plays a growing role in the production of synthetic drugs and opiates. Whether as producers of illicit crops, locations for the transshipment of narcotics, entry points to key markets, money-laundering locales, or large consumer markets, nearly all countries in the region take part in a drug trade that involves tens of billions of dollars a year. These money flows—and the sophistication of the criminal networks that sustain them—feed many other illicit activities—and thus have transformed the region's political and security landscape.

The funding of parties and candidates is merely one of the many fronts on which the battle between organized crime and democratic institutions is being played out, but it is an important one. Investing in politics is a natural step for an industry that, to thrive, requires weak law enforcement and a measure of control over crucial public institutions, such as customs. Helping to elect friends who can open doors and peddle influence through the state apparatus is often more efficient than other methods, such as bribery, blackmail, and threats of violence. Even for drug traffickers, the old rule applies: violence is not a sign of strength but of weakness. Better the softer approach.

Beyond the immense amount of funds available to drug traffickers, several political factors add to the vulnerability of Latin American democracies to the penetration of organized crime in campaign finance. Four such factors deserve mention: competitive elections, weak enforcement of campaign finance rules, political decentralization, and feeble political parties.

Competitive Elections

In most Latin American countries, elections are more competitive than ever. In forty-three presidential elections held in eighteen Latin American countries between 2000 and 2010, opposition candidates prevailed 53 percent of the time. Moreover, electoral volatility in the region is very high, comparatively speaking—and indeed reaches astonishing levels in countries such as Guatemala and Peru.[10] Competitive elections and viable opposition parties may enhance political transparency, but they also tend to raise the cost of politics.

---

9. "Blindan candidaturas" (2010). See chapter 6, this volume.
10. Madrid (2005, p. 6); Payne and others (2006, p. 183).

While reliable information on the cost of campaigns is notoriously difficult to come by, available data paint a worrying picture. In the case of Mexico in 2000 (according to data from the Federal Institute of Elections), paid advertising on television by the three main presidential candidates amounted to $70 million.[11] A similar estimate for the 2006 election puts the figure well above $100 million.[12] One should bear in mind that this number does not include all the other expenses inherent in a campaign, notably organizational outlays, which tend to consume the lion's share of campaign budgets in Latin America.[13]

Nor does it include the cost of elections at the subnational level, which is considerable in large federal countries such as Mexico, Argentina, and Brazil. In Brazil a rough estimation of the cost of the 1989 general election put it at about $2 billion. In 2006 it was $2.5 billion, according to Brazilian expert Bruno Speck, author of the country's case study in this volume (see chapter 3).[14] These sums are often higher for smaller countries, proportionally speaking. The current president of Panama, Ricardo Martinelli, a wealthy businessman, spent $19 million in his campaign, a remarkable figure in a country with barely 2 million registered voters.[15] In short, competitive elections are a wonderful thing for democracy, but they also offer irresistible opportunities for crime syndicates to make a political investment.

Weak Enforcement of Campaign Finance Rules

While Latin American countries have made significant strides toward regulating campaign finance, the enforcement of these rules continues to be extremely weak. Legal provisions are rife in the region. Every country has either banned certain kinds of political funding or introduced contribution limits. Likewise, in nearly every Latin American country, political parties must submit regular financial reports to the electoral authorities, an obligation that also covers individual candidates in several countries (Brazil, Chile, Colombia, Panama, Uruguay, and Venezuela).

Moreover, fines (in all countries except three) and penal sanctions (in seven of eighteen countries) have been introduced to back up existing political finance controls. Yet more often than not, this comprehensive legal apparatus means little in practice. The region is home to many examples of poorly designed political finance reforms and electoral authorities deprived of resources to enforce the law. As detailed by the chapter on Argentina in this book (see chapter 2), the comprehensive controls introduced by this South American country in 2002

11. "Elecciones 2000" (2002).
12. "Cada voto por Calderón" (2006).
13. Casas-Zamora (2005, pp. 117–23, 162–66).
14. Aguiar (1994, p. 84); Speck (2010).
15. "Gasto millonario" (2009).

lost all credibility when ten days before the 2003 election the leading candidate and eventual winner reported, without any adverse consequence, that his campaign expenses amounted to one dollar.[16]

Similarly, the experience of the Central American countries shows that despite numerous cases of blatant violations of political finance laws in the recent past, not a single criminal or electoral sanction has ever been meted out.[17] Mexico stands out as the only case in the region in which a powerful electoral authority has made a genuine effort to enforce campaign finance laws, in some cases with extraordinary severity. The weak enforcement of campaign finance controls in Latin America is old news for everyone, including crime syndicates.

Political Decentralization

Regardless of its merits, the regionwide trend toward political decentralization may be facilitating the penetration of organized crime, a point that the case studies in this volume convey repeatedly. On the one hand, decentralization processes open up new arenas of electoral competition that add to the cost of politics. Very often, these new layers of competition are outside the scope of the already lax campaign finance controls that operate at the national level.

On the other hand, the devolution of significant powers, even police powers, to local authorities creates an obvious incentive for the intervention of organized crime. Even in small countries, co-opting national institutions—through campaign contributions, bribes, or the threat of violence—is a much more difficult, expensive, and conspicuous option for drug traffickers than securing the cooperation of local authorities. Besides, the latter are often the ones with the power to disturb or shield criminal activities in a particular locale. The experience of Colombia, where vigorous decentralization has taken place since the 1980s, is particularly relevant in this regard.[18]

Weak Party Systems

The weakness of parties and party systems throughout the region also has troubling financial implications. The dearth of fee-paying party members and the modesty of most public funding systems in Latin America leave parties and their candidates vulnerable in two ways: they become dependent on private contributors and open to power grabbing by political outsiders, who may be supported by little more than a well-funded electoral machine. The cases of Panama's president Martinelli, Colombia's Alvaro Uribe, and Ecuador's Rafael Correa, among many

---

16. Ferreira Rubio (2005, pp. 10–11).
17. Casas-Zamora (2003).
18. See Mauricio Rubio's considerations on the *parapolítica* scandal in Colombia in the second half of the 2000s in chapter 4, this volume.

others, offer reminders of this shortcoming. The deficiency of parties points up a glaring risk: in many Latin American countries criminals don't need to buy off a national party structure in order to have a fighting chance at electoral success. All they need to do is bankroll an electoral machine, which can be surprisingly flimsy.

Why It Matters

Thus when it comes to investing in politics, organized crime has it relatively easy in Latin America. Does it matter? Yes, it matters a lot. The capture of parties and elected officials by moneyed interests is bad news for democracy in the best of cases. At a minimum, it compromises the premise of political equality that supports the whole edifice of democracy, reflected in the principle of one person, one vote, and stunts the ability of parties and leaders to channel their efforts toward meeting broader social demands. Such a loss of political autonomy is serious if it occurs vis-à-vis legitimate interests, business or otherwise. It is, however, devastating when it involves organized crime.

The encroachment on the autonomy of elected leaders by the financial participation of organized crime in their campaigns has peculiar traits. Insofar as they come from a donor with an uncommon ability to exert coercion, campaign contributions from organized crime are far more than a mere bid to buy influence with policymakers. The normal codes of etiquette and uncertainty that govern interactions between private donors and politicians, whereby quid pro quos are seldom articulated explicitly and elected politicians always retain the option of not fulfilling the donor's expectations, do not apply in the case of drug traffickers. In the classic formulation that became Pablo Escobar's trademark, *plata o plomo* (buck or bullet) are often the only choices public officials face. Given these options, once recruited, any politician finds it is exceptionally difficult to escape this dynamic. If he tries to do so, *plomo* (or something subtler) may come his way. Indeed, once a politician receives drug-related contributions, even if he does so unknowingly, this may be used to blackmail him once he is elected.

This is no Hollywood script. It is exactly what José Castrillón Henao, a Cali cartel associate who contributed generously to the campaign of President Pérez Balladares in Panama, attempted to do when arrested on drug-trafficking charges in 1996.[19] He failed to secure impunity for himself in this case, but others may have succeeded in similar circumstances. And of course, he made good on his threat: by going public with his contribution checks, he managed to embarrass the president well beyond the borders of Panama. Quite simply, Castrillón Henao and the likes of him are not your run-of-the-mill business donors.

---

19. "In Panama, Drug Money's Clout" (1998).

Relevant as the loss of the autonomy of elected officials may be, what is at stake in this story is even more fundamental. The capture of parties, leaders, and institutions by the perpetrators of illicit activities has one overarching goal: the hollowing out of the rule of law. This is the crucial difference between organized crime and nearly any other interest group. Legitimate interests that contribute to campaigns seek to shape the law in their favor. Organized crime normally seeks to prevent the law from being enforced altogether. Moreover, it does so by resorting to violence if necessary.

This distinction cuts to the heart of the threat that organized crime poses not just for democratic institutions but also for the state's very viability. Campaign contributions from organized crime enhance the power and influence of actors who, in many cases, actively dispute the state's sovereign control over a territory, as Colombians and Mexicans know well. They gain power not *through* the law but *outside* of it. In the worst cases of political penetration by organized crime, however, this distinction between institutions and crime, between the inside and the outside of the law, may itself dissolve. In those cases, the state and its authorities become participants in and abettors of criminal activities—and may even bet their future on them.[20]

The latter point is crucial. While most case studies in this book focus on a neat model of financial interaction between politicians and criminals, whereby the latter try to purchase political protection through campaign contributions and the former become purveyors of services instrumental to the development of illegal activities (chiefly, but not exclusively, impunity), relations between the political and the criminal world are often much more complex, nuanced, and counterintuitive. In certain circumstances, financial flows from the underworld into political campaigns are absent, indicative of the criminals' preference for intimidation (as in Escobar's case in Colombia) or, more interestingly, of a symbiotic relationship in which the provision of impunity and other goods by politicians is paid for not with money but with the crime kingpin's ability to mobilize voters in a certain territory.

Italy's case study in this volume (chapter 8) shows how, in some cases, the financial flows may even reverse, with politicians feeling compelled to purchase the electoral services of criminals. Similar interactions have been recorded in diverse settings, such as the favelas in Rio de Janeiro and the "garrison" neighborhoods in West Kingston, Jamaica, where territorial control by criminal organizations is a fact of life.[21]

20. Naim (2005).
21. Desmond-Arias (2006); Rapley (2006).

In other cases, the clear separation between criminals and politicians and the expected interaction between them are upended in different ways. Some of the experiences recounted in this volume show that politicians can turn state institutions into veritable criminal instruments, either through corruption so systematic and widespread that it can only be understood as a form of organized crime or by intimidating donors into contributing to the political boss's campaign or personal treasury. The case of Richard Nixon's infamous Committee for the Re-Election of the President (nicknamed as CREEP) suggests that the latter occurrence is not exclusive to developing or fledgling democracies.[22] In all cases, neat or otherwise, the financial links between criminals and politicians subvert the deepest purpose of democratic institutions, namely, to represent, channel, protect, and execute the public interest, difficult though the identification of the latter may be. This risk deserves to be taken very seriously by policymakers and scholars alike. Alas, scholarly research on this issue is nearly nonexistent.

The Gaps in Our Knowledge

The lack of studies of the link between organized crime and political finance is hardly mystifying. As a subject matter, political finance has only recently become a subject of interest to mainstream political science. For a long time the deregulation of the financial activities of parties and candidates, and the consequent lack of reliable information about them, made it nearly impossible to carry out empirical research on the issue.

Later, the proliferation of political finance regulations, and thus of publicly available information, had a positive impact on the field.[23] This progress is particularly salient in the United States. There, the enactment of comprehensive political finance regulations in the wake of the Watergate scandal of the 1970s, and their constant revision since then, has begotten a significant body of empirical literature.[24] Elsewhere, including Western European democracies, the situation is more precarious. Robust empirical studies on political finance *practices*, rather than merely their regulatory framework, remain scarce and are marred by the lack of a common set of concepts and methods to compare the information brought to light.

---

22. See Woodward and Bernstein (1994).
23. For good surveys, see Pinto-Duschinsky (2002); International IDEA (2003); Nassmacher (2009); Ohman and Zainulbhai (2010).
24. Corrado and others (2005) is a useful, if already dated, summary of the considerable literature generated in the United States and the main debates around campaign finance. A good historical overview of campaign finance in the United States up until the early 1990s can be found in the magnificent volume by Sorauf (1992).

If finding good data on political finance remains a challenge in the best of cases, the difficulties faced by anyone doing research on illegal or illegitimate funding practices—inherently concealed—are obvious. Whatever information makes it to the public domain does so, nearly always, as a result of scandals unearthed by the mass media. The crop of political finance scandals in contemporary democracies is, to be sure, anything but small. They range from the findings of the Watergate investigation in the United States to the illegal funding schemes periodically uncovered in countries as diverse as France, Germany, Italy, Spain, Israel, Japan, Brazil, Colombia, and Mexico, to name but a few.

The scholarly literature generated by these scandals is almost exclusively focused on financial contributions made in violation of the extant legal framework by otherwise legitimate business or government entities, either domestic or foreign, and how these contributions purchase political influence or skew the conditions of electoral competition.[25] While, as argued above, there is more than enough evidence of participation of organized crime in the funding of political campaigns in many countries in the world, academic works have done little more than mention the issue in passing. If illegal or illegitimate political finance practices remain rather arcane research subjects, the subset of cases in which criminal syndicates are a factor has barely been broached by the literature.[26]

The scholarly literature lacks a systematization of the publicly known cases of intervention by organized crime in elections. In some cases, the information already in the public domain, while incomplete, is not scarce. The use of funds from Colombian drug cartels in the 1994 campaign of President Samper in Colombia and the decades-long relationship between several Italian political parties and the Mafia are but two examples in which the role of organized crime in political finance is the subject of very detailed institutional probes. In most other cases, the workings of the press have uncovered a significant amount of relevant information that, unfortunately, has so far largely gone unused by academic researchers.

---

25. See, in particular, the case studies in Williams (2000) and Transparency International (2004, chap. 2). Also see Blechinger and Nassmacher (2001); Casas-Zamora and Zovatto (2010); della Porta and Mény (1997); Galiardo and Berbell (1995); Mendilow (1992, 1996); Mény (1996); Pujas and Rhodes (1998); Rhodes (1997); Smilov and Toplak (2007); Walecki (2005).

26. No book-length publication deals directly and exclusively with this topic. To the best of my knowledge, the study of Mexico by Curzio (2000) is the only article-length publication available in the literature. A small section in Heard (1960) deals specifically with the issue in the U.S. context. Casas-Zamora (2003, 2005) provide information on cases of political funding by organized crime in Central America. Studies on political finance in Colombia, such as De la Calle (1998) and Cepeda-Ulloa (1997, 2005), inevitably mention the issue, as does della Porta, Mény, and Vannucci (1999) in the case of Italy.

At this point, what the literature is missing is not a volume aimed at exposing the role of organized crime in political finance in all its lurid details but an initial systematization of the available information and what it shows through the lens of comparative political science and public policy.

The Book's Objectives

This volume thus includes national case studies on the role of organized crime in the funding of parties and candidates in a sample of countries in Latin America and, peripherally, other regions of the world. It aims to provide a comparative exploration of the subject matter and a set of tentative policy recommendations derived from the analysis of national experiences. More specifically, the volume intends to

—Shed light on the role and modus operandi of organized crime, particularly drug-trafficking organizations, in the funding of politics in Latin America and beyond

—Identify political, legal, and institutional weaknesses that facilitate the penetration of organized crime in the financing of political campaigns

—Suggest policy recommendations (for institutional design and political finance reform) to protect democratic systems from the dangers posed when organized crime, particularly drug-trafficking organizations, finances democratic elections.

Ultimately, the book's goal is to spark an empirically informed debate on the role of organized crime in the funding of politics in contemporary democracies and to open new avenues for empirical research on a topic highly relevant to the health of democracy.

Why These Cases?

The decision to give the research a regional focus on Latin America and to select certain cases has less to do with methodological strictures than with reasons of the information available for comparative purposes. As suggested above, Latin American democracies face peculiarly acute instances of organized crime's penetration. Money from the drug trade makes its way to Latin American political parties and candidates to a degree unknown to democracies elsewhere. This trait, plus the decades' long history of elections in Latin America, yields an uncommonly large body of evidence regarding the participation of crime syndicates in campaign finance. In addition, the region's democratic development, which includes a vigorous press and an active civil society, facilitates the discussion of complex and even opaque aspects of the functioning of democracy, such as political finance.[27]

The volume focuses on five Latin American cases: Argentina, Brazil, Colombia, Mexico, and Costa Rica—that is, the four largest democracies in the region plus one small one (Costa Rica), where the amount of information is unusually large and where the issue at hand has repeatedly surfaced in public debates. The latter also happens to be, alongside Uruguay and Chile, the most consolidated democracy in Latin America, according to almost any standard.[28] The Latin American cases are complemented by two extraregional case studies on Italy and Bulgaria, which add a global dimension to the analysis and allow for the teasing out of some general patterns from those that are specifically Latin American. In the Italian case, the political influence of organized crime has been widely and publicly discussed for decades, while in Bulgaria, as elsewhere in Central and Eastern Europe, it has been part of a broader debate on the capture and corruption of democratic institutions in the context of a turbulent transition away from authoritarian rule.

Such a selection of cases—which does not fall neatly within a "most similar cases" or "most different cases" comparative research design—do not yield generalizable conclusions.[29] It is nonetheless feasible from the practical standpoint (a difficult requirement, given the topic) for the volume to have heuristic value as an initial approach to an unexplored issue. This work thus is able to suggest not only new methods and lines of research on political finance and organized crime but also practical policies to deal with the problem.

Limits and Caveats

Four considerations ought to be made clear on what this volume is and is not about.

First, the cases included in this book provide merely an initial exploration of an issue beset by serious problems of information availability. As such, the

---

27. On the consolidation of democracy in Latin America, two good studies are PNUD (2004) and PNUD-OEA (2010). On freedom of the press in Latin America, see the reports by the Special Rapporteur for Freedom of Expression of the Inter-American Commission on Human Rights of the Organization of American States as well as the reports by Freedom House (www.cidh.oas.org/relatoria/index.asp?lID=1 and www.freedomhouse.org).

28. Costa Rica's current democratic cycle started in 1949, a sequence unparalleled in Latin America. According to Freedom House (2012), Costa Rica, Uruguay, and Chile are the only countries in Latin America with a score of 1 (highest) regarding the protection of political and civil liberties. Also, Costa Rica has consistently scored near the top of the region in terms of support for and satisfaction with democracy, as measured by Latinobarómetro, a regional opinion poll (Latinobarómetro, various years).

29. Sartori (1994).

aim here is not to offer conclusive validation or refutation of any hypothesis regarding the role of organized crime in political finance. We hope that this book will be the start of wider research aimed at arriving at more robust conclusions about the funding links between politicians and criminals and also about the policy instruments that might ameliorate the risks for democracy that these links present.

Second, this volume stands at the intersection of two strands of social research, that of political finance and that of organized crime. However, it should be regarded, primarily, as a collection of political finance studies rather than studies on organized crime, *tout court,* or even on the broader interaction between crime syndicates and politicians. While there is more than a hint of the latter subject matter in some of the chapters, the focus remains on those interactions with organized crime that have a bearing on the funding of the electoral activities of parties and candidates. As suggested above, it is this issue that remains a glaring gap in the literature on the role of organized crime in the corruption of democratic institutions. To be sure, some of the relations that lie at the heart of the following pages remain relevant for political finance purposes, even though very little money or few goods, if any, change hands. Often the participation of organized crime in funding politics cannot be understood without delving into the intricacies of the nature, activities, and conflicts of organized crime in a given context. But the focus of the case studies offered here remains firmly on political finance rather than organized crime.

Third, while this is a book on questionable political finance practices, it is not a treatise on the myriad kinds of corrupt funding practices that plague politics in many countries, ranging from vote buying to the abuse of state resources and the selling of appointments or honors by incumbents.[30] Here the emphasis is narrower: the use of proceeds from organized crime in the funding of political activities, which may or may not be illegal, depending on the country.

And last, to the extent that the regional focus of the volume is Latin America, most of the discussions here concern the funding of campaigns rather than the permanent activities of political parties. With few exceptions, parties in Latin America are poorly institutionalized.[31] Their structures exist largely to wage

---

30. Walecki (2004, p. 20) lists ten kinds of corrupt funding practices: illegal expenditures (including vote buying); funding from infamous sources; selling appointments, honors, or access to information; abuse of state resources; use of bribes or illicit commissions to pay for campaigns; demanding contributions from public servants; activities in violation of political finance regulations; political contributions made in return for favors, contracts, or policy changes; extortion of private sector actors by incumbents; purposefully limiting access to funding by opposition parties.

31. The best available study on the institutionalization of parties and party systems in Latin America is Payne and others (2006, chap. 6). See also Coppedge (2001) and the classic, if dated, study by Mainwaring and Scully (1995).

electoral battles and come alive just in time for the campaign season. To a large extent this is a result of the institutional design of presidential systems and, in particular, of fixed terms. The contrast could not be clearer with parliamentary or semiparliamentary systems, where elections may be called, in principle, at any time and where the survival of governments depends on parliamentary majorities composed of political parties. There, the nurturing of robust permanent parties is a systemic need of the highest order. Hence, to a remarkable degree, political finance in Latin America, as in the United States, *is* campaign finance.[32] This is balanced in the volume by the cases of Bulgaria and Italy; they are both parliamentary democracies, whose institutional design is conducive to permanent party structures, which need resources beyond just campaigns.

The Chapters That Follow

While united by common themes, the seven case studies in this book provide a tapestry of stories, often extraordinarily intricate, of the troubling links between politicians and criminal syndicates and their implications for democracy. In some cases, the dangers inherent in these interactions have been proven and realized for a long time, while in others they remain in the realm of allegations. Still, such allegations often reveal institutional vulnerabilities and a lack of robust transparency mechanisms.

The latter is true of Argentina, as analyzed by Delia Ferreira Rubio in chapter 2. There, a political system long affected by lack of transparency and high levels of corruption has nonetheless made an effort, especially in the past decade, to introduce fairly comprehensive political finance regulations. As elsewhere, the effectiveness of these rules has been undercut by the lack of political will to implement them. Despite the weakness of its transparency mechanisms, in Argentina at least two serious instances of alleged involvement of criminal syndicates in the funding of leading presidential candidates have made it into the public domain since 1999. In both of them the salutary role of the press in bringing the issue to light was followed by judicial interventions—with, however, inconclusive results. Ferreira Rubio makes the very important point that inoculating democratic institutions against the threat of organized crime demands far more than political finance rules, particularly if they are weakly enforced. Other peripheral reforms—such as placing campaigns and parties under the writ of anti-money-laundering rules, enhancing the autonomy of judges, and improving protections for whistleblowers—may be just as decisive.

---

32. See Casas-Zamora (2005, pp. 11, 14–15).

In chapter 3, Bruno Speck puts forward and then illustrates a more complex set of possible links between criminals and elected officeholders. Using a variety of examples, mostly revolving around the protection of the age-old gambling practice *jogo de bicho* and drug-trafficking activities, the author shows how those links may lead to three possible scenarios, depending on the criminals' expected rewards from their political involvement. By deploying the timely intervention of elected politicians, criminal syndicates may seek protection from law enforcement agencies, notably the judiciary. They may also try to influence policymaking more broadly, including rewriting the boundaries between legal and illegal activities. Finally, criminal rings may aim at capturing state institutions directly, with the purpose either of extracting rents on a grand scale or of securing impunity. Speck shows, interestingly, that while a culture of tolerance of corruption is an unfortunate part of Brazil's political system, the country's politicians continue to strongly reject links with drug traffickers. Echoes of this attitude (an imperfect but real protection for democracy) reappears in the Costa Rican case study.

Chapter 4 explores one of the key cases in this subject matter: Colombia. Mauricio Rubio offers a fascinating account of more than three decades of relations between drug traffickers and politicians, in which episodes of negotiation and financial dealings between them are interspersed with bouts of ferocious armed confrontation. As night follows day, connivance between criminals and elected officials gives way to political scandal, to an increase in law enforcement efforts against drug lords, and eventually to open conflict, only to come full circle back to the bargaining table and to a climate of coexistence between the actors. This cycle is also colored by the personal traits and styles of criminal bosses, by generational changes in the underworld, and, remarkably, by the criminals' permanent sense of betrayal after dealing with "dishonorable" politicians incapable of keeping their word. As in the Argentine case, the chapter on Colombia ends with a reflection on the limits of national political finance regulations and the need to mobilize public opinion and international intelligence cooperation to confront organized crime.

In chapter 5, Kevin Casas-Zamora traces the surprisingly long history of campaign finance scandals in Costa Rica, notwithstanding the country's precocious adoption, in the 1950s, of a generous system of direct state subsidies for political parties. As in other cases in this collection, for a long time state funding proved unable to single-handedly stem the reckless fundraising practices allowed by an otherwise deregulated political finance system. The result was a major political finance breakdown in the run-up to the 1986 election, tainted by the financial involvement of several questionable characters, including neighboring Panama's narco-dictator at the time, Manuel Antonio Noriega. The 1986 debacle proved a watershed, which introduced not just more rigorous regulation of private contributions but also, crucially, more selective practices on the part of fundraisers and politicians, who are loath to see their reputations soiled by links with drug traffickers. While the combination of stronger legal and reputational controls since 1986 has kept the role of organized crime in funding presidential campaigns in check (no small feat in the drug-infested Central American context), questions remain about the vulnerability of local elections. The latter is indeed one of the recurring themes in this book.

Local susceptibility is, for one, a critical concern in Mexico. In chapter 6 Leonardo Curzio provides an overview of a political system under a sustained assault by drug-trafficking organizations. This is the result of the troubling coincidence in time: on the one hand, Mexico's emergence as the center of gravity in the narcotics business and, on the other, a complex political transition that fragmented power and dislocated previous tacit accommodations between politicians and criminals. This convergence of issues compounds, in turn, the long-term effects of seven decades of one-party rule; these were phased out in 2000, but the stain from patronage and corruption remains. While the country has undergone several waves of political finance reform and introduced one of the world's most generous systems of public funding, escalating campaign costs provide an opportunity for the political penetration of illicit actors awash with cash. More important than risks at the federal level, however, are the dangers at the subnational level, where there is great heterogeneity in the links between criminals and politicians. As Curzio points out, and then illustrates with examples from the states of Tamaulipas and Quintana Roo, some Mexican states are well on their way to becoming "regional narcocracies." Protecting the vital role of independent media, which are subject to exceptionally intense pressures from drug traffickers, and bringing campaign costs under control are two of the measures that Curzio embraces as essential to preserve (or restore, depending on the region) the integrity of Mexican elections.

The five Latin American cases give way to the studies on Bulgaria and Italy. Chapter 7, on Bulgaria, tackles the issue from yet another angle: the discourse on the penetration of organized crime, its dissonance with reality, and its deleterious political effects. Daniel Smilov describes a country in which public debates have been dominated by the notion that criminal syndicates have captured state institutions wholesale, when the available evidence in fact points to specific interactions that may compromise but not negate the autonomy of political institutions. Even the latter type of link is not supported by robust evidence and remains, more often than not, fodder for political posturing and slanderous accusations among political actors. The evidence, Smilov posits, points toward a gradual but certain consolidation of political finance regulations, including a comparatively robust system of party subsidies, which have helped mitigate the reckless fundraising practices of the early days of the Bulgarian democratic transition. The author suggests an important point: that while the political influence of organized crime should remain a concern in Bulgaria, fixation on it may erode democratic institutions in ways that are every bit as damaging as the problem itself.

The last case study, on Italy, offers an engrossing and theoretically sophisticated analysis, impelled by an apparent paradox: despite the mountain of information uncovered by judicial investigations detailing the decades-long and pervasive links between criminal syndicates and politicians in Italy, there is very little evidence suggestive of financial contributions from the Mafia into the Italian parties' coffers. On the basis of that puzzle, Donatella della Porta and Alberto Vannucci develop, in chapter 8, an original typology of the possible interactions between the criminal and the political worlds, worlds in which the crucial variables are the stability and degree of control achieved by both sets of actors in a given context.

A high degree of control on both sides, as illustrated by the prolonged interaction between criminal organizations and the Democrazia Cristiana in southern Italy during the post–World War II era, allows for an iterated game in which political contributions become largely unnecessary. A generic pact in which both sets of actors agree to protect each other against the vagaries of elections and law enforcement replaces the flow of financial contributions. Votes, mobilized by criminals endowed with territorial control, become the currency that defines the relationship. In some cases, as alluded to above, this may even generate reverse money flows, in which politicians purchase the electoral services of criminals. Other situations, defined by the instability of one set of actors or both, lead to different types of links, in which the naked sponsorship of parties by criminals or their purchasing of specific political decisions become distinct possibilities. The analysis by della Porta and Vannucci opens new ground in political finance and poses fundamental questions as to the limits of campaign finance rules to protect democratic institutions from the threat of organized crime. Somewhat disturbingly, the absence of money, as with the absence of violence, is not to be equated with the lack of links between politicians and criminals. Indeed, in some cases, unobserved connections may be a sign of the opposite.

The following pages are an attempt to inject empirical content into a discussion that is as relevant for democracy as it is hitherto bereft of evidence. But they are also, in a way, a call to action. It is time to leave behind both indifference and political posturing with regard to the vulnerability of political finance to organized crime. This attitude ought to be replaced by a rigorous and sober effort to systematize the evidence and devise strategies to counter the dangers. To the extent that the proliferation of both democratic practices and transnational criminal activities are by-products of globalization, the problematic interaction between these domains is a sign of our age. The issue is not going away. And as this book will show, we hope, it is one that ought to be taken seriously in Latin America and beyond.

References

Aguiar, Roberto. 1994. "The Cost of Election Campaigns in Brazil." In *Comparative Political Finance among the Democracies*, edited by Herbert E. Alexander and Rei Shiratori. Boulder, Colo.: Westview.

Blechinger, Verena, and Karl-Heinz Nassmacher. 2001. "Political Finance in Non-Western Democracies: Japan and Israel." In *Foundations for Democracy: Approaches to Comparative Political Finance*, edited by Karl-Heinz Nassmacher. Baden-Baden, Germany: Nomos.

"Blindan candidaturas del PAN en Tamaulipas." 2010. *El Universal* (Mexico City), February 3.

Bowden, Mark. 2001. *Killing Pablo: The Hunt for the World's Greatest Outlaw*. New York: Penguin.

Browning, Frank, and John Gerassi. 1980. *The American Way of Crime: From Salem to Watergate, a Stunning New Perspective on Crime in America*. New York: Putnam's.

"Cada voto por Calderón costó en spots $45.46." 2006. *El Universal* (Mexico City), July 7.

Casas-Zamora, Kevin. 2003. "Estudio sobre financiamiento de partidos políticos en Centroamérica y Panamá." *Cuadernos de Capel* 48.

———. 2005. *Paying for Democracy: Political Finance and State Funding for Parties*. Colchester, U.K.: European Consortium for Political Research.

Casas-Zamora, Kevin, and Daniel Zovatto. 2010. "Para llegar a tiempo: Apuntes sobre la regulación del financiamiento político en América Latina." *Nueva Sociedad* 225 (January-February).

Cepeda-Ulloa, Fernando. 1997. *Financiación de Campañas Políticas*. Bogotá: Editorial Ariel.

———. 2005. "Financing Politics in Colombia." In *The Financing of Politics: European and Latin American Perspectives*, edited by Carlos Malamud and Eduardo Posada-Carbó. Institute for the Study of the Americas, University of London.

Coppedge, Michael. 2001. "Latin American Parties: Political Darwinism in the Lost Decade." In *Political Parties and Democracy*, edited by Larry Diamond and Richard Gunther. Johns Hopkins University Press.

Corrado, Anthony, and others, eds. 2005. *The New Campaign Finance Sourcebook*. Brookings.

Curzio, Leonardo. 2000. "Organized Crime and Political Campaign Finance in Mexico." In *Organized Crime and Democratic Governability: Mexico and the U.S.-Mexico Borderlands*, edited by John Bailey and Roy Godson. University of Pittsburgh Press.

De la Calle, Humberto. 1998. "Financiación de los partidos políticos y las campañas electorales en Colombia." In *La Financiación de la Política en Iberoamérica*, edited by Pilar del Castillo and Daniel Zovatto. San José, Costa Rica: IIDH-CAPEL.

Del Castillo, Pilar, and Daniel Zovatto, eds. 1998. *La Financiación de la Política en Iberoamérica*. San José, Costa Rica: IIDH-CAPEL.

Della Porta, Donatella, and Yves Mény. 1997. *Democracy and Corruption in Europe*. London: Cassell.

Della Porta, Donatella, Yves Mény, and Alberto Vannucci. 1999. *Corrupt Exchanges: Actors, Resources, and Mechanisms of Political Corruption*. New York: Aldine de Gruyter.

Desmond-Arias, Enrique. 2006. "The Dynamics of Criminal Governance: Networks and Social Order in Rio de Janeiro." *Journal of Latin American Studies* 38.

"Drugs Are Back." 1996. *The Economist*, May 25.

"Elecciones 2000: Cuánto gastaron los partidos en spots." 2002. *Etcétera* (Mexico City), November 1.

Ferreira Rubio, Delia. 2005. "El control del financiamiento de los partidos en Argentina: ¿Qué cambió con la nueva ley?" *Serie Documentos de Trabajo* 292: 10–11. Universidad del CEMA.

Freedom House. 2012. *Freedom in the World* (www.freedomhouse.org/sites/default/files/inline_images/FIW%202012%20Booklet–Final.pdf).

Galiardo, Juan Luis, and Carlos Berbell. 1995. *FILESA: Las Tramas del Dinero Negro en la Política*. Madrid: Ediciones Temas de Hoy.

"Gasto millonario en pasadas elecciones." 2009. *La Prensa* (Panama), November 9.

Griner, Steven, and Daniel Zovatto, eds. 2004. *De las Normas a las Buenas Prácticas: El Desafío del Financiamiento Político en América Latina*. San José, Costa Rica: OAS-IDEA.

Heard, Alexander. 1960. *The Costs of Democracy*. University of North Carolina Press.

"In Panama, Drug Money's Clout Outlives Noriega." 1998. *Washington Post*, November 19.

International IDEA. 2003. *Funding of Political Parties and Election Campaigns*. Stockholm.

Jordan, David C. 1999. *Drug Politics: Dirty Money and Democracies*. University of Oklahoma Press.

Kelly, Robert, and others, eds. 1994. *The Handbook of Organized Crime in the United States*. Westport, Conn.: Greenwood.

Latinobarómetro. Various years. *Informe Latinobarómetro* (Santiago) (www.latinobarometro.org/latino/LATContenidos.jsp).

Lupsha, Peter. 1986. "Organized Crime in the United States." In *Organized Crime: A Global Perspective*, edited by Robert J. Kelly. Lanham, Md.: Rowman and Littlefield.

Madrid, Raúl. 2005. "Ethnic Cleavages and Electoral Volatility in Latin America and the Caribbean." *Comparative Politics* 38 (October).

Mainwaring, Scott, and Timothy Scully, eds. 1995. *Building Democratic Institutions: Party Systems in Latin America*. Stanford University Press.

Maltz, Michael D. 1994. "Defining Organized Crime." In *The Handbook of Organized Crime in the United States*, edited by Robert Kelly and others. Westport, Conn.: Greenwood.

Mayorga, René. 1998. "El financiamiento de los partidos políticos en Bolivia." In *La Financiación de la Política en Iberoamérica*, edited by Pilar del Castillo and Daniel Zovatto. San José, Costa Rica: IIDH-CAPEL.

Mendilow, Jonathan. 1992. "Public Party Funding and Party Transformation in Multiparty Systems." *Comparative Political Studies* 25, no. 1.

———. 1996. "Public Party Funding and the Schemes of Mice and Men: The 1992 Elections in Israel." *Party Politics* 2, no. 3.

Mény, Ives. 1996. "Corruption French Style." In *Political Corruption in Europe and Latin America*, edited by Walter Little and Eduardo Posada-Carbó. Macmillan–Institute of Latin American Studies, University of London.

Naim, Moisés. 2005. *Illicit*. New York: Doubleday.

Nassmacher, Karl-Heinz. 2009. *The Funding of Party Competition: Political Finance in 25 Democracies*. Baden-Baden, Germany: Nomos.

Ohman, Magnus, and Hani Zainulbhai. 2010. *Political Finance Regulation: The Global Experience*. Washington: IFES.

Payne, J. Mark, and others. 2006. *La Política Importa: Democracia y Desarrollo en América Latina*. Mexico City: BID-IDEA-Editorial Planeta.

Pinto-Duschinsky, Michael. 2002. "Financing Politics: A Global View." *Journal of Democracy* 13, no. 4.

Posada-Carbó, Eduardo. 2008. "Democracy, Parties, and Political Finance in Latin America." Working Paper 346. Kellogg Institute for International Studies, Notre Dame University.

PNUD (Programa de Naciones Unidas para el Desarrollo). 2004. *La Democracia en América Latina: Hacia una democracia de ciudadanas y ciudadanos*. New York.

PNUD-OEA (Programa de Naciones Unidas para el Desarrollo–Organización de Estados Americanos). 2010. *Nuestra Democracia*. Mexico City: Fondo de Cultura Económica–PNUD–OEA.

Pujas, Veronique, and Martin Rhodes. 1998. "Party Finance and Political Scandal in Latin Europe." Florence: Robert Schuman Centre, European University Institute.

Rapley, John. 2006. "The New Middle Ages." *Foreign Affairs* 85, no. 3.

Rhodes, Martin. 1997. "Financing Party Politics in Italy: A Case of Systemic Corruption." *West European Politics* 20, no. 1.

Sartori, Giovanni. 1994. "Comparacion y metodo comparativo." In *La Comparacion en las Ciencias Sociales*, edited by Giovanni Sartori and Leonardo Morlino. Madrid: Alianza Editorial.

Smilov, Daniel, and Jurij Toplak eds. 2007. *Political Finance and Corruption in Eastern Europe*. Aldershot, U.K.: Ashgate.

Sorauf, Frank J. 1992. *Inside Campaign Finance: Myths and Realities*. Yale University Press.

Speck, Bruno. 2010. "Filiados deveriam financiar partidos." *O Popular* (Goiania, Brazil), February 16.

Transparency International. 2004. *Global Corruption Report: Special Focus–Political Corruption*. London: Pluto/Transparency International.

United Nations. 2000. Convention against Transnational Organized Crime (Convention of Palermo of December 2000) (www.unodc.org/documents/treaties/UNTOC/Publications/TOC%20Convention/TOCebook-e.pdf).

Vargas, Mauricio, Jorge Lesmes, and Edgar Téllez. 1996. *El presidente que se iba a caer: Diario secreto de tres periodistas sobre el 8000.* Bogotá: Planeta.

Walecki, Marcin. 2004. "Political Money and Corruption." In *Global Corruption Report: Special Focus–Political Corruption,* edited by Transparency International. London: Pluto–Transparency International.

———. 2005. *Money and Politics in Poland.* Warsaw: Institute of Public Affairs.

"Well I never, says the president." 1996. *The Economist,* June 29.

Williams, Robert, ed. 2000. *Party Finance and Political Corruption.* London: Macmillan.

Woodiwiss, Michael. 2001. *Organized Crime and American Power: A History.* University of Toronto Press.

Woodward, Bob, and Carl Bernstein. 1994. *All the President's Men.* 2nd ed. New York: Simon and Schuster.

Zovatto, Daniel, and Pablo Gutiérrez, eds. 2011. *Financiamiento de los Partidos Políticos en América Latina.* Mexico City: OEA-IDEA-UNAM.

DELIA M. FERREIRA RUBIO

2 Argentina: Two Cases

Money, politics, and crime are the main elements of power struggles in any society. They interact in a wide range of arenas, such as policy, public procurement, legislation, law enforcement, domestic politics, international relations, elections, and government management. These interactions and power struggles can have considerable consequences for government efficiency, the quality of democracy and political representation, the design of economic policies for sustainable development and social inclusion, and national and international security. Globalization exacerbates the influence of money and organized crime on politics and diminishes the capacity of individual states to respond to complex transnational challenges.[1] This chapter explores this issue—the role of organized crime in campaign finance—in a single country, Argentina. But first I examine the definition of organized crime.

What Is Organized Crime?

Organized crime is a rather nebulous phenomenon, but it can be characterized as being a structured and permanent group of persons with an agreement to commit crimes with the purpose of making money.[2] The crimes in which

---

1. UNODC (2010a).

2. The *UN Convention against Transnational Organized Crime* states that an "organized criminal group" is a "structured group of three or more persons, existing for a period of time and acting in concert with the aim of committing one or more serious crimes or offences established in accordance with this Convention, in order to obtain, directly or indirectly, a financial or other material benefit." The convention defines *serious crime* as "conduct constituting an offense punishable by a maximum deprivation of liberty of at least four years or a more serious penalty." See United Nations (2000). The Council of Europe defines organized crime as "illegal activities carried out by structured groups of three or more persons existing for a prolonged period of time and having the aim of committing serious crimes through concerted action by using intimidation, violence, corruption or other means in order to obtain, directly or indirectly, a financial or other material benefit." See Council of Europe (2002).

these groups engage include drug, human, and firearms trafficking; the smuggling of migrants, precious materials, and natural resources; money laundering; and piracy.

The associations stemming from these criminal activities ape the accepted business model and can thus be classified by sector. Borrowing the categorization from economics, P. Dreyfus identifies the following "industries" that organized crime is involved in: producing and distributing goods (for example, methamphetamine); delivering and selling goods (for example, drugs and firearms); growing and distributing agricultural products (for example, marijuana); extracting and selling minerals and natural resources; acquiring and selling art and archeological artifacts; providing security (such as the protection racket). To these industries Dreyfus adds cybercrime, adulteration of medicine, extortion, and trafficking in persons.[3]

Given the definition of organized crime, its relation to political campaign financing poses different challenges than those posed by legal corporate and private contributions. While corporate and private sector contributions seek benefits, advantages, privileges, and public contracts, contributions from organized crime come with the expectation of government passiveness in enforcing the law and impunity for organized crime. In the first instance, governments may face accusations of corruption; however, when it comes to rewards expected by organized crime, government corruption tends to be less visible. Government ineffectiveness could be portrayed and perceived as the result of lack of capacity or insufficient resources or simply the prioritization of other social problems, like public health, education, and poverty. Moreover, the link between corporate contributions and deals with public institutions is more traceable than the link between inefficiency and shady contributions because of the elusive nature of the underworld.

To design and implement efficient rules against contributions from illicit groups, it is essential to keep in mind both the nature of this kind of donation and the expected rewards. Rules designed to avoid undue influence by corporate groups or individuals may not produce the same results when applied to organized crime. For instance, laws that make certain contributions illegal may deter a corporate CEO, but would they compel a drug baron whose business is outside the boundaries of the legal system? When meddling in politics, organized crime may just be looking to benefit from impunity or the convenience that arises from lack of government control. More ambitious objectives include the co-option of public institutions and sometimes even state capture.[4]

---

3. Dreyfus (2009).
4. Garay Salamanca and others (2008).

State Capture and Organized Crime in Argentina

Certain institutional and social conditions make political involvement and state capture by organized crime more likely, and many of these are present in Argentina:

—Lack of transparency in the policymaking process

—Minimal supervision of public officials, elected or not

—High concentration of power, reducing the number of officials to be bribed or co-opted

—Institutional decentralization, which offers several entry points for organized crime

—Impunity as the result of ineffectual sanctions, noncriminalization of conduct, deficient law enforcement, and lack of witness and whistleblower protection

—Social tolerance for corrupt and illegal practices.

In the 1990s a key issue on the Argentinean political agenda was the undue influence of corporate money in campaigns. This preoccupation emerged mainly because donations by wealthy businessmen and prominent economic groups were increasingly perceived as the source of corruption and illicit enrichment, privileges, and favors. Legislative action, public contracts, and licenses were assumed to be the paybacks for campaigns contributions.[5] Lack of trust in the political system paved the way for a crisis within the government. In this context, proposals to reform the rules that govern party and campaign finance focused on avoiding the influence of the private sector in politics. Organized crime had not become an issue yet. The first serious allegations involving drug money in politics were made public after the 1999 presidential elections. Despite these charges, organized crime did not become a central issue during the 2001–02 debates over the comprehensive political finance reform.

Argentina's political units (twenty-three provinces and the city of Buenos Aires) are under a federal system, so they each pass their own laws that regulate elections and political parties. Some units do not regulate campaign finance, and those that do failed to include specific provisions on contributions from illicit groups. Although at least at the provincial and local levels there have been no allegations or investigations linking organized crime and electoral campaigns, there are rumors that in Buenos Aires there has been a relationship between drug dealers and some local politicians (*punteros*). Little or no evidence has been presented, and although there have been a few prosecutions, very few politicians have been convicted.

---

5. Ferreira Rubio (1997).

Political Finance Regulations in Argentina

Argentina was among the first Latin American countries to establish some control over money in politics. In 1945 the executive branch issued a decree prohibiting anonymous donations and requiring political parties and candidates to provide detailed reports on contributions and expenses. The law also limited campaign expenditure and made party accounts and campaign finances open to the public. Another innovative measure was that radio stations had to provide one hour a day of free airtime to competing parties during the last ten days before elections.[6] In 1957 the indirect public funding of electoral campaigns came into effect. This new provision also granted free access to the mail service and telegraph to political parties when running for membership in the Constitutional Reform Convention.[7]

Since 1983, when democracy was restored in Argentina, political finance regulation has been a topic of debate in Congress, leading to the initiation of hundreds of bills (many of which have not been brought to the floor). The following bills, however, were enacted. They mark the evolution of the rules governing money and politics, particularly campaign financing.

Act 23.298, 1985–2002

In 1985 Congress passed act 23.298, which—barring a few minor modifications—served as the regulatory framework of political finance until 2002. This legal instrument was in force during the 1999 presidential elections and the subsequent allegations accusing the Juarez cartel of making significant contributions to the campaign of one of the political parties.

Act 23.298 established very limited rules vis-à-vis political financing. Public funds, both direct and indirect, were given to political parties yearly for ordinary activities and during elections. Campaign public funding was distributed among competing parties in accordance to the number of votes they received in the previous election.

No ceiling was set for private contributions. Anonymous donations were forbidden, but the law allowed for two exceptions: money collected at public events and activities; and contributions that the donor gave conditioned on the political party's silence regarding their origin. These exemptions were glaring loopholes, and in practice all private contributions remained anonymous.

Disclosure and auditing requirements remained a mere formality. Political parties were expected to report ordinary contributions and expenses yearly and

---

6. Olivero (1994).
7. Ferreira Rubio (1997).

to submit a detailed account of campaign finances two months after the election. The electoral judges approved the balance sheets without effective audits. These reports were published in the *Boletin Oficial*, or official gazette, sometimes many years after the elections in question. Further, the information was aggregated without any donor names.[8]

Act 25.600, 2002–06

The economic and political crisis of 2001 increased the demand for more responsiveness and transparency on the part of political parties. In this context Congress passed act 25.600, the first comprehensive system to regulate party finances. The effort represented a turning point in terms of disclosure, despite President Eduardo Duhalde's decision to veto important parts of the bill.[9] Funding for political parties continued to come from both public and private sources: some public funds were distributed equally, and the rest—the biggest share—was distributed proportional to the number of ballots received in the previous election.

Act 25.600 also introduced ceilings for individual and corporate private donations and established limits on campaign expenditure. The statute applied to political parties and their candidates and even to third parties. In conjunction with this act, Congress passed an amendment to the electoral code fixing the duration of campaigns: ninety days for presidential elections and sixty days for legislative elections (act 25.610).

To improve transparency, act 25.600 presented interesting innovations in the Argentine context. Anonymous donations were completely banned. Each political party was asked to maintain a unique bank account for ordinary activities and another one devoted to political campaigns. The parties were required to present yearly detailed balance sheets and full lists of donors. They had to submit a preelection report on campaign finance ten days before the vote and a complete postelection report sixty days after the vote. Both reports were to be published on the Internet, with complete and detailed lists of donors, including name, identification number, amount of contribution, and date of donation. One important new policy was the introduction of an automatic suspension of any public funds for those parties that did not present the reports on time.[10]

When the government enforced these rules for the first time during the 2003 elections, only 28.76 percent of the parties presented preelection reports, and

8. Ferreira Rubio (1997).
9. Ferreira Rubio (2002).
10. Ferreira Rubio (2002).

some of those filed made a mockery of the process.[11] For instance, Néstor Carlos Kirchner (president 2003–07), who was elected after the former president Carlos Saúl Menem (1989–99) resigned his candidacy for the second round, filed a report declaring that he had received only two contributions of $80 each and that the total expenditure in the first eighty days of the campaign totaled $1.[12] His postelection report acknowledged a total of $884,766 in expenditures. An independent monitoring effort conducted by Poder Ciudadano found a total of $3,593,658.[13]

Although political parties had to publish their financial information on their website, by election day the majority of those pages showed the message "In Construction." The situation improved for the 2005 midterm elections, as the electoral judicial authorities applied pressure and threatened to impose sanctions against noncompliant political parties.

Act 26.215, 2007–09

Before the 2007 presidential election, Congress passed a new political finance regulation, act 26.215. The new bill was similar to the previous one regarding public and private funding; however, ceilings for private contributions were increased by 400 percent, while limits on campaign expenditure were increased by 50 percent. The most significant changes had to do with sanctions (repealing the automatic suspension of public funding for those parties who did not present reports on time) and media campaign advertisement (new rules stated that only political parties could buy time or space for campaign ads).[14]

The auditing capacity of the judiciary was reinforced, which resulted in more accurate crosschecks of the information presented by the parties. Thanks to some resolutions issued by the Electoral Appeals Court, the quantity and quality of available information increased considerably. As a result, media interest in these data also swelled, more information was published, and a new trend of investigative journalism appeared. For instance, provisions requiring full information disclosure played a key role in the investigation of the ephedrine-trafficking case and in the medicine mafia affair, which involved suspicious contributions for Cristina Fernández de Kirchner's (current president of Argentina) 2007 campaign.

---

11. Corcuera (2003). In 2003 there were 696 registered political parties at the national level in Argentina. All these parties could run in the national elections (senate, deputies chamber, and presidential) and were subject to the rules established by act 25.600.
12. Villosio (2003).
13. Ferreira Rubio (2004).
14. Ferreira Rubio (2007).

Act 26.571, 2010

In December 2009 Congress passed act 26.571, modifying not only political finance but also the rules governing the constitution, the operation of political parties, and the electoral code. The new rules reduced the duration of the campaign to thirty-five days before the vote, while media campaigning was cut to twenty-five days. In addition, the provision states that all candidates shall be selected through primary elections, which were to take place two months before the general election. A modification that has sparked concern on the part of small political parties is the severe requisites for the creation and maintenance of political parties as legal entities. This rule is seen as a way to recreate the bipartisan structure, a significant change for a country with more than 700 registered political parties able to run in national elections.

Act 26.571 also innovates on several fronts. Campaign contributions from legal entities are banned, although they are allowed for ordinary party activities. The criterion for public funding distribution is still a combination of equal and proportional considerations, but the portion of funds for equal distribution that was 20 percent of available resources has been increased to 50 percent. For the first time there is public funding for primary elections.[15] According to the new system, neither parties nor candidates are allowed to buy radio or TV time for campaign purposes; media time is given out by the government.

Unfortunately, the law includes some provisions that may undermine transparency. The separate bank accounts for ordinary party activities and for campaign financing are unified in the new statute, thereby making enforcement more difficult. For instance, contributions by legal entities are allowed for ordinary activities and banned for campaigns, but all the funds go to the same bank account. One antidisclosure measure is the drastic reduction in the penalty for noncompliance with the preelection campaign finance report: the sanction is now a fine up to a maximum of 0.18 percent of public funds for ordinary activities. The previous sanction system was mainly based on the suspension or loss of all public funds. (Table 2-1 summarizes the main characteristics of each of these moments in the evolution of political finance regulation in Argentina.)

Two Cases

The following section deals with the two cases in which organized criminal groups have been accused of meddling in campaign financing. The first case took place during the 1999 presidential elections and the second one surrounds the 2007 presidential elections.

---

15. Ferreira Rubio (2012).

Table 2-1. *Political Finance Regulation, Argentina, 1985–2010*

	1985–2002 Act 23.298 (First case study)	2002–06 Act 25.600	2007–09 Act 26.215 (Second case study)	2010 Act 26.571
Public funding				
Direct	For parties. Permanent and for campaigns. Proportional to votes in previous election.	For parties. Yearly and for campaigns. Not for primaries. Mixed allocation criteria (part equal, part proportional to votes in previous elections).	For parties. Yearly and for campaigns. Not for primaries. Mixed allocation criteria (part equal, part proportional to votes in previous elections). Extraordinary contributions discretionarily determined by government.	For parties. Yearly, for primaries and for campaigns. Mixed allocation criteria (part equal, part proportional to votes in previous elections). Extraordinary contributions discretionarily determined by government.
Indirect	Telephone lines, transport tickets, media time for campaigns. For printing ballots.	Media time for campaign purposes. For printing ballots.	Media time for campaign ads. For printing ballots.	For printing ballots. Media time during campaigns. Prohibition of private contracts.
Controls over private funding				
Anonymous	Allowed.	Banned.	Banned.	Banned.
Foreign	Banned for legal entities and governments.	Banned for individuals, legal entities, and governments.	Banned for individuals, legal entities, and governments.	Banned for individuals, legal entities, and governments.
Nationals	Allowed.	Allowed with ceilings.	Allowed with ceilings (higher than in previous act). Ceilings do not apply to party members.	Allowed with ceilings. Ceilings do not apply to party members. Legal entities can donate for ordinary activities but not for campaign finance.

(continued)

Table 2-1 (continued)

	1985–2002 Act 23.298 (First case study)	2002–06 Act 25.600	2007–09 Act 26.215 (Second case study)	2010 Act 26.571
Controls over expenditure				
Spending ceilings	None.	Determined in relation to number of registered electors.	Determined in relation to number of registered electors.	Determined in relation to number of registered electors.
Media advertising ceilings	None.	Media expenditures included in the general spending limit.	Media expenditures included in the general spending limit. Only political parties can buy time/space for campaign ads.	Only time and space freely distributed by government can be used. No one can buy time or space for campaign ads.
Duration official campaign	Not regulated.	90 days for presidential campaign. 60 days for legislative elections.	90 days for presidential campaign. 60 days for legislative elections.	35 days.
Transparency rules				
Contributions	Returns presented yearly by parties. Post elections campaign reports.	Pre- and post-election campaign reports, including list of donors. Ordinary reports yearly, including list of donors.	Pre- and post-election campaign reports, including list of donors. Ordinary reports yearly, including list of donors.	Pre- and post-election campaign reports, including list of donors. Ordinary reports yearly, including list of donors.
Expenditures	Returns presented yearly by parties. Post elections campaign reports.	Pre- and post-election campaign reports. Ordinary reports yearly.	Pre- and post-election campaign reports. Ordinary reports yearly.	Pre- and post-election campaign reports. Ordinary reports yearly.
Audit	Electoral judges. Only formal.	Electoral judges. Returns audited.	Electoral judges. Returns audited.	Electoral judges. Returns audited.
Publicity	Balance sheets published in *Boletin Oficial*	Returns published on Internet.	Returns published on Internet.	Returns published on Internet.

	1985–2002 Act 23.298 (First case study)	2002–06 Act 25.600	2007–09 Act 26.215 (Second case study)	2010 Act 26.571
Enforcement				
Sanctions	Fines. Suspension of political rights.	Fines. Suspension of political rights. Loss of public funding. Automatic suspension of public funds for not presenting returns on time.	Fines. Additional suspension of political rights. Loss of public funding. Sanctions for political parties reduced or mitigated in relation to previous act.	Fines. Additional suspension of political rights. Loss of public funding. Sanctions for political parties reduced or mitigated in relation to previous act.
Liable parties	Donors, party officials.	Donors, party officials, political parties.	Donors, party officials, political parties.	Donors, party officials, political parties.

The 1999 Presidential Campaign: Money from the Juarez Cartel

Since the mid-1990s the head of Mexico's Juarez drug cartel, Amado Carrillo Fuentes, invested in real state in Argentina: money from the cartel was sent via New York's Citibank to Mercado Abierto, an Argentinean financial firm. The owner of Mercado Abierto was Aldo Ducler, chief adviser to Palito Ortega, the Justicialist Party's vice presidential candidate, at the time.[16]

In December 1999, a few weeks after the presidential election was won by the Alianza candidate, Fernando de la Rua (1999–2001), the national newspaper *La Nación* exposed the activities of the Juarez cartel in Argentina.[17] On December 3 the same daily announced that Mexican authorities would bring criminal charges of money laundering against several people, among them Ducler. The case was presented before a criminal court; criminal judge Canicoba Corral was in charge of the procedure.

In the years following the scandal, the Juarez cartel's money-laundering activities in Argentina were part of a U.S. Senate inquiry into the participation of American banks in these illegal activities. The Argentine House of Deputies created a special inquiry commission to investigate the activities of Argentinean banks. Campaign finance was a secondary issue in these investigations.

16. Oppenheimer (2001, p. 56).
17. Morales Sola (1999).

In February 2001 *La Nación* reported that Interpol had found documents in Mexico that proved that the Juarez cartel had contributed to the Duhalde-Ortega presidential campaign in 1999. The journalist Andres Oppenheimer interviewed Mexican Interpol agent Juan Ponce, who told him that those documents revealed that Ducler had reported a $1 million contribution to the campaign and another $400,000 contribution for the purchase of a vehicle for the campaign. This last donation was subsequently reduced to $200,000 in the records, apparently because of complaints from the cartel about the amount spent. Duhalde, Ortega, and Ducler denied these or any other campaign contributions from the Juarez cartel.[18] In addition, during an interview with Oppenheimer in October 2000, Ortega denied any contribution from Ducler.

In his 2001 book, Oppenheimer suggests three possible explanations for what happened: contributions from the Juarez cartel did exist but were made through Fundación Sudamericana, a foundation created by Ducler and not reported in campaign registers; Ducler duped the Juarez cartel by reporting contributions that were not really made; someone from the cartel registered those contributions although they did not exist.[19] One may inquire about what happened with this information, but as in many other cases in Argentina, in the end nothing happened.

At that time, act 23.298 regulated campaign financing, and it allowed parties to receive anonymous contributions. The rules required no detailed report from political parties or from candidates. Electoral judges in charge of monitoring contributions performed a superficial review of the expenses reports of political parties and approved them without much hesitation.[20]

The 1999 campaign balance sheet presented by the Justicialist Party was approved by electoral judge Maria Servini de Cubria and was published in the *Boletín Oficial*. The accounts reveal the total campaign income to be of $3,619,438.60 and total expenses of $3,215,869.03. According to the balance sheet, the party received no private contributions—something very difficult to believe given the numbers.[21]

Before the October 24, 1999, presidential elections, no information had been published about the cartel's contributions. At that time, the only campaign finance disclosure mechanism was the disclosure pact implemented by Poder Ciudadano, a local nongovernmental organization, and Transparency International's Argentina chapter.[22] Although Duhalde and the other presidential

18. "Ortega negó aportes de Ducler" (2001).
19. Oppenheimer (2001, pp. 70–75).
20. Ferreira Rubio (1997, pp. 30–42).
21. *Boletín Oficial de la Nación*, April 18, 2001, 2nd section, pp. 34–35.
22. Ferreira Rubio (2004, pp. 97–98).

candidates had signed the pact, none of them disclosed the name of the donors but only the general campaign budgets. Duhalde, the Justicialist presidential candidate, told Poder Ciudadano that the total campaign expenses had been $26,000,000.[23] Although this amount differed considerably from that reported by the Justicialist Party, no investigation was initiated.

The 2007 Presidential Campaign: Ephedrine Traffic and the Medicine Mafia

As mentioned, in 2002 Congress passed act 25.600, legislation on party and campaign finance. The new statute improved disclosure mechanisms by establishing that parties should report in detail all contributions received and expenses incurred both before and after the elections. It also banned anonymous contributions and set limits on campaign expenditure and ceilings for corporate as well as individual contributions.[24]

These new rules were put into effect during the 2003 presidential elections and the legislative elections of 2005. During these two election cycles there were no allegations related to campaign contributions made by drug cartels or other criminal organizations.

In December 2006 legislation on campaign finance was again modified. One of the most important amendments had to do with the audit and judicial control procedure—act 26.215 now regulated the process to be followed by the electoral judges. According to the new rules, the Electoral Appeals Court (Cámara Nacional Electoral) improved its auditing authority and increased the quantity and detail of data requested from political parties. All the information presented by political parties was to be published on the court's website.

In October 2007 the presidential elections took place. Each party and alliance presented a detailed report on contributions received and expenses made. The Frente para la Victoria (FPV), the alliance whose candidate was Cristina Fernández de Kirchner, reported the highest income and expenses: $5,384,236 income and $5,405,183 expenses.[25]

The pre- and post-election reports filed by FPV soon brought about doubts and mistrust. The first scandal that ensued had to do with the exposure of illegal money from a Venezuelan businessman, who had arrived in Buenos Aires aboard a private flight hired by an Argentinean publicly owned company. The case, which involved Antonini Wilson as well as Venezuelan and Argentine public officials, is known as Valija-gate, because customs employees detected

23. Cassese (2000).
24. Ferreira Rubio (2005).
25. Poder Ciudadano (2008).

the money in a suitcase. It is suspected that the famous suitcase, with $800,000 inside, was only one of many that were introduced secretly to finance Kirchner's campaign. The case is still under investigation.[26]

In March 2008 the journalist María O'Donnell published an article revealing that many of the reported donors had given absolutely nothing to the campaign. The false donors reported by FPV were obviously a way of concealing the true origin of the money.[27]

According to FPV's reports, about 37 percent of the $4,272,112 in private contributions came from pharmaceutical companies, medicine brokerages (*droguerías*), health care management firms, or individual donors related to this economic sector.[28] The role of the health care sector in financing the campaign seemed clearly related to the fact that FPV's main fundraiser, Héctor Capaccioli, was in charge of the Superintendencia de Servicios de Salud at the Public Health Ministry. Among other functions, Capaccioli was responsible for the Administración de Programas Especiales, a special fund aimed at covering the costs of treatments of high-cost and low-incidence diseases (hemophilia, cancer, HIV, multiple sclerosis, among others). No allegations were made at that time regarding contributions related to criminal organizations.

In recent years, however, drug trafficking has increased in Argentina and with it suspicion of drug money in politics. According to data from the United Nations Office on Drugs and Crime (UNODC), cocaine seizures in Argentina increased 51 percent between 2007 and 2008 (from over eight tons to almost fourteen tons).[29] In 2008 the journalist Joaquín Morales Sola pointed out that drug cartels had increased their activities and presence in Argentina and stressed the fact that ephedrine trafficking was a very lucrative business, particularly because of the Mexican decision to close imports.[30] International agencies reported similar information.[31] By that time, the police had discovered a clandestine laboratory that produced ecstasy, and judicial investigators suspected that the Juarez cartel was behind the operation. UNODC reported that the illicit manufacturing of amphetamines was occurring in several Latin American countries and pointed out that the large quantity of precursor chemicals manufactured in Argentina was likely intended for other markets, like Mexico.[32] In 2008 ephedrine imports,

26. Alconada (2009).
27. O'Donnell (2008).
28. "Empresas de salud" (2008).
29. UNODC (2010b).
30. Morales Sola (2008).
31. International Narcotics Control Board (2009, paras. 49, 50); see also Bureau of International Narcotics and Law Enforcement Affairs (2010).
32. UNODC (2010b).

and the presence of Mexican and Colombian cartels in Argentina, emerged as prominent issues on the country's public agenda.

In August 2008 three young businessmen with ties to pharmaceutical companies and medicine broker firms were assassinated; the case came to be known as the *triple crimen*. The name of one of entrepreneurs, Sebastian Forza, appeared on FPV's donor lists. A judicial investigation led first to the connection between Forza, the drug cartels, and the alleged ephedrine trafficking, and then the inquiry uncovered the connection between Forza and a far-reaching network of firms related to medicine adulteration and robbery.

As the judicial procedure went on, other donors to the Kirchner campaign were investigated in relation to the *triple crimen*. Some of the donors that appeared in FPV's financial statements declared that they had really made no contribution but rather had sold or given bank checks to simulate campaign contributions.[33] The hypothesis was that these checks were never cashed but only used to conceal unreported contributions.[34] Thus the donors who appeared in FPV's reports were just a cover for the real ones. This case is probably related to Valija-gate, another unresolved affair, this one dealing with money from Venezuela that entered the country in mysterious suitcases.

Many of the persons involved in the *triple crimen* case were also involved in the medicine mafia case, a judicial investigation into the use of public subsidies to acquire medicines for the unions' health care system, or *obras sociales*.[35] The subsidies were distributed by one of FPV's fundraisers, Héctor Capaccioli, who was chief of the Superintendencia de Servicios de Salud at the Public Health Ministry. The lucrative operation included adulteration of medicines that were bought with public subsidies and then administered to terminal patients. The traffic in stolen and adulterated medications concentrated on expensive products, such as those used to treat cancer or HIV (figure 2-1).

As the medicine mafia case was apparently connected with campaign financing, a copy of the documentation and evidence gathered in the course of the investigation was sent to the electoral judge Servini de Cubria. On April 29 the electoral prosecutor issued an opinion against approving FPV's campaign reports and balance sheets.[36] FPV's campaign financial statements from the 2007 presidential elections had not been approved as of June 2013. Regardless of the decision of the electoral judge, what is clear beyond any doubt is that FPV's reports show serious irregularities. Although there are clear hints of illicit money in the campaign, there are also concerns about the electoral judges'

33. Cappielo (2010a).
34. Klipphan (2010).
35. Santoro (2010).
36. Cappielo (2010b).

Figure 2-1. *Medicines' Mafia, Triple Crimen, and FPV's 2007 Campaign Contributions*

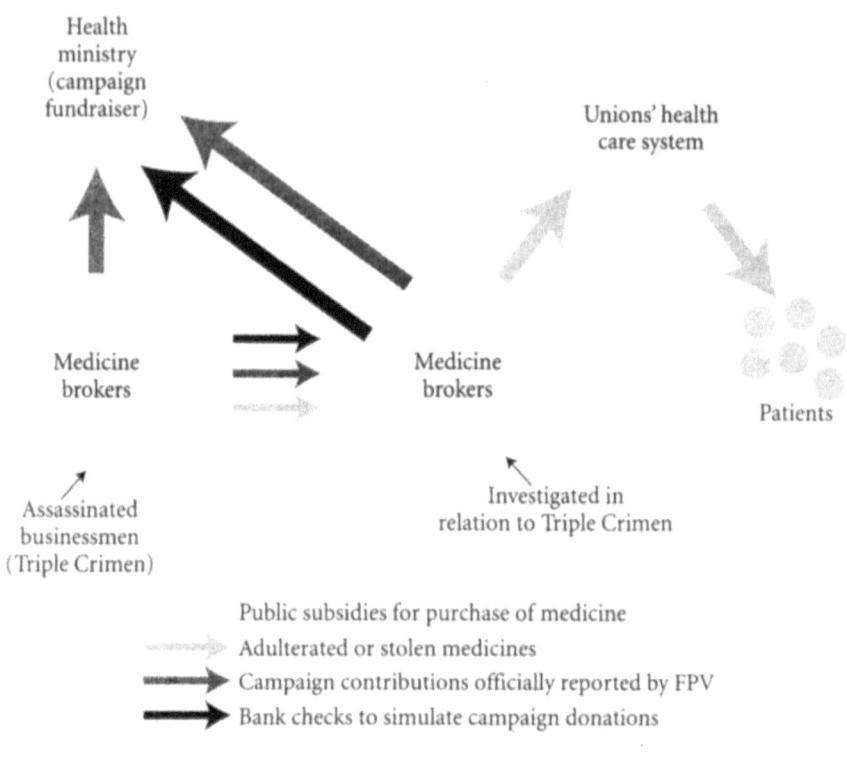

Source: Author.

jurisdiction over the case. These judges may not be entitled to reject campaign balance sheets on the basis of the criminal origin of political contributions. Act 26.215 does not contain any explicit prohibition of contributions with criminal or illicit origins.

Similarities and Differences in the Two Cases

Although two cases are not enough to draw conclusions on trends or patterns, one can point out some similarities and differences in the Argentinean experience. The Juarez cartel case and the medicine mafia case clearly differ regarding the actors involved. In the 1999 case, if the Juarez cartel in fact made those contributions, they followed a simple and direct pattern without involvement of public agencies. There was a donor and a fundraiser linked with one of the candidates. In the 2007 case, the medicine mafia connection, the fundraising scheme involved public authorities, criminal organizations, false donors, money laundering, and abuse of government resources. The cases also diverge in the organizational complexity required to conduct the activities.

The cases are similar in the way in which the scheme was discovered. Investigations started in both cases in relation to other issues—money laundering in the 1999 campaign and a criminal case during the 2007 campaign. In both cases information about suspicious campaign contributions was made public by the media and investigative journalists.

Disclosure can be identified as a key element in both the judicial investigation and media work. During these cases the rules in force regarding campaign financing were different. While there was no effective disclosure mechanism in place during the 1999 elections, there were detailed financial reports from political parties available on the Internet for the 2007 elections. It was in these files that the names of individuals and firms connected with the *triple crimen* and the medicine mafia were recorded as donors to Cristina Kirchner's campaign. The FPV had officially presented those reports, so there is no room for misleading explanations or justifications. These documents constitute evidence enough that the campaign received those contributions, or reported those contributions, as a way of concealing the real origin of the money.

An interesting question is, What were the direct consequences of these campaign contributions? We can only speculate. Three instances of government passivity are apparent:

—The lack of a radar system capable of tracking the whole national air space, a situation that facilitates the operation of clandestine airdromes.

—The lack of a centralized and coordinated policy regarding drugs, which slows decisionmaking and complicates implementation.

—The delay in the implementation of act 26.045, which created the National Registration for Chemical Precursors, ephedrine among them. Although the act was passed in 2005, the monitoring body was not fully in operation until December 2008 (after the *triple crimen*).

Policy Recommendations

Countries need a regulatory framework to help them face the challenge of the penetration of money from organized crime into politics. Rules may not be enough to address this problem, but they are certainly necessary. They should be tailored according to national context. In the case of Argentina, from the institutional point of view, I suggest the following measures:

—Reduce the margin for the arbitrariness that public officials have in the decisionmaking process. Arbitrariness facilitates abuse of state resources and corruption, particularly in the context of lack of efficient internal and external controls, which is an overall weakness of Argentina's institutional operation.

—Reinforce the independence of judges and prosecutors. In this vein, it is a priority to redesign the Council of the Judiciary, which is the body in charge of the selection and removal of national and federal judges who have jurisdiction over drug trafficking, elections, political parties, and national public officials.

—Strengthen the operational capacity of the agencies charged with intercepting and preventing money laundering. Although Argentina passed an act against money laundering (act 25.246), the agency in charge of implementing the preventive controls, Unidad de Investigaciones Financieras (UIF), has not been effective. The UIF is responsible for analyzing, handling, and disclosing information for the purpose of preventing and deterring the laundering of assets arising from crime as well as for the analysis of suspicious terrorist financing transactions (act 26.268).

—Establish whistleblower protection mechanisms.

—Reinforce collaboration among public control and auditing agencies (money laundering, tax and bank monitoring). Crosschecking information is essential in the fight against corruption and particularly in the field of disclosure of campaign and party finance.

—Enhance transparency and access to information mechanisms. Secrecy significantly facilitates concealing the origin of resources and the links and relations among politicians, party officials, candidates, and donors.

Regarding party and campaign finance regulation, it is necessary to reinforce disclosure measures as well as to facilitate access to complete, up-to-date, and timely information on income and spending. Transparency increases the risks and costs faced by those involved in corrupt and illegal transactions. Disclosure is also essential for investigative journalism and the media in general, which are key allies in the fight against this kind of illicit conduct.

For this reason, some rules included in act 26.571 should be reviewed. The unification of bank accounts for ordinary and electoral party finances makes it difficult to audit campaign contributions. Compliance with information rules should be enforced through strict penalties instead of minor fines, such as those in force now. Sanctions should take into account the financial worth of organized crime. Fines may be discouraging for individual or corporate donors, but they seldom deter the boss of a cartel. In these cases, fines should be high and combined with asset recovery mechanisms.

It is advisable to close windows of opportunity for illicit money to penetrate politics. If only campaign periods are subject to monitoring, illicit money may be introduced before the election season to avoid controls. In presidential systems with fixed time mandates, as in Argentina, limits on the campaign's duration do not really restrict campaign activity but create an obstacle for comprehensive control, because from the legal point of view campaign finance is reduced to the legal campaign period.

The prohibition or criminalization of contributions coming from or related to illicit activities might not be efficient as a deterrent for donors, but they are important because they grant electoral judges the authority to investigate and apply sanctions if such a contribution is proved. The law should grant electoral judges not only the authority to investigate these cases but also the resources needed to do the work. Bank and tax secrecy should not stand in the way of electoral judges' investigations.

Another window of opportunity for illicit money to penetrate politics is local and provincial elections, particularly in those districts that have feeble or nonexistent campaign finance regulation. According to the constitution of Argentina, elections and political party regulations are the exclusive jurisdiction of the provinces. In this context, NGOs have an opportunity to analyze the situation in the provinces, set some best practices and standards, and work with local authorities to improve regulations, strengthen enforcement, and enhance transparency and the disclosure of money in politics at both provincial and local levels.

The globalization of organized crime poses extra challenges for the design and enforcement of rules related to foreign resources and political finance. It is not enough simply to ban foreign contributions. Authorities in charge of controlling and auditing political finances should explore the feasibility of efficient and quick international cooperation when investigating the origin and route of money. At the same time, domestic laws against money laundering should include political parties in the group of individuals and legal entities that have to report suspicious transactions.

These measures might not be enough to tackle the risks of organized crime meddling in politics unless we reduce the social tolerance of corruption, which undoubtedly entails much more than passing new laws.

References

Alconada Mon, H. 2009. *Los secretos de la valija. Del caso Antonini Wilson a la petrodiplomacia de Hugo Chávez.* Buenos Aires: Espejo de la Argentina-Planeta.

Bureau of International Narcotics and Law Enforcement Affairs. 2010. *2010 International Narcotics Control Strategy Report.* Vol. 1, *Drug and Chemical Control, Country Reports* (www.state.gov/p/inl/rls/nrcrpt/2010/vol1/137194.htm).

Cappielo, H. 2010a. "Investigan a 25 empresas que aportaron fondos." *La Nación*, May 21.

———. 2010b. "No aprueban los gastos de campaña." *La Nación*, April 30.

Cassese, N. 2000. "Dudas por los gastos de campaña." *La Nación*, June 12.
Corcuera, S. 2003. "Evaluación de los procesos electorales recientes 2002–2003 y de la primera aplicación de la Ley 25.600" (www.observatorioelectoral.org).
Council of Europe. 2002. "Crime Analysis: Organised Crime—Best Practice Survey no. 4." Strasbourg.
Dreyfus, P. 2009. "Vino viejo en odres todavía más viejos: Tendencias regionales del crimen organizado en Latinoamérica en la primera década del Siglo XXI y más allá." In *Seguridad Regional en América Latina y el Caribe, Anuario 2009,* edited by H. Mathieu and P. Rodríguez Arredondo. Bogotá: Friedrich Ebert Stiftung.
"Empresas de salud, principales aportantes del kirchnerismo." 2008. *La Nación,* August 25.
Ferreira Rubio, D. 1997. *Financiamiento de Partidos Políticos*. Buenos Aires: KAS-Ciedla.
———. 2002. "La nueva ley argentina de financiamiento de los partidos: mucho ruido y menos nueces que antes." In *Dinero y Política. El financiamiento de los partidos en la democracia,* edited by G. Caetano and others. Montevideo: Ediciones de la Banda Oriental–Goethe Institut.
———. 2004. "Financiamiento político: rendición de cuentas y divulgación." In *De las normas a las buenas prácticas. El desafío del financiamiento político en América Latina,* edited by S. Griner and D. Zovatto. Costa Rica: OEA-IDEA.
———. 2005. "El control del financiamiento de los partidos en Argentina." Documentos de Trabajo 292. Buenos Aires: Universidad del CEMA.
———. 2007. "Financiamiento de los partidos políticos en Argentina, Ley 26.215." Montevideo: Seminario organizado por Uruguay Transparente. "La legislación comparada sobre financiación de los partidos políticos" (www.deliaferreira.com.ar).
———. 2012. "Financiamiento de los partidos políticos en Argentina. Modelo 2012." *Revista Elecciones* 11, no. 12. Lima: ONPE.
Garay Salamanca, L., and others. 2008. *La captura y reconfiguración cooptada del Estado en Colombia*. Bogotá: Método.
International Narcotics Control Board, United Nations. 2009. *Report on Precursors, 2008*. New York.
Klipphan, A. 2010. *Remedios que Matan. La mafia de los medicamentos*. Buenos Aires: Aguilar.
Morales Sola, J. 1999. "El lavado de dinero llegó a la Argentina. EEUU denunció la operación entre el Bank of America y una financiera." *La Nación*, December 2.
———. 2008. "Un país demasiado fácil para el narcotráfico." *La Nación,* August 20.
O'Donnell, M. 2008. "Los desconocidos de siempre." *Crítica de la Argentina,* March 8.
Olivero, R. 1994. *El financiamiento de partidos políticos en la Argentina*. Buenos Aires: Ediciones i4.
Oppenheimer, A. 2001. *Ojos Vendados*. Buenos Aires: Editorial Sudamericana.
"Ortega negó aportes de Ducler. Una investigación revela que el narcotráfico le envió dinero." 2001. *La Nación*, February 27.
Poder Ciudadano. 2008. *Informe de monitoreo del financiamiento de la campaña presidencial 2007*. Buenos Aires.
Santoro, D. 2010. "Levantan el secreto bancario de cuentas de 25 aportantes a la campaña K." *Clarin*, May 21.

United Nations. 2000. Convention against Transnational Organized Crime (Convention of Palermo of December 2000) (www.unodc.org/documents/treaties/UNTOC/Publications/TOC%20Convention/TOCebook-e.pdf).

UNODC. 2010a. *The Globalization of Crime*. Vienna.

———. 2010b. *HONLAC/20/2: Report of the Secretariat on Statistics on Drug-Trafficking Trends in the Americas and Worldwide*.

Villosio, F. 2003. "Kirchner presidente prematuro. Hacé cargar el matafuego." *TXT Revista Textual*, May 16, pp. 22–23.

BRUNO WILHELM SPECK

3
Brazil: Crime Meets Politics

In Brazil the public debate on the role of organized crime has been coming to a head for the past decade. Public attention to organized crime has focused on urban gangs, such as the PCC (Primeiro Comando da Capital) and the CV (Comando Vermelho), that are involved with the trading and distribution of illegal drugs. These gangs epitomize the threat that organized crime poses to ordinary Brazilians. The criminal activities of these groups—whether it is distributing drugs in schools, conducting abductions, or holding people for ransom—affect the daily lives of millions of people.[1]

However, organized crime in Brazil goes even deeper, as shown by the intelligence gathered by special groups within law enforcement agencies as well as congressional hearings and state legislatures. These criminal webs engage in the trafficking of drugs, humans, and arms; robberies of trucks, cars, and shipments; illegal mining; the lodging and trading of animals; kidnapping, protection, and extortion; and forgery, software piracy, and trademark violations. A growing number of scholars analyze the nexus between organized crime, the economy, politics, and society in Brazil.[2]

Law enforcement officers and economists have adopted the model of viewing crime and law enforcement as two separate spheres. According to law enforcement agents, organized crime typically exploits illegal markets through entrepreneurial organization and, when confronted with law enforcement by the state, resorts to violence and the corruption of public officeholders.[3] The connection between the growth of organized crime and the outlawing of markets is

---

1. Cavallaro and Dodge (2007).
2. See Mingardi (1996); Procópio (1999); Misse (1999); Zaluar (2004); Arias (2006); Oliveira and Zaverucha (2006). For comparative research projects see Geffray, Fabre, and Schiaray (2002); Garzón (2008).
3. United Nations (1975). An excellent compilation of definitions of organized crime is provided by Klaus von Lampe on the website www.organized-crime.de/OCDEF1.htm.

epitomized by the Prohibition era in the United States (1920–33). The demand for alcohol remained despite the outlawing of production and distribution by the Eighteenth Amendment to the U.S. Constitution (ratified in 1919 and revoked in 1933). Legal businesses were not allowed to meet the demand, so organized criminals stepped in and exploited the illegal market.

Economists regard organized crime as a business venture with special challenges. As an economic activity, organized crime extracts rents, deals with competitors, maintains profit margins, manages supply chains and vendors, adapts to changes in the environment, and explores new business opportunities.[4] Like any other business, organized crime has to deal with the regulatory environment defined by the state. Rather than guaranteeing property rights, the state—responsible for outlawing markets and enforcing the law—is the natural adversary of organized crime. In both views, law enforcement constrains the exploitation of illegal markets. But this interaction with public officials is seen by organized crime as nothing more than damage control and ultimately represents simply a business tax.

Social scientists view the interaction between organized crime and law enforcement through a different prism—one that puts the symbiotic relationship between criminals and state agents at the core of the problem. Organized crime becomes a topic for politicians and political scientists when criminals challenge the authority of the state, either by committing isolated but symbolically significant acts or by substantially undermining the central functions of the state.[5] Evasion, corruption, and confrontation have been identified as the three main strategies that organized criminals use against the state.[6] It is probably safe to assume that criminal organizations generally prefer to avoid confronting the state, as it involves the risk of law enforcement agencies disrupting their business. Evading law enforcement is difficult when the exploitation of illegal markets becomes entrepreneurial. It is in the intermediate space of *coexistence*, as the exploitation of illegal markets corresponds with inefficient implementation of the law, where a complex system of symbiotic relationships between organized criminals and civil servants emerges. This chapter explores different forms of coexistence between organized crime and the state, focusing specifically on the role of elected officeholders.

Building on this latter approach, this chapter replaces corruption with a broader concept of coexistence, one that covers a broad range of interactions between organized crime and the state. Scholars identify forms of contact between criminals and the state that go beyond bribery and that result in law

4. Reuter (1983).
5. Godson (2003).
6. Bailey and Taylor (2009).

enforcement agencies turning a blind eye to organized crime.[7] Organized crime protects its activities by recruiting state agents, typically the police, to escort drug transports through the country. These agents may threaten or eliminate people who are willing to cooperate with clean law enforcement agents. In some cases, police agents actually control criminal groups. The picture changes when organized crime taps into state resources, thereby shifting the business from rent extraction in private markets to illegal rent extraction from the state. This type of relationship yields a more complex system of interaction between organized crime and public officials.

While the economic approach is based on a model of two separate spheres with sporadic and specific interactions, the political science approach explores the plethora of connections between organized crime and public officials, which can reach the point of a symbiotic relationship. Interaction between public officials and crime is not simply a tax on business better to be avoided. It can rather be an essential part of a joint venture that opens markets and spurs profits.

The purpose of this chapter is to make a contribution to our understanding of the interaction between organized crime and politics, starting with a brief analysis of two forms of organized crime in Brazil: the traditional gambling business going back to the early twentieth century and illegal drug trafficking starting in the 1970s. Then, shifting the focus to the political arena, the chapter provides a brief synopsis of the laws and practices of campaign financing in Brazil, which gained relevance during the second half of the twentieth century and end with state-of-the-art regulations today. An analysis of the interaction between organized criminal groups and state agents follows this discussion.

While most analysts do not discriminate among offices, this chapter focuses solely on the relationship between elected representatives and criminal organizations and excludes the role of civil servants or appointed officeholders. This narrower focal point allows for a more in-depth analysis of this group, including the electoral connection. A model of the main forms of this relationship comprises two dimensions. The first dimension is the perspective of candidates and the benefits they expect from interacting with criminal groups. Noting the difference between private and political benefits, this section discusses the role of campaign financing as a key form of political support. The second dimension covers benefits that organized criminals expect from interacting with elected officials. Representatives can protect criminals from law enforcement by making use of institutional privileges, their political power, or social networks. Furthermore, the legislature may pass laws and implement policies that favor the

---

7. Pinto-Duschinsky (1999).

interests of criminal groups. Last, kingpins may decide to enter politics themselves. In this case, the focus of rent extraction shifts from illegal markets to the siphoning away of state resources.

The sections that follow discuss examples drawn from the last two decades of Brazilian political history using this model of interaction between organized criminals and elected officeholders as a heuristic tool. This allows us to identify expected benefits and risks for each group and to pay particular attention to campaign financing. The chapter ends with remarks on the role of institutional mechanisms and political culture to either promote or hinder the connection between elected officials and criminal groups. Specific recommendations are put forth on campaign finance reform, the strengthening of law enforcement agencies by ensuring their independence, the vetting process of electoral candidates, and the privileges given to elected officeholders.

Organized Crime in Brazil

While this chapter does not aim at an in-depth analysis of the various forms of organized crime in Brazil and cannot provide a detailed discussion of shortcomings and advances in the country's political financing regulations, a basic understanding of both is necessary to gauge the electoral connection between organized crime and political candidates. The following sections are a peek into two markets exploited by organized crime: the *jogo do bicho*, a popular form of gambling, and drug trafficking.

Jogo do Bicho

The classic image of organized crime in Brazil harks back to the first decades of the twentieth century, when the *jogo do bicho* started in Rio de Janeiro.[8] As legend has it, the municipal zoo, in order to attract visitors, organized a daily raffle, drawing the daily winner of a small prize from that day's admissions tickets. This raffle soon became a lottery, and because of the link between the animals in the zoo and the numbers, the lottery became known as the *jogo do bicho* (the animal lottery). The *jogo do bicho* became a public issue once the state changed its policy toward gambling and outlawed the game based on moral objections. The Getúlio Vargas presidency (1930–45) was keen to present Brazil as a modern nation based on a workforce with a strong work ethic. The bohemian lifestyle of urban gambling bosses and the mystique surrounding the *jogo do bicho* were seen as undermining the morality of the people.

---

8. Magalhães (2005).

The prohibition of gambling under the new criminal code of 1941 led to police prosecution of urban entrepreneurs involved in organizing the *jogo do bicho*, very much as the rum runners of the Prohibition era in the United States were targeted. However, gambling was not defined as a felony under the law; rather, it was a misdemeanor, and prosecution was ambiguous. Based on this semitoleration policy, and because of its enormous popularity, the *jogo do bicho* would expand during the twentieth century into virtually all urban centers in Brazil.[9] Today the *jogo do bicho* is organized by a small group of entrepreneurs in each state. The "tellers" are to be found accepting bets several times a day in all of Brazil's cities. One estimate puts the daily turnover in São Paulo at $500,000 a day, for a monthly turnover of $15 million.[10] At an estimated rate of 10 percent net rent extraction, the business generates $1.5 million a month in the city of São Paulo. With such profits, the *jogo do bicho* has a strong influence on law enforcement, politics, and society.[11] To avoid repression by police and other law enforcement agencies, entrepreneurs of this oldest branch of organized crime are suspected of bribing law enforcement agencies and politicians.

The *jogo do bicho* is a territorial crime, with local bosses fighting for control over turf. The leaders of the criminal organizations running the *jogo do bicho* are called *bicheiros*. Their power goes far beyond the use of violence against rival entrepreneurs and the corruption of public officials. Thousands of employees make a living from the business, and millions of Brazilians place daily bets. These criminal entrepreneurs enjoy social esteem, especially in Rio de Janeiro, as they finance samba schools and philanthropic organizations and provide support to certain of those in need. In their interaction with elected officeholders, *bicheiros* can use their money, social recognition, and violence to influence the outcome of political campaigns.

Cocaine Trafficking

In addition to the classic form of organized crime, other illegal activities gained prominence during the twentieth century. Drug trafficking, specifically cocaine, became one of the most profitable. Large-scale cocaine trafficking dates back to the late 1970s, as the Brazilian government expanded its frontiers westward to the vast and unexplored Amazon region. This project, which includes building infrastructure and settlements, resulted in a closer connection to the neighboring states of Bolivia, Peru, and Colombia. These countries became drug

---

9. Misse (2007).
10. Mingardi (1996).
11. Garzón (2008).

production centers. The cocaine production and refinery hubs are often located near the Brazilian border, so that drug dealers can cross into Brazil to escape law enforcement. In addition, the supply of chemicals for cocaine production comes from Brazil's industrial plants.

In addition to providing the chemicals for cocaine production, Brazil is the transit route to its ports, from which cocaine is exported to its final destinations. Brazilian settlers engage with their cocaine-producing neighbors by supplying the materials needed to refine raw cocaine into cocaine powder and also by buying cocaine for their own use, to withstand the harsh working conditions of gold mining in the rivers. They also participate in money laundering.

As drugs began to be transported from the northwestern frontier states to coastal cities in the southeast, urban crime became part of narcotics trafficking. Urban gangs are an important link in the chain of cocaine trafficking, as they distribute the drug to the growing market of urban consumers in Brazil. Organized drug gangs are based in urban squatter settlements. Groups like the PCC in São Paulo and the CV in Rio de Janeiro are well known to the Brazilian public. They command their activities both from within and from outside prison and have an ambiguous relationship with law enforcement agencies.[12] On the one hand, they have penetrated law enforcement and corrupted law enforcement officers. On the other hand, law enforcement has remained the main enemy of organized crime—it is a threat to urban gangs and to their profits. Urban gangs have repeatedly challenged the power of the state in urban areas by launching prison strikes, imposing curfews on businesses, or openly confronting the police.[13]

Political Financing in Brazil

The rules of political financing in Brazil, inherited from the military government (1964–85), were designed for a context of limited political competition. Legislative elections were held regularly, but the military government would routinely interfere with the results to guarantee the success of the ruling National Renewal Alliance Party (ARENA) against the opposition, the Brazilian Democratic Movement (MDB).[14] In addition, direct elections for president, governors, and mayors were replaced by indirect elections, following the model of parliamentary democracies. Direct elections were maintained only for legislative bodies that had limited power under military rule, though. In addition, the

12. Zaluar (2004).
13. Bailey and Taylor (2009). In 2006 a curfew was imposed in São Paulo, followed by a series of attacks against police stations; in 2009 a helicopter was shot down in a police raid in Rio de Janeiro.
14. Fleischer (1994).

Table 3-1. *Enfranchised Citizens, Brazil, 1970, 1990, 2010*

Year	Population (millions)	Enfranchised population (millions)	Percentage of enfranchised population
1970	92.6	28.9	31
1990	146.8	83.8	57
2010	190.7	135.8	71
Percentage increase	106	368	

Source: Tribunal Superior Eleitoral.

government reduced the multiparty system to a two-party system (1965–79), forcing politicians to join either ARENA or MDB.

In short, political competition was kept on the back burner by the military government for the sake of legitimizing democracy sui generis. As a consequence elections would require limited resources, for ultimately the allocation of political power was not to be decided upon in the voting booth. The rules on financing politics designed during this period would cover the funding of parties, mostly with a focus on strengthening control on income and expenses, and would not make any reference to the funding of elections.[15] In addition, corporate money was excluded from financing political competition, and media ads were regulated.

Brazil's transition from authoritarian to democratic rule was an incremental process. The country underwent gradual political change, including the reintroduction of a multiparty democracy (1979) and the direct elections of governors (1982), mayors of large cities (1985), and the president (1989). The extension of voting rights hitherto excluded illiterate and young citizens. In 1985 the minimum voting age was reduced to sixteen years and illiterate citizens were allowed to vote, which enfranchised a large part of the citizenry (table 3-1). During the decade of transition, elections underwent a profound change, from being a façade designed to legitimize an authoritarian government to a mechanism that effectively decided on the allocation of political power. Also during this period a new multiparty system emerged.

Campaign finance quickly became a sensitive issue in the incipient democracy, as it became clear that the influence of unregulated and unchecked money on politics could undermine the values of free and fair elections. The public was initially mesmerized by the sheer amount of money involved in political

15. Speck and Campos (2011).

elections. But the gap between the strict rules from the past military government that had outlawed private donations, on the one hand, and the emerging practice of raising funds from corporate donors, on the other, would soon result in political scandals. The impeachment of President Fernando Collor de Mello in 1992, based on accusations that involved his campaign manager Paulo César Farias, revealed the central role of campaign finance in the evolving Brazilian democracy. Collor's impeachment, however, was not based on illegal campaign financing only. Accusations extended to kickbacks that his office and cabinet members received from contractors with the state.

The Pau-Brasil scandal the following year, regarding the illegal private funding of Governor Paulo Maluf's campaign in São Paulo, again crystallized the breach between the rules inherited from the past and the reality of Brazil's post-authoritarian campaign financing. In the following years, lawmakers would redefine the country's system of political financing and make such changes as allowing companies to make substantial contributions while asking parties and candidates to report them.[16]

New Party and Campaign Finance Rules

In response to the series of scandals, Brazilian legislators reframed the rules of political financing in the 1990s. Party and campaign financing were now addressed by separate sets of rules. The overhaul was profound. The Law on Party Financing (1995) and the Law on Campaign Financing (1997) are the legal framework of money in politics, and they remain unchanged.[17] Private donations, including corporate money that had previously been banned, became legal sources for both campaigns and political parties. No absolute ceilings were placed on the amount of donations that could be received by candidates or given by donors. Only companies that depend on public subsidies (such as media companies) or providers of public services (such as public transport and waste removal) remained banned from making donations. Campaign donations could not exceed 10 percent of an individual contributor's annual income and, in the case of corporate donations, 2 percent of the company's annual turnover. While such rules do not level the playing field for private donors influencing the electoral process, they do allow for some control over the origin of donations from lawful sources.[18] These regulations can help keep money from organized crime away from the political process.

---

16. Speck (2005).
17. Minor changes were made in 2006 and 2009.
18. The drawback of these very specific limits on private donations is that they make donors unequal by law, which goes against the right of equal participation in the election process.

Table 3-2. *Funding of Political Parties, Brazil, by Source, 1999 and 2009*
BRL except where indicated

Source of funds	1999	Percent	2009	Percent
Public	112,408,223.00	78	161,235,070.27	75
Private	30,934,307.73	22	53,141,234.27	25
Total	143,344,529.73	100	214,378,313.54	100

Source: Tribunal Superior Eleitoral.

Another important change in the political financing system in Brazil has to do with direct public funding. Although introduced in the 1970s, public funding remained insignificant until the reforms of the 1990s. The 1995 reforms included an increase of the party public fund, which would distribute roughly BRL100 million among all political parties. Today, the fund is the most important source of financing for political parties at the national level (table 3-2). National party headquarters have managed to cover approximately BRL3 out of every BRL4 of their expenses from this source, making public funding the dominant source of financing for political organizations. No direct public funding for elections is available, however.

Another key resource for campaigning of political parties and candidates is airtime on radio and TV. Free airtime for candidates during election season was introduced in 1962. During the military government—specifically, 1974—the law was complemented by a ban on paid advertising. The rule was then meant to control electoral dynamics and to contain the role of opposition parties. In the context of a multiparty democracy, with increased campaign costs, free access to media and the ban on paid advertising gained a different raison d'être. Today, free airtime and the ban on paid TV ads help counterbalance the extremely unequal market of private resources, as the state provides political contenders with airtime depending on their past electoral record rather than on their fundraising capacity.[19]

The last innovation that came with the reforms of the 1990s was the requirement that parties and candidates render public accounts of both income and expenses. Such reports need to include information about financial and in-kind contributions, with details such as the amount of the donation and the identity of the donor. In addition, the law established that financial reports rendered to the electoral authority had to be made available to the public. Since 2002 the electoral authority has made these data available in a user-friendly format,

---

19. Free airtime extends to both private and public media channels and is allocated among political parties based on equitable and proportional distribution.

Table 3-3. *Campaign and Party Finance, Brazil, Select Years*[a]

Source of finance	Campaign finance (every 2 years)	Party finance (annual)[b]	Total (4-year cycle)
Private	BRL800 million (2006)	BRL40 million (average 1998–2009)	BRL1,760 million
Public	None	BRL160 million (average 1998–2009)	BRL640 million
Total	BRL800 million	BRL200 million	BRL2,400 million

Source: Adapted from Speck and Campos (2011).
a. All numbers are adjusted to the values of November 2010. The average exchange rate in November 2010 was BRL1 = US$0.58.
b. Twelve-year averages differ slightly from selected years in table 3-2.

resulting in media and civil society using the information to conduct oversight of the bureaucracy and legislature.[20]

Historically, the electoral authority responsible for adjudicating conflicts has enjoyed great independence in Brazil.[21] Such autonomy has contributed to the cleanup of the electoral process and the implementation of a number of reforms (such as electronic voting) between 1996 and 2000. The technological knowledge and infrastructure acquired to make this change has led to the modernization of the electronic reporting system and to more public access. The main shortcoming in the Brazilian system of political financing is weak oversight and impunity in the face of noncompliance.

Hidden Money in Election Campaigns

Today, as a result of the new dynamics of political competition and the adoption of a new legal framework, the financing of political parties and election campaigns in Brazil is a mix of private and state resources (table 3-3). Eighty percent of the annual expenses of national political parties are covered by public funds. Election expenses, on the other hand, come from private sources.

Corporate donations represent the lion's share (65 percent) of electoral campaign funds, and there are only a few major donors. Banks and construction companies contribute up to BRL100 million. Under the Brazilian electoral system, the need for funds is pressing because of the high correlation between amounts raised and votes won. The open-list system puts the responsibility for raising campaign money on the candidate rather than on the party. Victorious

---

20. One example of the tracking of campaign finance by civil society is the website www.asclaras.org.br maintained by Transparencia Brasil.
21. Sadek (1996); Marchetti (2008).

candidates regularly outspend their opponents by large sums. As a consequence, the candidates' links to individual donors may compete with candidates' relationship with the political party or constituency, a factor that reinforces the personalist culture in Brazilian politics and the risk of campaign donors receiving kickbacks in exchange for their support.

The fact that private donations are so highly coveted makes them perfect entry points for organized criminal groups hoping to get access to officeholders. There are other ways of supporting candidates besides fundraising, such as electioneering in organized crime strongholds. However, monetary contributions do not leave as many traces as campaigning for candidates, bribing people, and intimidating voters or opposing candidates.

Brazilian laws require parties and candidates to account for all sources and expenses. Anonymous donations are not allowed. Despite efforts by the electoral authorities to improve oversight by filing expenses electronically and publicly disclosing data, the system still has room for underreporting. Both candidates and donors keep part of their campaign donations off the books (*caixa dois*), as campaign spending often involves unregistered expenses, such as vote buying and other unethical practices. Another layer of complexity comes with the fact that donors resort to money—from informal activities, for instance—that is not declared to authorities for tax purposes. Where donations from the private sector enter campaigns unchecked, absorbing contributions from organized criminal groups becomes an easy task.

Interaction between Organized Crime and Elected Officials: A Typology

Organized crime frequently co-opts law enforcement officers, as they are the first point of contact that criminals have with the state. Interaction at this stage may involve bribery, the use of personal connections, or extortion. Members of the police are also frequently hired to protect narcotics shipments, a troubling inversion of roles between the government and criminals. Similarly, criminal rings can also corrupt prosecutors, judges, or members of other law enforcement agencies. What kind of exchanges come into effect when organized crime deals with elected officeholders? What are the benefits to candidates and elected officials? And what do members of criminal organizations expect from these officeholders?

Organized Crime Conveying Political Benefits to Candidates and Elected Officials

For elected representatives, involvement with organized crime can result in personal and political benefits. When it comes to pocketing money, the benefits are no different for elected officials than for other public servants who accept money in exchange for favors. Politicians may receive bribes either on a case-by-case basis or in the form of regular payments from criminal networks. Alternatives to bribery are sharing in an existing illegal business and taking advantage of a new illegal business opportunity in partnership with a criminal group.

The financial power and other resources of criminal organizations can be used to influence voters and to intimidate the political opponents of the favored candidate. This financial power can become the basis of a symbiotic relationship between elected officials and the criminal organization not only during election season but also afterward, when the elected official is making policy. After candidates have been elected, the calculation may become one of using the power of criminal organizations to, say, implicate political opponents in scandals or create a climate of public insecurity so as to weaken and destabilize the government. Further, once elected, officials may receive money from organized crime to cover routine costs. In short, there are numerous opportunities for organized crime to take advantage of the greed or political ambition of candidates and elected officials.

The bribes paid to public officials fill campaign coffers for future election cycles. When members of criminal groups themselves run for office, they naturally use their own financial resources. In this scenario of the self-funding of election campaigns, the distinction between private and political benefits tends to fade. The connection between organized crime and political financing therefore transcends the question of hidden donations to parties and candidates. Thus organized crime can undermine fair competition in a variety of ways: by rigging the process of the election administration, from registration to vote counting; by invoking its network of influence to garner votes for a candidate; by using muscle to threaten or hinder the campaigns of opposing candidates; and by enabling candidates to self-finance their campaign using funds from criminal activities.

Benefits that Organized Crime Receives from Elected Officials

The barons of criminal organizations have an interest in protecting their business from law enforcement, in managing their ongoing activities, and in finding new business opportunities. Elected officials can contribute to these objectives by intervening administratively or through policymaking and legislation.

First, these officials can protect criminal business ventures from harm when evasion, bribery, and defiance of law enforcement agencies fail. They can also intervene to solve problems for organized crime when administrative protections cannot. Lawmakers who support the sitting government have considerable influence on the administration. The trading of favors for continued political support, which in Brazil as in many other countries is business as usual, may effect law enforcement agencies' handling of specific cases.

Second, lawmakers can draft bills that weaken law enforcement agencies so as to protect the interests of their organized crime associates.

Third, criminals can run for elected office. While they can use career politicians to achieve their objectives, they may also opt for cutting out the middleman and running for elected office themselves. This is a double-edged sword, though: public office comes with benefits such as immunity from prosecution, but there are risks, too, including extended public scrutiny.

INFLUENCE PEDDLING IN LAW ENFORCEMENT AGENCIES. Organized crime can hide under the radar of law enforcement agencies or attempt to co-opt law enforcement officers. When this fails, a relationship with elected officials can make a difference. These officials have close connections to the administrative branch and, if they are members of the ruling coalition, have a strong influence with police, prosecutors, and judges. In the fragmented Brazilian party system, governors and even the president depend on members of the ruling coalition to back the government. Party discipline in Brazil tends to be weak, so the government has to negotiate with individual lawmakers.

These individuals often control key positions in the government bureaucracy. These personal ties can be activated when a lawmaker needs to honor a request from a member of his constituency or a campaign sponsor, both of whom might be members of criminal organizations. A head of a police department nominated by a politician would have a double loyalty, to his superiors and to his political patron. Based on these ties, elected representatives can solve a number of problems for organized crime when nonconfrontation and bribery have not succeeded. Criminals may benefit from these networks when a shipment of illegal narcotics or weapons is confiscated during a police raid or members of gangs get arrested in the course of an investigation. The intervention by an elected official can result in the release of criminal goods or of arrested members of criminal gangs. There is a short window for these interventions before other agencies become involved and things get beyond the reach of influence of the co-opted officials.

Elected officials possess resources in addition to their connections to the government and administration. Their social networks can be called upon to provide kickbacks to organized crime. Lawmakers are part of the political elite that is often closely connected to members of the justice system by family, friendship, or business ties. Such connections do not represent a corruption risk per se, but they do offer valuable information and access to possible business partners for organized criminal groups.

Besides family ties and friendships, many legislators have close links to members of law enforcement agencies. Policemen and -women, attorneys, and judges frequently run for office; once elected, they use their networks to favor members of criminal organizations. The social capital of state representatives makes them important figures even for members of the justice system who are formally independent of the legislature. The link with the judiciary also has political dimensions, as legislators set the budget of the judicial system, which in turn influences remuneration and promotion.

Another means of protecting organized crime is through the use of special rights and privileges that are attached to the office of an elected representative. Elected lawmakers in Brazil are constitutionally immune to investigation and sanctions. These special rights were added to the constitution of 1988 in reaction to the censorship against lawmakers during military rule. Elected representatives have repeatedly used this position to add members of organized criminal groups to their staff or to transport shipments of illegal goods in official vehicles. As a result, legislators are approached by kingpins because of their lawmaking role—to broker deals with law enforcement agencies and to use their office as safe havens.

POLICYMAKING AND LAWMAKING. Criminal organizations also use elected representatives for their policymaking and lawmaking roles. The national and state police forces are the key institutions for law enforcement. The national police, which are under the command of the president, are responsible for interstate crimes, for crimes with international connections, and for crimes that involve drug trafficking. The civil and military branches of the state police, both commanded by governors, do the bulk of crime prevention and investigation.

Thus governors and the president have great authority over the design and implementation of law enforcement. Their decisions may have an effect on the allocation of budget resources, the selection of cabinet members, and the development of intelligence to fight organized crime. A governor who is on the payroll of criminal groups may cut the budget for combating crime, select cabinet members and heads of law enforcement agencies who will not take a hard stance against illicit markets, shut down investigations that would inconvenience organized crime, and dismiss public servants who insist on conducting such investigations.

Even where access to the head of government is blocked, state and national elected officials who are part of the ruling coalition have significant influence over public administration. Since governments in Brazil are built on fragile coalitions, political support by influential lawmakers is often offered in exchange for nominations to top positions in the administration. State representatives might, for example, press for the nomination of a head of the highway police in frontier states, a position that can affect the transport of illicit goods between the western border and urban centers on the Atlantic coast.

The influence of governors and the president extends to the prison system, which is under the control of the Justice Department. The management of prisons is a central issue for organized crime, since many members sentenced to long prison terms continue their illegal activities behind bars. Corrupt prison directors make such internal businesses possible. Governors also have a say in the nomination of state attorneys and members of state tribunals.[22] Similarly, the president nominates the attorney general, in addition to federal and Supreme Court judges.

National and state representatives are also targets of organized crime because of their role as lawmakers and watchdogs. Illegal markets are by definition a product of past lawmaking—specifically the criminalization of such activities. When co-opted by organized crime they can soften the legislation on the fight against criminal activities. Such lawmaking may involve blurring or shifting the line between legal and illegal activities when issues like the legalization of drug consumption or other illegal markets are under debate. Another area of potential interest for organized crime is the investigative role of the legislature. When parliamentary investigations on organized crime are held, legislators have a say in the use of subpoenas for witnesses, the lifting of bank secrecy, the verification of phone records, and the assessment of ongoing investigations by other law enforcement agencies. The co-option of lawmakers by criminal networks can contain the damage from such activities.

The influence of elected officials goes beyond executive and the legislative power. Since Congress sets the annual budget of law enforcement agencies, judges and prosecutors are susceptible to the demands of state and federal deputies. The unique position of lawmakers enables them to establish a link between criminals and members of the judiciary. Being connected to both low-level civil servants and the higher echelons of government makes elected representatives potential brokers between organized crime and potentially corrupt officials.

---

22. The governor selects the attorney general from a triple list based on a vote-based selection process among attorneys. The governor confirms judges for the state tribunal as suggested by a board of peers. However, the governor also nominates an additional 20 percent of judges recruited externally among lawyers and attorneys.

CAPTURING THE STATE. Elected officials in Brazil enjoy a number of special rights and privileges designed to protect them from harassment by the government. While immunity from criminal prosecution in advanced democracies is meant to protect the lawmaker from retribution because of his or her political actions or beliefs, in countries with an authoritarian past, accusations of wrongdoing have been used to threaten elected representatives. The postdictatorship Brazilian constitution (1988) protects elected representatives from prosecution. They cannot be investigated by law enforcement agencies without oversight by the court. In addition, any criminal accusation has to be previously authorized by a decision of the majority of the legislature. Since then the National Congress and state legislatures have maintained a strong esprit de corps and refused to authorize investigations against lawmakers who were involved in traffic accidents, economic crimes, bureaucratic crimes, extortion, and even murder. At times, as many as half of the representatives in a legislature stood accused of crimes for which they would never be prosecuted.[23]

Elected officials are also protected from prosecution by the *foro privilegiado*. With the exception of municipal councilors, all representatives enjoy the right to be judged only by higher courts, which makes prosecution unlikely.[24] Thus in addition to the difficulty of investigating and prosecuting elected officeholders, cases would often be delayed for years. Elected office has therefore proven to be an efficient way to avoid criminal sanctions. Since the homes, vehicles, and airplanes of elected officeholders cannot be searched by law enforcement agencies, they can be used to transport or hide narcotics. Some lawmakers have therefore added members of criminal organizations to their staffs to protect them from police raids. It did not take long before drug traffickers themselves ran for elected office, given the legal protections they would have if elected.

Scenario 1: Elected Officials Protecting Illicit Businesses

Drug money influences electoral campaigns along the border region, which is where cocaine enters Brazilian territory. Political contributions made by drug traffickers go unreported but sometimes surface in investigations by law enforcement agencies or by journalists. There are only a few documented cases of political contributions from organized crime to candidates or elected

---

23. Transparencia Brasil keeps a record of pending criminal investigations against lawmakers with its ongoing project, Excelencias.
24. Mayors of municipalities and members of state parliaments cannot be judged by ordinary courts but only by the Tribunais de Justiça. For governors, the responsible court is the Superior Tribunal de Justiça. Members of the national parliament can be prosecuted by the Superior Tribunal Federal.

officeholders. Donations from organized crime may also enter a campaign's coffers via middlemen or be declared as the candidate's personal funds. In short, there are myriad ways to circumvent reporting requirements, and the dearth of reliable data surrounding these activities only compounds the problem.

While it is difficult to track down individual transactions, campaign costs tend to be high in drug-trafficking regions. Looking at the numbers of political financing in Brazil, the pattern observed in the border region (the mideast and the north) is that, compared to other regions, there is higher expenditure per vote during elections. This fact can serve as support for the hypothesis that drug money is involved in electoral campaigns. However, the finding does not constitute hard evidence of the connection between candidates and drug syndicates. Candidates' links to organized crime are but one factor to explain the data on campaign expenses. There might be other reasons for increased costs, such as economies of scale, increasing campaign costs in states with a small electorate, and difficult access to remote regions. Probing the hypothesis that the presence of organized crime drives up campaign costs requires further statistical analysis.

Criminal Activities and Damage Control

While it is hard to prove organized crime's financial involvement in politics, certain such cases have surfaced in Brazil. A main concern of drug dealers who are working with representatives of the state is damage control following the seizure of illicit commodities or detention of members of criminal rings. When law enforcement officers have not been bought off by organized crime, elected representatives can step in and provide specific services to drug dealers. State legislators may have the ability to convince the police officer in command to reverse the arrest of members and return the illegal shipments, for example. Such intervention is based on personal networks within the administration that subvert the division of powers and the system of checks and balances. During the congressional hearing on drug trafficking held in 2000, several witnesses reported that elected officeholders made attempts to influence law enforcement agencies in favor of organized crime.[25]

Protection of criminal activities by elected representatives is not limited to damage control. Lawmakers can legally protect members of criminal gangs. Jabes Rabelo, the national representative for Rondonia, was suspected of involvement with criminal organizations, but there was no evidence against him. His brother, Abidiel Rabelo, was a well-known drug dealer, but although such a family connection was embarrassing for the legislator, it could not be held against him.

25. Torgan (2000).

In 1991 Abidiel was arrested in São Paulo for transporting 400 kilograms of cocaine. However, Abidiel and his aides were using documents identifying them as members of Jabes Rabelo's congressional staff. Such identification would usually deter police from searching a place or making arrests. However, the protection given by Jabes Rabelo backfired. Congress opened proceedings against the representative, and Jabes Rabelo was eventually expelled from office for violating the parliamentary code of ethics. He had been in office only nine months.[26]

Compared to the slaps on the wrist that Congress has given lawmakers for bureaucratic crimes, tax fraud, or manslaughter, the expulsion of Rabelo reveals how seriously national lawmakers take accusations of involvement with organized crime.[27] By the end of the decade, protecting criminals from the police would cost another legislator his public office. In 1999 it became known that Hildebrando Pascoal, a national representative from Acre, was closely connected with organized crime in his state. Pascoal's association stunned the Brazilian public.[28] He had been a member of the military police force in Acre and was elected to the state legislature in 1994. In 1998 he was elected to the national legislature. Even after entering politics, Pascoal led a group of corrupt police officers that shielded the cocaine shipments crossing Acre. He murdered with a chain saw those who were going to testify against them. Pascoal's nickname was the "chain saw deputy."

Despite rumors about his role in the killings, there was no evidence against him. The state police conducted investigations, but Pascoal had excellent connections with them. He was acquitted because of a lack of evidence. During congressional hearings on drug trafficking in Brazil, a witness was murdered before testifying. Federal police began an investigation. Pascoal admitted to his colleagues in the legislature that he had issued papers that would allow policemen to identify themselves as being under his protection. After finding such papers with members of the organized crime group, Pascoal was expelled from office by his colleagues for colluding with criminal rings and abusing his political power. He had been in the national legislature for less than eight months.[29]

As with the case of Rabelo, the Pascoal case showed that Congress took accusations of involvement with organized crime seriously, required accountability, and dealt out appropriate punishment. Once removed from office, Pascoal lost his immunity; evidence of a series of additional crimes that he had masterminded

---

26. National representatives are elected in October and sworn in on February 1 the following year. Rabelo took office on February 1, 1991, and was expelled November 7 the same year.

27. For an analysis of the different rationale behind expelling lawmakers in Brazil, see Teixeira (2001).

28. Torgan (2000).

29. Pascoal took office on February 1, 1999, and was expelled the same year, on September 22.

surfaced. The federal police issued an order of arrest against him for orchestrating death squads and taking part in drug dealing in Acre. In the course of the investigation and prosecution more witnesses were murdered. He was convicted of murder and other crimes in 1996 and sentenced to sixty-five years in prison.

Brokering Deals with the Justice System

In addition to providing a safe haven for illegal activities, Brazilian lawmakers broker deals between criminal gangs and the justice system. The connection between the former congressman Francisco Pinheiro Landim from the state of Ceará and drug trafficker Leonardo Dias Mendonça shows the kind of service that representatives can provide to drug traffickers. A federal police investigation in 1999 uncovered Landim's trading of habeas corpus to drug-dealing entrepreneurs. Habeas corpus is a measure granted by courts to protect citizens against the abuse of power by the state. Landim would set up the negotiations between the members of the court and criminals in custody. Once settling the amount of the bribe to be paid, the judge would grant a writ of habeas corpus to a criminal, guaranteeing his release until a future trial.

At the time of the scandal, the group around Mendonça was the largest drug-dealing enterprise in the country—a Brazilian version of Colombia's Pablo Escobar.[30] Landim was wiretapped when making use of his position as a lawmaker and of his personal network to influence judicial decisions on granting habeas corpus to Mendonça, who had been arrested. The investigation revealed Landim's scheme of leveraging sentences to his or his friends' advantage and a long history of helping criminals deal with the judiciary: he would demand that a bribe, of a certain amount, be delivered by a certain time to a certain bank account (belonging to one of his underlings—for his later collection). The media gave BRL650,000 as the amount paid by Mendonça for using habeas corpus, which was finally granted by the courts.[31]

Though lawmakers do not have formal power over the judiciary, their personal connections with the political elite allow them to establish the link between members of criminal groups and members of courts whose decisions are for sale. Landim enhanced his social network by hiring the sons of two of the judges involved in the case. After the scheme was exposed, Landim and three justices were investigated. The justices were investigated by the correctional authority and forced to retire, while Landim faced an investigation by his colleagues in the legislature.

Landim, who had recently been reelected to a fourth term, used a legal loophole to escape punishment. He had not yet been sworn in for the new term

---

30. Silva (2002).
31. Lima (2003).

(starting in February 2009) and was technically serving his third term. By resigning in January from the mandate that was coming to a close, Landim was able to abort an ethics committee investigation. The bylaws of the Brazilian Congress do not allow for an investigation of a member who has left office.[32] The scandal did not prevent him from taking office again and then from resigning just a few days later. With this maneuver, Landim managed to avoid any investigation and public exposure of his case.

The dealings with court sentences did involve bribes, but there was no reference to criminal money entering Landim's electoral campaign. The payments actually ended up in private bank accounts, which can enable candidates to fund their own campaigns. Indeed, Landim's 2002 election was mainly self-financed, according to the records of the Electoral Court. A total of 77 percent of the money raised, which amounted to BRL162,000, came from his personal accounts (34 percent) and from family members and his businesses (43 percent).[33]

Unlike Jabes Rabelo and Hildebrando Pascoal, Landim had a long political career before he became involved in organized crime. He had been in politics in the northeastern state of Ceará since his early twenties, was elected municipal councilor in 1966 and 1970 for MDB, and then became deputy mayor of his hometown (Solonopole) and state legislator in 1982 and 1986. He was president of the state legislature in Ceará during his last two years in office. He then ran successfully for National Congress in 1990 and was reelected in 1994, 1998, and 2002. The scandal of 1999, though, brought this long political career to an abrupt end.

Scenario 2: Organized Crime Influencing Policymakers and Legislation

The financing of electoral campaigns by gambling entrepreneurs has always been an open secret in Brazil. Several politicians have even admitted accepting money from the patrons of the gambling business. Federal representative Agnaldo Timoteo from the state of Rio de Janeiro acknowledged in an interview that he had taken campaign donations from Castor de Andrade, a major force in the gambling business of Rio de Janeiro.[34] A note found during a police raid in 1994 in the offices of Castor de Andrade confirmed these and other donations to politicians. The investigation requested by the state prosecutor, Antonio

---

32. The bylaws had already been changed because the earlier version (before 2003) would foresee immediate suspension of ongoing investigations in case the elected officeholder would renounce the position. Current bylaws do not abort ongoing investigations but still do not allow measures against members who step down before formal accusations are initiated.

33. Data from the election authority (www.tse.gov.br).

34. *O Globo*, April 1, 1994, quoted in Mingardi (1996, p. 90).

Biscaia, revealed a widespread net of bribery of *bicheiros* in all sectors of society. The amount spent on each election campaign in Rio de Janeiro by the gambling business alone is estimated at US$2 million.[35]

Buying Coexistence with the State

The support by *bicheiros* of candidates for elected office is not limited to financial contributions. Organized crime's social recognition and credibility as well as its wide spread allow it to directly influence voters. During the 1986 campaign prominent members of the gambling business supported the gubernatorial candidate Moreira Franco by personally and publicly asking voters for their votes. According to newspaper reports, during the 1990 elections gambling bosses in Rio de Janeiro printed the names of the candidates that they supported on the back of betting slips, thereby reaching thousands of voters on a daily basis.[36] Such voting campaigns are built on the social roots and credibility of *jogo do bicho* in their communities.

In return for their electoral services, *bicheiros* expect the political elite not to enforce the gambling prohibition. Governors take part in this tacit protection, specifically in nominating chiefs of police who can be trusted to turn a blind eye to gambling activities in territories of those *bicheiros* who support electoral campaigns.

Shifting the Line between Legal and Illegal

The protection of gambling interests also extends to the lawmaking capacity of federal representatives. This reach was preceded by a changing legal environment vis-à-vis gambling activities. Compared to the first half of the twentieth century, the state's stance on gambling has transformed from moral condemnation to pragmatic acceptance. In 1967 sports lotteries managed by state agencies became legal. In 1971 the legalization of lotteries for philanthropy followed, and then in 1984 it became permissible to bet on horse races. These decisions were serious blows to the economic activities of the gambling business, as legal competition absorbed part of its market share.[37] In response, the bosses of *jogo do bicho* had to find other illegal businesses or lobby for legalizing gambling. To undertake the second option they needed the support of lawmakers. Since the state was now organizing lotteries, the context of gambling was ripe for change, and the *bicheiros* maintained a vital interest in influencing the regulation of *jogo do bicho* as a legal business.

---

35. According to the *Folha de Sao Paulo*, quoted in Mingardi (1996, p. 90).
36. Newspaper reports according to Mingardi (1996, p. 91).
37. Misse (2007).

The discussion on new varieties of gambling and the regulation of such activities in Brazil brought renewed attention to the role of elected officials. Such changes in gambling regulation signaled that hiding in the underworld and bribing law enforcement officials were not the only ways for gambling entrepreneurs to survive. The purpose of co-opting lawmakers was no longer to secure protection from law enforcement agencies but to shape the political debate on the legalization and regulation of gambling activities.

Arguments for and against the legalization of bingo were put forth in Congress. Entrepreneurs involved in gambling stressed the social benefits of legalization, arguing that the activity would generate jobs and tax revenue in a country that lacked opportunities for employment. The estimates published by the bingo association illustrate the economic power of this business—within a few years it yielded an annual profit of BRL27 billion and tax revenue of BRL7 billion.[38] While official disapproval of gambling in the early twentieth century had been based on moral grounds, state-organized lotteries undermined such an argument. The case against legalization was made mainly by law enforcement agencies. One of the main concerns with the legalization of bingo was that the games could provide a loophole for money laundering, as the proceeds from gambling activities are not traceable.

The 1988 constitution of Brazil made the regulation of gambling a congressional prerogative. Discussions over the legalization of *jogo do bicho* in Congress began in 1994.[39] A project on the exploration of this form of gambling by a state institution was submitted by the national legislator José Fortunati.[40] Fortunati's project included organizing *jogo do bicho* as a public system, similar to the model of the sports lottery. More than twenty projects were presented by national lawmakers. Ivo Mainardi, another national representative, suggested, in an amendment to Fortunati's proposal, that private management of *jogo do bicho* would replace public management, thereby giving priority to entrepreneurs. Mainardi's amendment was clearly in defense of the business interests of *bicheiros* who wanted a share of the legal business.[41] However, there is no proof linking the lawmaker to the *jogo do bicho* business.[42]

---

38. Weber (2010).
39. Iunes (2010).
40. Projeto de lei (draft law) 4652/1994, the first proposal to legalize *jogo do bicho*, was discussed in Congress but was finally archived in 2003. See www.camara.gov.br.
41. In 1995 fifteen amendments to Fortunati's initial proposal were presented in Congress. The text of his amendment said, "Those entrepreneurs who have been engaged in *jogo do bicho* for at least five years will be granted a concession for legal engagement before other competitors" (translation by the author). See www.camara.gov.br.
42. Mingardi (1996, p. 92).

The lobbying surrounding the gambling regulation debate extended to other policy areas, like the financing of sports and the question of tax revenues, and in 1993 the government finally legalized bingo. Part of the rents from this activity, which was to be organized by private entrepreneurs, was to be collected in the form of national taxes and allocated to fund the new Ministry of Sports. From that point on, regulations over bingo have continually changed, and the statutes have still not been consolidated. In 2000 a new regulation cancelled the legalization process and made bingo subject to a permit to be issued by the state agency Caixa Economica Federal. Bingo games that had started operating based on the previous rule remained legal, however. In 2004 another regulation banned all bingo games and imposed fines on entrepreneurs who defied the law. In 2009 a law to regulate bingo was introduced in Congress. As of this writing, this last piece of legislation has not passed Congress.

The assumption that bingo entrepreneurs were trying to influence the policymaking process was eventually confirmed. Waldomiro Diniz was taped extorting financial contributions for the 2002 elections campaign from the *bicheiro* Carlinhos Cachoeira.[43] At the time of the extortion, Diniz was in charge of the state-run sports lottery in the state of Rio de Janeiro. The tapes were released in 2004, when he was senior adviser to the Lula government on the regulation of gambling. Diniz was quickly dismissed so that the political crisis could be contained. Despite the swift response, the scandal was a major blow to the new government, and it ended in congressional investigations.[44]

During the investigations it became resoundingly clear that the regulation of new varieties of legal gambling attracted the lobbying efforts of businessmen. While Diniz was thought to have raised funds for the 2002 gubernatorial candidate Antony Garotinho, another key figure, Rogério Buratti, revealed that businessmen involved in bingo had financed the campaign of President Lula and his party to the tune of BRL2 million. In the course of these investigations, law enforcement agencies found bingo regulation to be a coordinated strategy of the Italian and Colombian mafias to launder dirty money. According to Garibaldi Alves Filho, the rapid expansion of bingo in Brazil was based on an investment by the Italian Ortiz Group, which had imported and set up videopoker machines.[45]

During his campaign, Lula had announced his plans to legalize and regulate gambling. The Diniz scandal exposed the link between illegal bingo entrepreneurs and campaign finance and suggested that the political initiative to regulate

---

43. The Diniz scandal was largely covered by Brazilian newspapers. See Meireles and Krieger (2012a, 2012b).
44. Alves Filho (2006).
45. Alves Filho (2006).

gambling had been infiltrated by, or even driven by, criminal entrepreneurs. The political consequences of this scandal included the abandonment of all plans to legalize and regulate gambling activities. The issue had become damaging to the image of the government and policymakers.

Scenario 3: From Safe Havens to Capturing the State

Several members of organized criminal groups have tried to enter politics, the most important reason being protection from investigation, prosecution, and sanctions by law enforcement agencies. The case of Espírito Santo, one of the smallest units of the federation situated just north of Rio de Janeiro, illustrates this. A former *jogo do bicho* entrepreneur, who had entered politics in 1990 and ascended rapidly to become one of the most important politicians in the region, ended up capturing the state and using it as a source of rent extraction. He was taken out of office through federal police intervention in 2003.

José Carlos Gratz was a self-made businessman who began his career at a low-income job in the region of Espírito Santo, picking crustaceans in the mangroves.[46] Later he worked as an accountant for a local *jogo do bicho* boss. In the years that followed, Gratz ended up controlling the gambling business in the state. The police arrested Gratz after an investigation requested by Governor Max Mauro—a man who would become Gratz's archenemy.[47] After being arrested several times, Gratz decided to protect himself by running for the state legislature. He was elected in 1991 and became president of the Assembleia Legislativa in 1997, a position he would keep for three consecutive terms, until 2002. During his six years as president of the Assembleia, Gratz would pull the strings on numerous schemes of illegal rent extraction from state resources.

Targeting State Resources

State lawmakers supporting Gratz used the legislature to illegally extract private rents as well. The Assembleia Legislativa started sponsoring nonprofit associations dedicated to social work. Such transfers were made by check and amounted to BRL5,000 to BRL10,000 each. Subsequent investigations revealed that many of these checks ended up in the pockets of politicians.[48] The nonprofit destination was just a façade, as the checks were actually cashed by lawmakers,

---

46. The following biographical sketch is drawn from "Defesa aberta" (1999).
47. For the testimony of Mauro, see "O caso Maura Fraga" (2001).
48. A series of articles published in the local newspaper *A Gazeta* on October 19, 2005, reveals details of an investigation conducted in 2004 and 2005 by the federal revenue service and the federal police into the financial transactions of the state legislature (Assembleia Legislativa de Espírito Santo).

their relatives, or their political aides. Another way to divert resources from the Assembleia included payments to the printing house Lineart. The printing house earned contracts amounting to BRL4.6 million between 1998 and 2002. This printing house would also make regular transfers to lawmakers, thus giving cover to the illicit use of state funds.

Family connections, public office, and criminal joint ventures overlapped in the Gratz plot. The Lineart printing house was owned by Cezar and Flavio Nogueira. Flavio Nogueira was the head of the state attorney's office. Another brother, André Nogueira, was the chief manager of the Assembleia and ordered the transfers. The total resources diverted by such schemes were BRL10 million, with illegal transfers being made to 140 people. Gratz, the central figure in the scheme, had signed the checks in his capacity of a president of the Assembleia.

Gratz's rise illustrates the metamorphosis that criminal entrepreneurs go through when they enter politics. Looking at the state apparatus from the perspective of seizing opportunities for rent extraction, Gratz did not stop at the Assembleia's budget. The state legislature approves state budgets, oversees the nomination of candidates for the state accounting office, and can support the governor in exchange for controlling parts of the state apparatus or using its veto power. Under Gratz, the Assembleia maximized its political power for the purpose of private rent extraction. The scheme involved blackmailing the governor, and lawmakers in Espírito Santo started charging for their political support of the governor. They would receive regular payments in exchange for voting in support of government proposals. Twelve parliamentarians were accused of cashing checks from the legislature to supposedly support non-profit organizations.

The Gratz group also expanded the power of the legislature by usurping government functions. The Assembleia issued regulations for several businesses in the state as a pretext to extort payments from such companies or to sanction those that did not pay the bribes. One of the most important mechanisms used to put pressure on local businesses was the tax regime. The Assembleia approved more than 300 tax regimes, granting exemptions to businesses that colluded with them. The Xerox Company famously withdrew from Espírito Santo after high-ranking politicians asked for extra payments. The incoming government, after the fall of Gratz in 2002, raised tax income by 20 percent by cancelling tax exemptions and unifying the tax code.[49]

Gratz's scheme increased the reelection rate of members of the Assembleia so as to avoid reversing the patronage system and destabilizing the scheme. Gratz

---

49. *Valor Economico*, April 26, 2005.

himself boasted that reelection of state legislators had increased significantly.[50] Again, some of the illegal payments to state legislators were reinvested in the reelection campaign coffers of incumbent candidates.

Gratz's career is a glimpse into how former members of criminal rings change once they enter politics. Instead of using elected office for protection from criminal investigation and as a safe haven for exploiting illegal markets, they resort to embezzlement. In that way elected office becomes more than a useful tool for personal protection. From the perspective of criminal groups that feed off of state resources, staying in office enables them to engage in other extractive activities. Clinging to office becomes more important in light of media exposure, public awareness, and scrutiny by law enforcement agencies. Once politicians are stripped of their privileges, their illicit businesses tend to collapse.

Criminal activity in the state of Espírito Santo reached its peak in 2002, when it became known that the organization Escuderie LeCoque was a death squad, which forced those who resisted their game to acquiesce and intimidated law enforcement agencies. When a lawyer was murdered in the state in April 2002, the Brazilian Bar Association asked for federal intervention in Espírito Santo, characterizing the state as a "land without law."[51] The elections in October 2002 would help clear the political landscape. The electoral justice invalidated Gratz's reelection on the grounds of vote buying. In addition, many state lawmakers under investigation did not run for reelection, and the new governor, Paulo Hartung, helped purge rogue politicians.

Gratz's empire crumbled rapidly once the main figures behind the scheme were removed from office. As soon as Gratz lost control of the assembly, his sphere of influence shrank. He had also, of course, lost his parliamentary immunity. Gratz's fall shows how organized crime feeds off abuse of public office and resources. Staying in office ensures the flow of illegal profits and protection from sanctions. Ending this flow tends to destroy the bases of organized crime.

The Moral Decay of Traditional Politicians

In the course of a single decade, at least three states in the Brazilian federation have fallen victim to an orchestrated effort by members of the political elite to exploit public treasure for personal benefit. In 2002 investigations in Espírito Santo revealed that this region had been plundered by a group of state legislators. Similar situations were uncovered in the state of Rondonia in 2006 and in the federal district of Brasilia in 2009. In the latter case, the force behind the plot was the governor, with the support of legislators. In all three cases, the network that

---

50. Gratz (2002).
51. "Entenda a crise no Espírito Santo" (2003).

worked to siphon off state resources and protect the scheme from investigation extended to the state audit office, the attorney general, and the justice tribunal.

Criminal embezzlement from the state does not necessarily originate with criminals. Traditional politicians may experience a slow but constant decay in their ethical and moral standards, as they cease to represent public interests in order to enrich themselves. José Ignacio Ferreira, a politician with a political career spanning more than three decades, was elected governor of Espírito Santo in 1998.[52] Ferreira would soon become a lame duck, following a scandal that involved the financing of his electoral campaign. An investigation by the electoral justice discovered that Ferreira had granted himself a loan by the state-owned bank Banestes to cover the deficit of his campaign for governor in 1998. He had also abused state resources to back "his" candidates during the 2000 municipal elections. He managed to elect seventy-six of the seventy-seven mayors in Espírito Santo. Once the investigation against Ferreira's campaign financing began, he lost the power to oppose Gratz.

The Double-Edged Sword of Entering Politics

Corporatism has prevented the legislature from imposing sanctions on its members. In the case of the *mensalão*, where forty members of the ruling coalition of the Lula government were accused of having received monthly payments for their support of the government, only three were expelled from congress, despite protests by the media and civil society. In addition, several drug barons have run for election in order to avoid prosecution. However, election to office is a double-edged sword. Parliamentary hearings, investigations by the federal police, and the collection of data on cases pending against national legislators by civil society organizations have dogged some of these political elites. When it comes to accusations of involvement with organized crime, the political elite in the legislature has been more sensitive. In the past twenty years four federal representatives allegedly connected to organized crime have been forced from office; three of them were in their first term.

During the 1990 runoffs in the gubernatorial race in Rondonia, a state bordering Bolivia, the leading candidate, Senator Olavo Pires, was killed by a hired gunman before speaking at a rally in the capital. He was rumored to have been involved in drug trafficking; pamphlets saying "Do not vote for the drug trafficker" were anonymously distributed during the campaign. Pires, a

---

52. Ferreira was a municipal legislator (1963–67), a state legislator (1967–69), a senator (1983–91 and 1995–98), and governor of Espírito Santo (1999–2002). He was a founding father of the Partido da Social Democracia Brasileira (PSDB) when it moved out of the Partido do Movimento Democrático Brasileiro (PMDB) in 1988 and was the leader of the government in the Senate during the Collor government (1991–92).

businessman who entered politics in 1982, when he was elected national representative, remained in the national legislature until 1994. He always denied any links to organized crime. Investigations into his murder did not confirm his innocence or identify the people who hired the assassin. The behavior of the political elite immediately before and after his assassination made it clear that any connection to Pires was politically toxic.[53]

A year later Jabes Rabelo was forced from office in the same state, and in the following years two national lawmakers from the same state, Nobel Moura (1993) and Rachel Candido (1994), were forced to resign for allegedly taking part in organized crime. Although Rondonia had the highest concentration of scandals, other frontier states faced similar problems. The sacking of Pascoal in the state of Acre for involvement with organized crime occurred in 1999, for example.

In other states, the penetration of criminals into elected office seems to be limited to the state legislature. In 2009 Wallace Souza, a representative from the state of Amazonas, was charged with leading a criminal organization that was involved in drug trafficking, assassinations, and other crimes. Souza, a former police officer who had been expelled from the forces to later start a career as a TV reporter, aimed at creating a climate of political instability, just to be appointed head of the police forces himself.[54] The following year, two of Wallace's brothers, Carlos and Fausto Souza—deputy major and municipal councilor, respectively, in the capital city of Manaus in the state of Amazonas—lost their positions based on a judicial order. They were accused of being involved in criminal rings and of obstructing investigations while in office.[55]

In 2010 the electoral justice charged Luiz Claudio de Oliveira, a local councilor in the city of Rio de Janeiro, with elections tampering in 2008. He was accused of having close ties to the local drug traffickers in Rocinha, the largest favela in Rio de Janeiro, of colluding with the drug kingpins to force voters to elect the candidate, and of preventing candidates from campaigning in the neighborhood. Luiz Claudio eventually earned 73 percent of his votes in the Rocinha. In 2010 Luiz Claudio was campaigning for a seat as a state representative when he suddenly died of a heart attack.[56]

The infiltration of organized crime in Brazilian politics has advanced more rapidly at the municipal and state levels, as these seats often go unchallenged by insiders and are ignored by institutional checks and balances. In addition, local

---

53. According to Sardinha (2009), there were no senators at Pires's funeral except his colleagues from the state of Rondonia. This was considered an affront by Pires's family, which refused to have the corpse brought to Congress for official mourning.
54. "Deputado do Amazonas é investigado" (2009).
55. "Fausto Souza será afastado amanhã" (2010).
56. "Leslie Leitão e Paula Sarapu" (2010).

media are less independent, and civil society tends to be weaker. Local and state authorities and law enforcement agencies are often involved in a dense network of organized crime. Intervention by federal agencies is often the only way to fight organized crime as it takes hold.

At the national level, investigative journalism, strong civil society organizations, and peer pressure by representatives from other states who want to protect their reputations have cut short the political careers of several criminals. Institutional reforms, discussed in the section that follows, have also made it more difficult for corrupt elected officials to conspire with organized crime.

Institutional Reforms and Policies

Given the variety of motives and markets for the nexus of politics and organized crime to thrive, reform policies and institutional remedies require attention to many topics. The following recommendations focus on cross-cutting and overlapping fields. These recommendations include political finance rules that sanction false statements about campaign funding, law enforcement agencies that are independent enough to withstand external interference, and accountable political institutions.

Political Finance Rules

The system of election and party financing in Brazil emphasizes reporting and public disclosure of income and expenses. While public oversight by the electoral justice has improved step by step in the last decade, Brazil's Electoral Court still lacks the capacity to audit the information submitted by candidates. Electoral authorities need to upgrade this capacity so as to detect fraudulent reporting on the financing of parties and elections campaigns.

There are no severe penalties for the accountants and authorities responsible for signing off on reports that are incomplete or fraudulent. In the case of inconsistencies, election authorities simply request that the information be corrected. This system does not guarantee accurate information on income and expenses during elections. Full transparency is essential for detecting inconsistencies in income and expenses of campaign funding. Where large amounts of donations can flow unchecked through the system, it is easy for hidden donations from organized crime to blend in. Only when campaign funding became subject to accounting standards and gross misstatements were treated as a criminal offense were state oversight institutions and civil society able to detect large donations from organized crime.

In addition to strengthening the investigative capacity by sanctioning misreporting, the information on political financing must be released so that the citizenry can cast informed votes and withdraw support from parties that do not abide by such standards. The current system of rendering accounts on campaign expenses is based on ex-post information.[57] The information on campaign donations should be available during the campaign. Such a system would make it harder to tamper with the numbers after the accurate reporting of income and expenses.

In addition, caps on campaign expenses would make oversight for both state agencies and watchdogs more feasible. The Brazilian system of ceilings allows each party to set the ceiling on the campaign expenses of its candidates. Limiting campaign spending to a ceiling valid for each candidate would limit the race to outspend rivals and therefore lessen the role of money in election campaigns. In addition, politicians whose campaign activities are incompatible with the ceiling would be easier for the media and civil society to detect and question and for law enforcement agencies to sanction.

Self-financing campaigns can imply that a candidate has private wealth or is using illegal funds. It is easy for a candidate to receive money and then channel it into his or her own campaign war chest. To close this loophole, the ability of candidates to fund their own campaigns must be limited. There are also reports of campaign donations being used to launder money. Measures strengthening accurate reporting can limit the flow of dirty money into politics.

Independent Law Enforcement Agencies

Legislators are able to negotiate favors from law enforcement agencies—namely, the police—because of these agencies' lack of independence. Strengthening the independence of the police chiefs is an important measure to keep parliamentarians from peddling their influence with the police to criminals. A national correctional authority for police forces, such as Brazil's oversight agencies for judiciary and prosecuting agencies, would introduce national standards of investigation and training and help fight corruption.[58]

One of the prime objectives of organized criminals seeking access to elected officeholders is to intervene in law enforcement agencies. Individual legislators' influence on governments and law enforcement agencies goes back to weak political parties. Strong political parties can efficiently oversee the government and support independent law enforcement institutions.

---

57. In 2006 an amendment to the 1995 election law required candidates to provide public information on campaign expenses before election day. However, candidates must submit detailed information on the sources of campaign donations not earlier than one month after the election.

58. The Conselho Nacional do Judiciário and the Conselho Nacional do Ministerio Público are two correctional institutions created in 2004 by Constitutional Amendment 45 (December 30, 2004) that have contributed to investigating and punishing the misbehavior of corrupt officeholders.

Accountable Political Institutions

In the aftermath of authoritarian rule, safeguards against abuse of government power have been in the forefront of the discussion. Since then, the focus has shifted to accountability. The practice of parliamentarians policing themselves has been of limited usefulness in Brazil. The cancellation of a congressional investigation when a representative resigns before the investigation has started and the suspension of investigative procedures by Congress when a mandate expires have allowed many representatives who have behaved questionably to escape sanctions.

Lawmakers are also well protected from external control. Institutions like the *foro privilegiado* (the right to be sentenced by higher courts only) and the immunity of officeholders have come under public criticism. There have been significant adjustments in the way that law enforcement agencies initiate procedures against lawmakers. In the past, Congress had to agree with requests by the Supreme Court to accuse a member of Congress, and by endlessly postponing the decision it would de facto deny these requests. Although the rule introduced in 2005 grants the Supreme Court the right to open accusations against a member of Congress, Congress can stop such procedures at any time.[59] In practice, however, this minor change has had a significant impact on investigations against lawmakers. It has enabled the Supreme Court to prosecute an increasing number of parliamentarians, since Congress could no longer delay investigations simply by taking no action.

Brazilian lawmakers have been pressured to pass legislation with stronger criteria for eligibility for office. A law requiring a "clean record" (*ficha limpa*) for candidates standing for elected office precludes anyone with criminal convictions from running.[60] The new law was approved after intense pressure from civil society organizations. This rule, which was partially in effect during the 2010 elections, should have a positive impact on the selection of political candidates.[61] The *ficha limpa* requirement should prevent members of criminal organizations from running for office. The ban is limited to a conviction in a state court in the three years preceding the election. It reflects a new balance set by

---

59. Dantas (2005); Constitutional Amendment 35, December 20, 2001.

60. The Clean Record Law (*lei da ficha limpa*) is an amendment to the law on ineligibility (Law Complementar 135, June 4, 2010).

61. Some candidates excluded from running in 2010 questioned the validity of the law for the 2010 elections. The Brazilian constitution prohibits changes in the electoral rules starting one year before election day. In a decision delayed until March 2011 (six months after the election), the court suspended the validity of the law for the 2010 elections, thus upholding the rule for upcoming elections.

the election law between the right of citizens to run for office and the right of the community to be represented by people of integrity.

Summing Up

Campaign finance is not always the channel that links criminal groups to elected officeholders, and if such a connection exists, it is hard to prove. Fighting organized crime requires taking into account many economic and social factors involving criminal enterprises. This chapter suggests ways to sever the links between organized crime and elected officeholders, based on a careful analysis of their symbiotic relationship. In Brazil protection and business opportunities are traded for personal benefit and for supporting election or reelection.

The complicity of Brazilian lawmakers with organized crime has reached a critical point. At the national level, both the political culture and checks and balances have exposed and expelled lawmakers with criminal connections. At the state level, however, there are close connections between organized crime and elected politicians, and lawmakers tend to intervene in favor of organized criminals on a case-by-case basis. There are also signs of lawmakers influencing law enforcement and protecting criminal entrepreneurs. In a number of cases, both institutional and cultural mechanisms in defense of integrity have failed, and federal intervention has been necessary to oust corrupt politicians who had managed to capture the state. Organized criminals who have got into politics have caused some of these situations. In other cases the moral standards of members of the traditional political elite had collapsed.

Going forward, however, the signs are hopeful. The clean record law (*ficha limpa*) is a case in point, supporting as it does the right of the people to be represented by law-abiding citizens.

References

Alves Filho, Garibaldi. 2006. "CPI dos Bingos." Final report. Brasilia: Senado Federal.

Arias, Enrique Desmond. 2006. *Drugs and Democracy in Rio de Janeiro: Trafficking, Social Networks, and Public Security*. University of North Carolina Press.

Assembleia Legislativa do Estado de São Paulo. 1999. "Relatório Final da CPI do crime organizado."

Bailey, John, and Matthew M. Taylor. 2009. "Evade, Corrupt, or Confront? Organized Crime and the State in Brazil and Mexico." *Journal of Politics in Latin America* 2: 3–29.

Cavallaro, James Louis, and Raquel Ferreira Dodge. 2007. "Understanding the São Paulo Attacks." *ReVista: Harvard Review of Latin America* (Spring): 53–55.

Dantas, Adriano Mesquita. 2005. "A imunidade parlamentar formal: uma análise crítica da Emenda Constitucional 35." *Jus Navigandi, Teresina*, August 19.

"Defesa aberta." 1999. *Istoé,* November 6.
"Deputado do Amazonas é investigado por envolvimento com crime organizado." 2009. *Globo,* August 2.
"Entenda a crise no Espírito Santo, chamado de Estado sem lei." 2003. Redação Folha Online. Folha de São Paulo, March 24.
"Fausto Souza será afastado amanhã." 2010. *A Crítica,* July 20.
Fleischer, David Verge. 1994. *Manipulações casuísticas do sistema eleitoral durante o período militar, ou como usualmente o feitiço voltava contra o feiticeiro.* Brasília: UnB.
Garzón, Juan Carlos. 2008. *Mafia & Co. The Criminal Networks in Mexico, Brazil, and Colombia.* Washington: Wilson Center.
Godson, Roy, ed. 2003. *Menace to Society: Political-Criminal Collaboration around the World.* Piscataway, N.Y.: Transaction.
Gratz, José Carlos. 2002. Interview. *Vida Brasil,* August 15.
Iunes, Ivan. 2010. "Lobby forte pela legalização dos bingos." *Correiro Brasiliense,* March 10.
"Leslie Leitão e Paula Sarapu: Vereador Claudinho da Academia morre de enfarte." 2010. *O Dia,* June 19.
Lima, Maurício. 2003. "Falta de decoro." *Veja,* March 5.
Magalhães, F. Ganhou. 2005. "Leva, só vale o que está escrito. Experiências de bicheiros na cidade do Rio de Janeiro: 1890–1960." Ph.D. dissertation, Universidade Federal do Rio de Janeiro.
Marchetti, Vitor. 2008. "Governança Eleitoral: O Modelo Brasileiro de Justiça Eleitoral." *Dados: Revista de Ciências Sociais, Rio de Janeiro* 51, no. 4: 865–93.
Meireles, Andrei, and Gustavo Krieger. 2012a. "Bicho de campanha." *Weekly Journal.* February 16.
———. 2012b. "Redação: Waldomiro Diniz é condenado a 12 anos de prisão." *Weekly Journal,* March 3.
Mingardi, Guaracy. 1996. "O Estado e o crime organizado." Ph.D. dissertation, Universidade de São Paulo.
Misse, Michel. 1999. "Malandros, marginais e vagabundos & a acumulação social da violência no Rio de Janeiro." Ph.D. dissertation, Instituto Universitário de Pesquisas do Rio de Janeiro.
———. 2007. "Mercados ilegais, redes de proteção e organização local do crime no Rio de Janeiro." *Estudos Avançados* 21, no. 61: 139–57.
"O caso Maura Fraga." 2001. *Observatorio da Imprensa,* January 29.
Oliveira, Adriano, and Jorge Zaverucha. 2006. "Tráfico de Drogas. Uma Revisão Bibliográfica." *Revista Brasileira de Informação Bibliográfica em Ciências Sociais* 62, no. 2: 5–17.
Pinto-Duschinsky, Michael. 1999. "Organized Corruption, Corruption, and Political Financing: A Foreign Perspective." Washington: IFES.
Procópio, Argemiro. 1999. *O Brasil no mundo das drogas.* 2nd ed. Petrópolis: Vozes.
Reuter, Peter. 1983. *Disorganized Crime: The Economics of the Visible Hand.* MIT Press.
Sadek, Teresa. 1996. "Justiça eleitoral." São Paulo: Fundação Konrad Adenauer.
Sardinha, Edson. 2009. Series of articles on Senator Olavo Pires. *Congresso em Foco,* March 2–5.

Silva, Allesandro. 2002. "Investigação da PF revela poder do ex-garimpeiro Leonardo Dias." *Folha de São Paulo*, December 15.
Speck, Bruno Wilhelm. 2005. "Reagir a escândalos ou perseguir ideais? A regulação do financiamento político no Brasil." *Cadernos Adenauer* 6, no. 2: 123–59.
Speck, Bruno Wilhelm, and Mauro Macedo Campos. 2011. "The Impact of State Funding and Private Funding on the Brazilian Party System: An Analysis of Rules and Practice on the National Level." Paper prepared for the IPSA-ECPR Joint Conference, Whatever Happened to North-South? University of São Paulo, February 16–19.
Teixeira, Carla Costa. 2001. "Os usos da indisciplina, Decoro e estratégias parlamentares." Série Antropologia 307. Departamento de Antropologia, Universidad de Brasília.
Torgan, Moroni. 2000. "Relatório da Comissão Parlamentar de Inquerito destinada a investigar o avanço e a impunidade do narcotráfico." Brazil Congresso Nacional, Camara dos Deputados.
United Nations. 1975. "Changes in Forms and Dimensions of Criminality: Transnational and National." Fifth United Nations Congress on the Prevention of Crime and the Treatment of Offenders.
Weber, Demétrio. 2010. "Em discussão na Câmara, proposta de legalização do bingo é criticada por integrantes do governo." *Globo Agencia Camara*, March 30.
Zaluar, Alba. 2004. *Integração perversa: pobreza e tráfico de drogas*. Rio de Janeiro: Editora da FGV.

MAURICIO RUBIO

4
Colombia: Coexistence, Legal Confrontation, and War with Illegal Armed Groups

Efforts to regulate campaign financing and political parties in Colombia came relatively late in the country's history. Despite early discussions and proposals in the 1950s by both major parties—the Liberals and the Conservatives—and the Alberto Lleras Camargo administration (1958–62), Congress failed to pass any legislation on the matter. During this period, as Eduardo Pizarro (1998) argues, representatives in Congress made it clear that they were unwilling to rein in political parties.[1] There was also a profound lack of interest in key aspects of party organization, given the traditional emphasis on democracy as a system to deliver social equality rather than a set of procedures for the establishment of government.[2]

But by the mid-1980s Colombia could neglect the issue no longer. Two threats to the system, namely drug-trafficking money in politics and the demands of the *guerrilleros*, helped usher in, for the first time in the country's history, political financing regulations defining the role of the state in funding electoral campaigns. While these crises served as a catalyst for reform, the political turbulence they caused also hampered progress.

In the years before the first set of reforms, it was evident that Colombian democracy was tainted by drug money. In 1983 Pablo Escobar had managed to infiltrate Nuevo Liberalismo (NL), a dissident party whose platform was the fight against corruption. After being expelled from NL, Escobar joined Alternativa Popular, a faction of the majority Liberal Party, which led him to win a seat in the House of Representatives. While in Congress, Escobar promoted debates against the NL, because that party had received checks from drug traffickers. In addition to the drug lord's infamous role in politics, the murder of Rodrigo

---

1. Pizarro (1998).
2. Posada-Carbó (2008).

Lara Bonilla, minister of justice at the time, was still fresh and deeply troubling to politicians and the general public. The incident was the apex of a series of disagreements, mutual breaches, and retaliations between the Belisario Betancur administration (1982–86) and the drug cartels that allegedly had supported his campaign. Following Lara's assassination, the government intensified the war against the drug lords, including enforcement of the extradition treaty with the United States.

Although under immense pressure from powerful drug cartels to turn a blind eye to their meddling in politics, the establishment pressed ahead with discussions on a political financing framework in the context of the war it was waging against left-wing *guerrilleros*. Interestingly, electoral financing and political parties emerged as top issues of a common agenda between the government and the *guerrilleros*, contained in President Betancur's ambitious program of peace negotiations. The government was primarily interested in weakening the role of drug cartels in politics and ending embarrassing scandals, but it also understood that the two-party system was broken and that the *guerrilleros* wanted to create a more participatory regime that moved Colombia beyond the hegemony of the two major parties. As corruption eroded the administration's legitimacy and the government fought drug traffickers, the *guerrilleros* sought legal recognition of nontraditional parties and movements.

It was in this context that in 1985 the Congress passed the first law to regulate political parties in Colombia. Law 58 introduced partial and indirect public financing of election campaigns and revamped the old Electoral Court, whose mandate had until then been limited to elections. The Electoral Court became the National Electoral Council, or NEC, and its new responsibilities included legally recognizing political parties as well as regulating their activities and funding. Law 58 focused on private contributions and only included indirect public funding, such as free access to the state media, financial help for advertising, and free postage and printing services.

With respect to private funds, the new legislation allowed individuals and corporations to make contributions both in cash and in kind. A cap was imposed on private contributions as well as on the amount that a presidential candidate could spend on his campaign from his own assets. In addition, the campaign period was limited to ninety days, and parties were required to register their accounting books with the electoral authorities and to make this information public.

By 1991—during the second phase of electoral finance reforms—the political landscape had significantly changed, with the integration of a former guerrilla organization into mainstream politics. But the pressure on the government—from both drug traffickers and guerrillas—remained unabated just as in the 1980s. The Alianza Democrática M-19, a political party that resulted from the peace agreement with the guerrilla group that, at that time, was closest to the drug lords, won a substantial fraction of the National Constituent Assembly delegates. The government conducted part of the discussion on political reform while at the same time negotiating Pablo Escobar's arrest conditions. Indeed, Escobar surrendered the same day the assembly approved the ban on extradition of nationals. Corruption allegations, including bribery of delegates by the Cali cartel, remained common.

In 1991, also to combat corruption and promote wider political participation, the assembly took action on the need to expand the public financing of political parties and campaigns. Public funding was seen as a way to mitigate the *auxilios parlamentarios*, a patronage system whereby members of Congress can assign infrastructure projects at their discretion to areas with influence. These government appropriations, which turned into massive pork barrel projects, reached 1 percent of the national budget and became a major source of corruption. As a result the 1985 rules governing indirect funding remained the same, including candidates' access to public television, but new legislation introduced direct, albeit partial, public financing of parties and campaigns.

Significantly, the new political finance laws were elevated to the constitutional level and became enshrined in the 1991 constitution. The legal framework was designed to overhaul the entrenched bipartisan structure of politics that the guerrillas often denounced. One of the constitution's pillars, which arose from efforts to negotiate with the insurgency, was the understanding that Colombian democracy needed to include a wide range of political parties and movements. Concretely, this meant a move from representative democracy to a more participatory model. In redefining Colombian democracy, the constitution introduced electoral rules that, in fact, weakened an already fragile party system and undermined several mechanisms of direct democracy.[3] The result was a very fragmented political landscape.

It was not until 1994, with the Basic Statute of Political Parties and Movements, or Law 130, that Congress translated the constitution into clear and enforceable legal provisions. The lag of almost three years is testament to the difficulties that the constitutional guidelines encountered in Congress. But more important, the timing of the passage is telling of the influence of drug money in Colombian politics. Three months before the approval of Law 130, a presidential campaign-funding scandal broke out concerning an agreement that was forged between the government and the Cali cartel in Madrid a year earlier. Even after the adoption of the law, the NEC played no role in solving the scandal, thereby exposing some of the shortcomings of the reform effort.

3. Posada-Carbó (2008).

Although the aforementioned scandal shook Colombians and prompted extended discussions on the topic of political finance once more, the crisis did not lead to congressional action. A few months after taking office, Ernesto Samper Pizano (who stood accused of illegally financing his presidential campaign) created the Commission for the Reform of Political Parties. One of the key proposals of this commission was precisely to amend the current provisions regarding political financing. The NEC proposed legislation, and the administration that followed also proposed political reform bills, but Congress failed to pass them. The main argument was that the proposals did not address the fundamental problems of the country.[4]

Quite apart from the need for new legislation, enforcement has also been a challenge in Colombia. For one, the National Electoral Council, which is responsible for the regulation of political parties and electoral campaigns, has always been a precarious institution. The fact that the NEC has scarce resources and limited power, in addition to having a partisan structure and membership, has made it impossible to control parties' resources. As it stands today, the NEC is better endowed "to resolve conflicts of interest between the parties than to monitor their excesses."[5]

The extreme fragmentation of parties—a consequence of both the new constitutional framework of 1991 and the steady decline in party loyalty—only compounded the problems associated with a weak NEC. The number of players eligible for public funds multiplied, and naturally, the cost of campaigns increased. By allowing not only parties but also associations, movements, and even individual candidates to receive electoral funds, including public subsidies, and by granting full discretion in the expenditure of these resources, the legal regime unraveled. Party anarchy and the virtual privatization of electoral campaigns were the result. With hundreds of lists of candidates for the Senate and the House, the supervisory and management role of the NEC became untenable.[6] In short, campaign finance reforms until the 1990s proved to be detached from the practical considerations of implementation and enforcement.

In 2005 Law 996 was passed to regulate the election of the president, but it dealt mostly with hiring by the government before the elections, not with the financing of campaigns. Today Colombia has a mixed political finance system. Both the state and individuals channel funds to political parties and electoral campaigns. In addition, there are limits to the amount that parties can spend and the private contributions they can accept. For presidential campaigns, there

4. Posada-Carbó (2008, p. 14).
5. Pizarro (1998, p. 36).
6. Pizarro (1998, p. 39).

is an overall cap on private funding, as well as a ceiling on individual contributions, of 2 percent of total campaign expenditures. The bulk of the funding—approximately 80 percent—must come from the public treasury. While a fragment of the money is disbursed before elections, the number of votes determines the amount that parties and candidates ultimately receive. There are similar ceilings and controls for those running for Congress. The state also partially funds internal party referendums for candidate nominations.

The National Electoral Council allocates and administers these public resources. All political organizations financed with taxpayer money must report their annual income and expenses as well as the specific allocation of public funds. Once the NEC reviews and approves the reports, national newspapers make them public. It is worth underscoring that the legal system of political finance in Colombia is still based on the legislation and decisions of the NEC and, since 1991, on the constitution.[7] The privileged status that political finance laws have in Colombia is unique in Latin America and is a product of its turbulent history.[8]

The arguments for regulating political finance in Latin America as a whole are varied. Apart from those related to ensuring competition, eliminating financial barriers to political activity, and achieving more transparency, a recurrent concern has been to avoid "what happened in Colombia." The region now understands quite well that "dirty or illicit money corrupts the system and undermines the rule of law."[9]

This chapter puts forth the argument that the idea of a criminal organization corrupting a democratic system by seeking legal benefits is overly simplistic. This caricature of reality ignores the fact that not all drug lords are created equal: some provide financial support to politicians, others resort to direct proselytizing, and still others show a total disregard for public life. In addition, one cannot overlook the symbiotic and long-standing relationship that exists between the Colombian elite and illegal actors. Indeed, a fraction of the political class has had a long tradition of partnerships with informal and illegal activities.

The account of the relationship between political finance and organized crime in Colombia over the past four decades reveals that the dynamics of illegal political finance can be understood only in the wider context of political negotiations, nonfinancial agreements, legal confrontations, and all-out war between organized crime and the political establishment.

---

7. Law 58 of 1985, Law 130 of 1994, and Law 996 of 2005. See also Montoya and Navarrete (2009); de la Calle (1998).

8. According to Pizarro (1998), the other exception is Brazil.

9. Payne and Cruz Perusia (2007, p. 78).

Finally, the chapter draws testable hypotheses from the Colombian experience, discusses the public policy implications, and captures the lessons learned from the Colombian case.

Organized Crime and Political Finance: The Actors

Colombia's illegal armed actors exhibit two styles over two generations. Colombian armed barons of the first generation, roughly extending from the 1980s to the end of the century, generally fit one of two styles: the entrepreneur or the political warrior. Among the entrepreneurs were drug traffickers and emerald traders. Guerrillas fall into the political warrior category, while the paramilitaries are a mixed group, with both business and political elements. These distinctions are widely recognized by the general public and even acknowledged by drug traffickers. Virgina Vallejo, a former anchorwoman, Pablo Escobar's lover, and close friend of Gilberto Rodriguez Orejuela (head of the Cali cartel), summed it up: "I cannot help thinking that those surrounding Pablo are always talking about politics, while those surrounding Gilberto only talk about business."[10]

The second generation—composed of the descendants, lieutenants, employees, and persecutors of the first *capos*—is far more varied and less visible. They have become more specialized and focused on the business of drug trafficking and generally show less interest in politics. Without attempting to provide an exhaustive account of how these actors support and interact with politicians, the rest of the chapter shows the diversity of approaches that Colombian *narcos* have taken toward politics.

The Medellin Cartel: Business, Politics, and War

Pablo Escobar, the head of the Medellin cartel, had a long criminal career that started at a young age.[11] While in school, he had many followers and commanded respect—his popularity being partly due to his money, which he began to earn by distributing smuggled cigarettes in neighborhood shops. It was with Alfredo Gomez, an influential local politician, that Escobar and his cousin Gustavo Gaviria became serious criminals. Gomez, popularly known as The Godfather, made a fortune as a smuggler while maintaining his status as a respected public figure in Envigado, a small town near Medellin. Pablo Escobar also took notice of his grandfather, Roberto Gaviria, who had chosen a similar

---

10. Vallejo (2007).
11. Based on Castro Caycedo (1996); Salazar (2001); Bowden (2001); Legarda (2005); Salazar Pineda (2006); Vallejo (2007).

lifestyle. According to Doña Hermilda, Pablo Escobar's mother, her father lived in Cañasgordas and became mayor of the town, but "above everything, he was a smuggler."[12] Escobar first learned the tricks of the trade from his grandfather's practice of transporting liquor in coffins. Later, while working as a bodyguard for Gomez, Escobar met weapons experts and others who formed part of his web of illicit activities.

Unlike the Rodriguez Orejuela brothers of the Cali cartel, whose links to politics came later in their careers, Escobar showed talent and ambition for public life from an early age. He spent his childhood at the estate of Joaquín Vallejo, his real godfather, a wealthy politician from Antioquia and a former state minister. At school, Escobar was elected president of the Student Welfare Council and was known for stealing answers to tests and distributing them to his classmates. He had leftist leanings but mainly wanted to be rich.

By age twenty-five, and while working for Gomez, Escobar was deeply involved in illicit trade but was also interested in his boss's political activities. During the 1974 elections, Gomez supported the Conservative Party's presidential candidate, Belisario Betancur, as well as several candidates for the Senate and House of Representatives. Even though Betancur lost, several individuals on Gomez's payroll won congressional seats. This incident became public and prompted a debate in Congress, which Escobar followed in great detail by collecting press clippings. A skilled lawyer, Guido Parra, defended Gomez in these proceedings, and Escobar became ever more mesmerized by his boss's power. That same year, the novice kingpin was arrested for stealing a vehicle, and he shared his time in prison with Gomez, who had been arrested for carrying smuggled goods in military trucks. Gomez's generosity toward poor prisoners—and the fact that politicians of national stature, such as Alberto Santofimio, visited him—also made an impression on Pablo Escobar.

Shortly after being released from the penitentiary, Escobar became a populist local leader and surrounded himself with powerful leftists. He organized and funded nearly a hundred neighborhood committees to undertake community projects. He sought to eradicate the slums of Medellin with the construction of 5,000 homes, partnering with the former director of city planning, who offered a plot of land for each house. (Later he would serve as intermediary for a negotiated solution to the confrontation between the government and the drug traffickers.) Escobar's political vocation was further buttressed by the influence of an uncle, who was a union leader, and by the alliance with Carlos Lehder, a drug lord from Armenia, a nearby city of coffee growers. Lehder, also a member of the Medellin cartel, had his own political party, edited a newspaper, and aligned

---

12. Salazar (2001, p. 37).

himself with some members of the M-19 guerrilla group. He was famous for his radical speeches and for giving a plane to the governor of his *departmento*, or district. With a blend of fascism, Marxism, antiimperialism, and patriotic doctrine, Lehder boasted that he used an island in the Bahamas as a base for flooding the "American enemy" with cocaine.

Social work in poor neighborhoods led Escobar to dig deep into politics, and in 1982 he campaigned for a seat in the House of Representatives. The presidential contenders were Alfonso López Michelsen and Alberto Santofimio, from the Liberal Party, and Belisario Betancur, a Conservative Party candidate. Representing Nuevo Liberalismo, an antipatronage movement, the nominee was Luis Carlos Galan, a scrupulous man. Jairo Ortega, a former lawyer for Gomez, wanted to join Galan and invited Escobar to run for Congress. At a rally in Medellin, however, Galan and one of his closest collaborators, Rodrigo Lara Bonilla, publicly rejected Ortega and Escobar—an affront that the drug lords would never forgive. They then joined Santofimio, who encouraged Escobar's political career, noting that "with your money and intelligence it is certain that you will be president of Colombia."[13] Ortega ended up winning the congressional post, which he alternated with Escobar. A few months later, the Spanish Socialist Party officially invited Escobar and Alberto Santofimio Botero to Madrid for the inauguration of Felipe Gonzalez as president of the Spanish Government. That same year, *Semana* magazine devoted a lengthy cover story to Pablo Escobar, calling him Antioquia's Robin Hood.

Another outcome of the 1982 elections was the rise to the presidency of Belisario Betancur, who then appointed Rodrigo Lara Bonilla as his minister of justice. Lara Bonilla then decided to wage war against drug traffickers. Irritated, Ortega and Escobar prepared congressional hearings against Lara Bonilla. Ortega accused him of receiving dirty money to finance the Nuevo Liberalismo campaign with Galan, presenting as evidence a copy of a check drawn by the drug trafficker Evaristo Porras to finance the campaign and a video recording of Porras's meeting with Lara Bonilla. It was all a trap, which Escobar had planned in retaliation for his public expulsion from Galan's movement. Lara Bonilla's response, when faced with the scandal, was to step up action against drug traffickers.

Lara Bonilla managed to lift Escobar's parliamentary immunity to reopen proceedings against him for murder, and Escobar publicly renounced politics. An arrest warrant for extradition was issued against Lehder, and in March 1984 government authorities destroyed Tranquilandia, a large cocaine-processing center. In May of that year Lara Bonilla was murdered, in Bogota. A couple of

---

13. Salazar (2001, p. 92).

months following the assassination, an important meeting between Colombian politicians and drug traffickers took place in Panama.

Excluding the plan to frame Lara Bonilla and the support of a few political friends, little is known about Escobar's financing of campaigns or political parties. It is likely that he considered this kind of support ineffective. Indeed, his major achievements—and there were many of them—resulted from kidnappings rather than from bribing politicians.[14] As an example of his influence, Escobar even managed, through his lawyers, to make contact with the U.S. attorney general and offer information against the guerrillas in exchange for amnesty.[15]

Escobar claimed to be the ruler of the underworld, and as such, he collected taxes from other drug traffickers and earned a unique level of financial and political autonomy. Out of fear of retribution, many drug dealers would make the payments.[16] Escobar also believed, up until the end, that he held sway over mainstream society. In an interview days before his death by shooting—which resulted from one of the darkest alliances between the mafia and the Colombian and U.S. governments—Escobar said, "I do not think it was a mistake [to go into politics]. I am sure that if I had participated in the next election I would have won overwhelmingly over all politicians in Antioquia."[17]

Mostly Business: The Cali Cartel

In sharp contrast to Pablo Escobar, the leaders of the Cali cartel led mostly apolitical careers, managing parallel legal and illegal businesses.[18] Gilberto Rodriguez started as a drugstore messenger, moving thereafter to own a pharmaceutical empire. Behind the façade of a legal and successful business lay links to the Cali underworld. Along with his brother, Miguel, he headed a gang called Los Chemas, supposedly left-wing revolutionaries, and generated money by abducting people.

In 1972 the brothers founded Drogas La Rebaja, a drugstore chain that would eventually handle about half of the pharmaceutical market in Colombia. This business, which sold medicine at prices up to 30 percent less than its competitors, served as a money-laundering machine but also as a charitable front, seemingly committed to the health of the poor. The cartel acquired 66 percent of Banco de los Trabajadores, and although it was never proven, this was apparently the first major financial institution to wash drug dollars. In the mid-eighties, the cartel sold this stake to the corrupt politician Rafael Forero Fetecua. By 1978 the Cali cartel had gained control of a bank in Panama. In addition to having a foot in

14. Rubio (2005).
15. Bowden (2001, p. 68).
16. Reyes (2007, p. 54).
17. Bowden (2001, p. 192).
18. Based on Chaparro (2005); Téllez and Lesmes (2006).

the drug and bank markets, it bought a chain of radio stations, which went on to become the third biggest chain in Colombia.

Following the assassination of Minister Lara Bonilla and the Betancur government's decision to enforce the extradition treaty, Gilberto Rodriguez fled to Brazil and then to Spain, where he was arrested along with Jorge Luis Ochoa, a colleague of Pablo Escobar's in the Medellin cartel. Rodriguez managed to avoid extradition to the United States through legal loopholes. In the end, he was sent to his own country and soon set free. This episode shows the immense power and legal muscle that drug lords commanded.

Suspicion about Drogas La Rebaja's ties to drug trafficking arose in the late 1980s, when bombs attributed to Pablo Escobar destroyed almost a hundred stores of the chain. Despite these attacks and several criminal investigations, a sophisticated legal team managed to keep the business running. By this time, the magnitude of the illegal business was such that Miguel Rodriguez conceived a kind of OPEC to regulate the world price of cocaine. Through taxes on all dealers, he wanted to fund payments to politicians who would help legalize their fortunes as well as to finance campaigns to take on common enemies. It was not until then that the Rodriguez Orejuela brothers began to seriously consider forging high-level political alliances to avoid extradition to the United States and to ensure that their businesses and lives ran smoothly.

By the time that the Cali cartel financed the 1994 presidential campaign, this organization was already well established. This was almost a textbook case of organized crime financing politicians in exchange for legal benefits. This instance of political involvement differed from the stereotype in that it was also a long-term personal investment for retirement and was partly motivated by philanthropy. For years, the kingpins of the Cali cartel treated politicians no differently than they did businessmen: they did not trust either. The Rodriguez brothers understood that their money would not guarantee any particular outcome, which became clear when they were subsequently arrested, and they seemed to have been aware of the diminishing marginal returns of electoral expenditure.[19] In its war against the Medellin cartel, the Cali cartel's territorial control and sophisticated intelligence network proved to be more successful than political clientelism.

Global Technocrats or Warlords: The Snitches' Cartel

The second generation of illegal armed actors in Colombia is far more diverse, complex, and inconspicuous than the first. From what is known about the heirs of the great bosses, one could conclude that the business-oriented strategy and the policy of discretion were more effective than all-out war and direct

---

19. Casas-Zamora and Zovatto (2010).

participation in politics. While the children of Escobar and Lehder completely dropped out of illicit trade, those of the Rodriguez brothers continued the model of trafficking with a veneer of legal activities.

Many of the new drug lords learned from their former bosses, while others learned about trafficking by combating it as members of security forces. Second-generation drug barons generally kept a low profile, away from politics and even from their country. Agustin Caicedo Velandia, a powerful contemporary narcotics trafficker and a former agent of the Fiscalia, or prosecutor's office, alternately lived in Argentina and Central America and sponsored drug shipments from abroad.[20] In the Drug Enforcement Agency operation in which he was captured, a former officer from the Administrative Department of Security also fell. An ex police officer who worked with the traffickers provided key information for their arrest.

A detailed description of a couple of kingpins of this new generation suggests several features. In general, we can observe a trend toward the specialization and sophistication of the business. The educational level of drug lords is also higher: there are engineers, medical doctors, professionals in finance, and even specialists in law. William, the son of Miguel Rodriguez, studied law at Harvard, for example. An extensive network of highly skilled professionals in Colombia and abroad allowed them to outsource part of the business. The owner of a route may subcontract the production of raw materials as well as the processing, transporting, and distributing of drugs. He may also export money laundering.

It is also clear that technological advancements have facilitated these and other transformations in the illicit trade. Indeed, the very changes that have eased legal trade and enabled globalization have also boosted illicit trade. New telecommunication media, vessels with global positioning systems, submarines, and the availability of synthetic cocaine are just some of the inventions from which drug dealers have greatly benefited. It is no longer necessary for the boss to have a militia, because he can purchase protection and debt-collection services in the marketplace. As a consequence, alliances with politicians have become rare. Only two politicians are known to have been involved with the notorious *neocapos* from Medellin, Juan Ramon Zapata and Gabriel Usuga, known as Los Cíclopes. The first public figure was a man from El Salvador with diplomatic status who leased his plane to transport money to Panama, and the second was an Arab prince who partnered with the kingpins to export a huge amount of cocaine from Venezuela to France.[21]

---

20. "Ex agente de CTI" (2010).
21. Reyes (2007). On the partnership between the Arab prince and the Colombians, see also Monti (2004).

The other players that gained prominence in this period were the paramilitary groups that sold protection and debt-recovery services. With the end of the Medellin and Cali cartels, most of these private armies retreated to rural areas and maintained tight political control over some villages. The leader of one of those paramilitaries is Cuco Vanoy, the Lord of Bajo Cauca, who has been compared to Pablo Escobar for his weight in the drug market and philanthropy toward the poor. Vanoy has "built playgrounds, two clinics with sophisticated equipment, community kitchens; paved roads; gave groceries, fans, chairs, sheets of zinc roofing; remodeled asylums; made donations to the Catholic, Christian, and Evangelical Churches; created the Tarazá Without Hunger program, which benefited 100 families; and paid for the tubal ligation surgery of 270 women. Populism has been his most effective strategy for conquest."[22]

In terms of organizational structure, drug-trafficking organizations went from being very hierarchical to having a fragmented and more elusive composition. This new feature had political implications and may explain the diminished interest in public life. Some argue that the motivation for engaging with politicians went from a desire to influence national decisions to a desire to tap into local power networks. This move, and the fact that scattered cells could be more easily kept clandestine, offered greater protection from the authorities.[23]

While some illicit armed actors signaled a retreat from politics, others had political ambitions—but of a different nature from those of the first generation. In the case of Los Chamizos in Santa Marta, the military leader himself became a political candidate.[24] There have also been mayors who, harassed by the guerrillas, sought protection from the paramilitaries. These paramilitaries, in turn, earned prestige, power, and political allies. The heirs of the first cartels were also willing to deal directly with the U.S. justice system and are thus known as the *cartel de los sapos* (snitches).

Politicians: Anything Goes

Traditionally, those involved in dealing with issues of organized crime and political finance have operated under the presumption that the link between drug trafficking and politics can be boiled down to bad guys corrupting mostly honest guys. The fact is, however, that the empirical record does not justify this assumption: opportunistic politicians, seduced by the profits associated with all types of contraband, plague Colombia's history.

---

22. "Cuco Vanoy" (2007).
23. Duncan (2006).
24. Zuñiga (2007, p. 243).

Background: Smuggling and Clientelism

It would be impossible to go into detail about Colombia's century of civil wars, uprisings, rebellions, violence led by politicians from the capital, amnesties, betrayals, and military dictatorships. What is critical to point out is that they all suggest a long history of weak democracy.[25] It is also worth mentioning that the rise of the M-19 urban guerrilla—a major player in drug trafficking and politics—was the result of electoral fraud in the 1970 presidential election. Indeed, some of the illegal armed actors at least initially had genuine and legitimate political grievances.

Political clientelism, understood as the granting of favors with public resources in exchange for electoral support, has a long tradition in Colombia, especially in the border cities and ports.[26] Some of Colombia's first rumors of illegal money in election campaigns emerged among the *marimberos*, the smugglers and exporters of marijuana who operated on the north coast. Several of the first congressmen accused of having links to drug traffickers were from the coast or from the departments at the border with Ecuador and Venezuela, the traditional places for smuggling.[27] A president of the Senate in the early 1970s, for instance, was the partner of a powerful smuggler and marijuana czar.

This alliance between politicians and smugglers dates back to the beginning of the nineteenth century. In a sample of sixty criminal investigations of smuggling during the first half of the 1800s, the businessmen involved were found to be "very close to the most influential politicians of the time."[28] The case of Pablo Escobar, the grandson and pupil of a smuggler, also confirms that illegal markets were training grounds for the first generation of Colombian armed actors. Another example is Santiago Ocampo, mentor of the leaders of the Medellin cartel, who began his career as a customs agent on the border with Venezuela. He was the first to establish contact with Omar Torrijos, commander of the Panamanian National Guard and de facto leader of Panama at the time, for the transit of cocaine. The first series of vendettas in Medellin, at the start of Pablo Escobar's career, was the "Marlboro war" among cigarette smugglers.

Ernesto Samper, whose presidential campaign in 1994 would be financed by the Cali cartel, began his political career in a movement made up of merchants from *sanandresitos*, or shopping centers that sold contraband goods. A speech he gave at the time perfectly illustrates the nature of his dealings: "I was with the *sanandresitos* before being a councilman. . . . Thanks to you I was taken to

---

25. See Ronderos (2003).
26. Archer (1990).
27. Castillo (1987, p. 231).
28. Meisel (2009).

the Council of Bogotá and managed to get the necessary funds for the paving of these streets.... From 1982 *sanandresitos* began to be respected. From this year on we showed that the only sin committed by *sanandresitos* is the sin of selling good, nice, and cheap products."[29]

The motivation behind dirty money in politics has not always been to protect illegal businesses, although that has certainly been important. Drug dollars have also been channeled to populist causes or used in more autonomous forms of clientelism. To illustrate this point, note the perspective of Alvaro Jimenez, a former member of the M-19, on how drugs furthered nonviolent politics:

> The conversation with people at the corner of the square or on the sidewalk was not enough to maintain the tie with the peasants. So we bought the Caracol radio station. We wanted to go into politics directly, as *autodefensas*; we did not want politicians to win our reputation. We also overhauled the stadium, financed football teams of guys who wore t-shirts, and sponsored beauty contests. And people knew it was our doing, without any help.[30]

Unreliable Partners

A recurring theme among narco-traffickers is their deep distrust of politicians and, in some cases, even open contempt toward those whom they have funded. In the speech announcing his retirement from politics—when he lost immunity in Congress and resigned his seat—Pablo Escobar declaimed against politicians and complained about politicking. He berated public servants for focusing on "the narcissistic retouch of their damaged image and ... their tottering and rotten feuds."[31] During Lara Bonilla's funeral, when President Betancur announced that he would revive extraditions to the United States, Escobar felt betrayed by what he believed to be a breach of election promises and even considered making public the evidence of tainted political contributions. Pablo Escobar and the Medellin cartel generally retaliated by killing or kidnapping those who betrayed them, and Federico Estrada's story is a case in point. Escobar demanded that Estrada, a senator, promote a favorable law; Estrada refused and, months later, was assassinated.

The leaders of the Cali cartel were no different from Escobar and the Medellin cartel in their disdain for politicians. They believed that candidates made empty promises and that, once in office, they might or might not honor agreements.

---

29. Quoted by Villar Borda (2004, pp. 289–90).
30. COPP (2002, p. 67).
31. Salazar (2001, p. 121).

In response to the criticism that he was spending too much money on bribes, Gilberto Rodriguez said: "Politicians are bandits, but you have to have them as friends or you are fucked."[32] When the journalist who served as intermediary for the financing of the 1994 campaign said to Rodriguez that Ernesto Samper was evidently a good friend, he answered: "Let's hope that the heart of that sonofabitch won't be spoiled."[33] Unlike Escobar, however, the Rodriguez brothers would usually expand bribes to reduce defections.

The Cali cartel developed two lists of politicians: in one list were their friends, which included all those who had been tested for several years and deserved their trust. In the second they placed "undesirable politicians," who were deemed unreliable but necessary. This second list also included members of Congress who they thought would align with the highest bidder. A prosecutor of the judicial trial that followed the 1994 campaign financing scandal said that the Cali leaders "knew that politicians are today with you and tomorrow with someone else. So they decided that it was best to take control by buying the largest possible number of congressmen, and the most influential."[34]

An episode that perfectly illustrates the precarious relationship between politicians and drug lords occurred in 1996, when Congress decided to debate the forfeiture law. Congressional hearings were set to find out how a vote on the law of forfeiture could have been influenced by the Rodriguez brothers, who were in prison. To prevent the investigation, the brothers sent the sponsor of the congressional debate a copy of a letter signed by him, thanking Pastor Perafan, a known drug dealer, for the financing of his campaign. The drug barons also reminded the transgressor that he was "not the only person in public life from whom they have documents and testimonial evidence of his double standards."[35] It is clear that business deals between representatives and drug lords—essentially, political finance—were characterized by constant bribes and blackmail.

Dealings with Organized Crime

The first known incident of drug-trafficking money in politics was in 1976, when a provincial deputy got arrested for trading thirty kilos of cocaine.[36] Later that year, Luis Carlos Galan said that mafias involved in the business of smuggling drugs and emeralds had "reached the point of placing their own

32. Chaparro (2005, p. 77).
33. Chaparro (2005, p. 90).
34. Chaparro (2005, p. 80).
35. Chaparro (2005, p. 300).
36. Castillo (1987, p. 225).

agents in the state administration and in Congress."[37] From then on, cases of compromised politicians came to light relatively often and involved both major parties. In 1978 members of the Conservative Party reported drug influence in the competitive race for the presidency between Liberal Julio Cesar Turbay and Conservative Belisario Betancur. The influence went beyond presidential elections: according to the U.S. ambassador, the drug traffickers "may have already bought and paid ten members of the legislature."[38] The alleged support came from the *marimberos*, the marijuana *capos* on the Atlantic coast, who were notorious for their unruly behavior and frequent vendettas. Turbay was elected, and as a consequence of pressure from the media—CBS's *60 Minutes* dedicated a report linking the new leader to drug trafficking—and the U.S. government, he ordered the destruction of crops and signed, at the time without major reactions, an extradition treaty with the United States.

The debate over narco-dollars in politics intensified during the 1982 presidential elections. The Conservative candidate, Belisario Betancur, who joined the race for the second time, was accused of having received some $300,000 for the 1978 elections from a confidant of the Ochoa brothers, who were associated with the Cali cartel.[39] For the elections that were in progress, Gustavo Gaviria—Pablo Escobar's cousin—financially supported Betancur and became part of the candidate's elections committee. Betancur responded in kind by publicly pledging not to extradite Colombians. Once elected, Betancur sent a letter to Hernando Gaviria, Escobar's uncle, thanking him for the decisive contribution to the Movimiento Nacional.

The Liberal Party showed no more respect for the rule of law during these elections. The official candidate, Alfonso López Michelsen, appointed as campaign manager his former mentee, Ernesto Samper, known for his political clientelism and links to *sanandresitos*. While touring Medellin, the two politicians and a few colleagues from Antioquia gathered at the Intercontinental Hotel with the leaders of the cartel in a meeting that lasted several hours. At the meeting the group agreed to finance the elections through a car raffle, with drug dealers buying $350,000 worth of tickets. According to one of the Ochoa brothers, contributions in fact amounted to approximately $800,000.[40] López Michelsen purportedly agreed to visit Escobar at his ranch, Nápoles, as the *capo* was interested in forging a relationship with an important and clever statesman. Despite the ruinous publicity, there are photographs of renowned politicians, including Alberto Santofimio, at the ranch and also using Escobar's Cheyenne II aircraft.

37. Quoted in Salazar (2001, p. 72).
38. Castillo (1987, p. 225).
39. Salazar (2001, p. 93).
40. Salazar (2001, p. 95).

The Liberal campaign in Medellin, however, ended up with an official deficit of about $200,000. When local politicians asked the campaign manager, Samper, for funds, he responded that he would pay when he became president. After the campaign, Samper founded a think tank, the Instituto de Estudios Liberales. It was in that same year that Escobar was expelled from the party of Luis Carlos Galan. Allied with Alberto Santofimio, he was elected to the House of Representatives.

An important feature of Colombia's story about drug money in politics is its back and forth between affability and war. During periods when rapprochement efforts collapsed, usually due to the killing of a prominent figure on either side, the parties declared open battle. To highlight this dynamic and Colombia's struggle against corruption, this section summarizes several important events: three episodes of the war on drugs, two major summits in Panama, and two scandals of narcotics financing elections.

War on Drugs: The Raid of Tranquilandia, 1984

Just two years after the 1982 scandal surrounding both the Liberal and Conservative candidates for the presidency, which suggests a cozy relationship between the government and the major cartels, members of the National Police in cooperation with the United States Drug Enforcement Agency raided and destroyed a major cocaine-processing center called Tranquilandia. The offensive occurred during the presidency of Belisario Betancur, who allegedly received campaign funds from the Cali (via the Ochoa brothers) and Medellin cartels. However, the relationship between the president and drug cartels deteriorated soon after the election period, as Betancur appointed Lara Bonilla as minister of justice and, as previously noted, the latter declared war on the illegal armed groups. Betancur himself began to treat drug traffickers with an iron fist in response to the assassination of Lara Bonilla in 1984, which explains the raid and his decision to reconsider extraditing criminals to the United States.

The complex of Tranquilandia, which belonged to the Medellin cartel, was located in the jungles of Caqueta, near several clandestine runways. According to authorities at the time, the Fuerzas Armadas Revolucionarias de Colombia (FARC) protected both the runways and the laboratories; however, evidence of this partnership between drug traffickers and the guerrillas was thereafter deemed questionable.[41] The possible link between drugs and the left-wing revolutionaries added another layer of difficulty to a government that vacillated between negotiations and military approaches to tackle illegal armed groups. At this time, the Betancur government was actually having peace talks with the FARC, and they became formalized with the signing of the Acuerdos de la

---

41. Salazar (2001, p. 122); Lee (1989, p. 171).

Uribe. Against this backdrop, one can presume that the first summit in Panama between government officials and drug kingpins was the latter's last attempt at dialogue before going to war against the state. Both the betrayal of Betancur and the political rapprochement with the rebels exasperated the *capos*.

Negotiations: First Panama Summit, 1984

In mid-1984 Alfonso López Michelsen, who was defeated by Betancur and was now leader of the Liberal Party, and the attorney general, Carlos Jímenez Gómez, held two meetings in Panama with the most visible leaders of the Medellin cartel. According to one of Escobar's lieutenants, the first meeting was organized by Alberto Santofimio, a politician and member of the Liberal Party. The purpose of the summit was to convince President Betancur, through López Michelsen and Jímenez Gomez, to put the threat of extradition definitively to rest.[42] Claiming to control 80 percent of Colombian cocaine exports, the drug traffickers offered to withdraw from the business, reveal their routes, and invest the money in the country. The main obstacle to the negotiations was the recent murder of the justice minister, Rodrigo Lara Bonilla, as the Medellin cartel was the suspected orchestrator. Nonetheless, López Michelsen and Jiménez Gómez committed to consult with the Colombian government and the U.S. embassy about a possible deal.

Two incidents in the war on drugs jeopardized further negotiations. First, General Noriega of Panama, yielding to U.S. pressure, raided the Medellin cartel's laboratories in the Darien zone. The kingpins vacated their refuge in Panama and emigrated to Nicaragua. Having lost the opportunity to negotiate, the smugglers returned to Colombia to start a war on behalf of the *extraditables*, who were led by Escobar. Before this confrontation the very Santofimio who had organized the summit in Panama confided to Escobar that threats would be more effective than bribes for avoiding extradition.

It was in this context of failed talks and renewed conflict that Liberal Virgilio Barco, a man by temperament and conviction not prone to crooked schemes, won the presidency in 1986. His administration was particularly hard on illegal armed groups and illicit trade; hence the period from 1986 to 1990 brought perhaps the worst level of narco-terrorism—in retaliation for government policies.

Barco's successor, Cesar Gaviria, inherited the Liberal candidacy after the assassination of Luis Carlos Galan. Galan's battle against drug traffickers made any electoral agreements with drug barons highly unlikely. During the Gaviria administration, the Cali and Medellin cartels, locked in a fierce war, made a truce to gain legal benefits in the National Constituent Assembly. The division

---

42. Legarda (2005, p. 55).

of labor was clear: Cali would put up the money for political campaigns and the bribing of delegates, and the Medellin cartel would take care of kidnappings.[43]

War on Drugs: The Pepes, 1993

There is no doubt that one of the saddest chapters of the war on drugs in Colombia is the unusual alliance of the *perseguidos por Pablo Escobar*, or people persecuted by Pablo Escobar, known as the *pepes*. They set out to kill the powerful *capo* after his escape from the prison La Catedral.[44] Several factors contributed to the consolidation of this ruthless vigilante group. The trigger was the assassination of the Galeano and Moncada brothers, valued members of the Medellin cartel, who refused to pay the contribution required by Escobar to keep his war going. To avenge their deaths, a group of convicts freed in exchange for information about Escobar joined together in what came to be called the Dirty Dozen.[45] Escobar's escape from *La Catedral,* a prison that had been built to his own specifications, also contributed to the emergence of the *pepes*, as his transgression ended the justice system's quiet acquiescence.

Confrontation was back. In 1992 President Gaviria created the Bloque de Búsqueda (Search Bloc), a division of the armed forces with the sole objective of apprehending Pablo Escobar. The United States welcomed the initiative, with the DEA and the CIA joining forces.[46] After several months of searching to no avail—even with the assistance of informants—the government began relaxing the boundaries of the law to intensify the hunt. As the *pepes* morphed into a death squad, the paramilitary troops of the Castaño brothers, who also sought to take vengeance for the death of the Moncadas and Galeanos, joined the hunt. Finally, there was the Cali cartel, which partly funded the venture, as it also sought to end the long-standing feud with Escobar.

In January 1993 two car bombs exploded in Medellin, confirming that Escobar would pursue the feud using the same tactics he had used to wage war against the state. The *pepes* murdered collaborators, harassed family members, tortured potential informants, threatened Escobar's lawyers, and even killed Guido Parra, Escobar's main lawyer, along with his son. The chief hit man of the *pepes* was Adolfo Paz, commonly known as Don Berna. He was soon to be a key paramilitary figure and an assistant to one of the Galeano brothers. After several months of fighting, with its death toll of approximately 3,000 people,

---

43. Chaparro (2005, p. 84).
44. For details of this operation, see Bowden (2001). For a short summary, see "Pacto con el Diablo" (2008).
45. Salazar (2001, p. 299). The list of the twelve is supplied in Reyes (2007, p. 56).
46. Bowden (2001). See also declassified information from the National Security Archive (www.gwu.edu/~nsarchiv/NSAEBB/NSAEBB243/index.htm).

they managed to kill Escobar on December 2, 1993. The *pepes* disintegrated after they achieved their goal; many of them later became part of the AUC (United Self-Defense Forces of Colombia).

Negotiations: Pact of Recoletos

To the chilling story of the *pepes*, it is necessary to add a less bloody but equally embarrassing episode that helps place the 1994 presidential election financing scheme in context. Given a truce between the government and the drug lords and a combination of threats, kidnappings, and bribes, the Cali and Medellin cartels were able to ensure that the ban on extradition of nationals was included in the 1991 constitution. Their victory is testament to the control that drug cartels possessed in Colombia during this period.

After the *pepes* killed Pablo Escobar, Cali cartel leaders changed their business strategy. They wanted to quietly retreat and surrender to authorities in exchange for mild sentences and the guarantee of no extradition to the United States. To that end, Cali drug barons decided to strengthen their relationship with Congress and to the possible next president. A coalition of dealers managed to put together $15 million to fund the election campaign.[47] This scandal, essentially over the Cali cartel financing the 1994 presidential election, is known in Colombia as Proceso 8000.

According to Santiago Medina, treasurer of the campaign, the deal began to take shape a year before the election.[48] A journalist and a politician, both in the cartel's payroll, traveled to Madrid to meet with the then ambassador of Colombia, Ernesto Samper. There, in a well-known coffee shop, the three formalized the general terms of the financing scheme in an agreement called Pacto de Recoletos. The candidate intended to support a process of surrender to justice without the risk of extradition, and the Rodriguez Orejuela brothers and Medina agreed. For the first round of elections $1 million of drug money entered the campaign, and an unspecified sum was paid directly to different leaders and political *caciques* in Cali. For the second round, the situation was thornier because of quota limits, which were then around $5 million. The Rodriguez Orejuela brothers in the end agreed to send the money. They received, as a receipt, a signed document listing the proposed expenditures of the funds.

Not surprisingly, with such a history of corruption and violence, especially following the episode of the *pepes*, those who took part in the Recoletos pact perceived what they were doing as a small, venial sin. In fact, the signatories were either so pleased or so unconcerned about their commitment that they left

---

47. Chaparro (2005, p. 78).
48. Medina (1995).

a photographic record of it.[49] At the same time, the Rodriguez Orejuela brothers of the Cali cartel—and a few years later, paramilitary leader Carlos Castaño—hoped that the Colombian establishment and the United States would show their appreciation for their valuable contribution to the downfall and death of Pablo Escobar. Indeed, the death squad had operated with the support of citizens, the government, national security forces, and U.S. agencies.

War on Drugs: Millennium Operation, 1999

At the end of 1999, in a joint effort of the Colombian National Police and U.S. agencies, more than thirty drug heavyweights were captured in several cities across the country. Alejandro Bernal, a typical second-generation drug lord, and Fabio Ochoa, an old member of the Medellin cartel, both fell in the raid. Known as the Millennium Operation (Operación Milenio), this action is considered one of the most important of the war on drugs, similar to the fall of the Cali cartel. As important as the drug traffickers who were caught are those who managed to flee, thanks to their contact with Baruch Vega, an asset of the FBI, the CIA, and other agencies. Many drug lords and paramilitaries, frightened by the blow, rushed to the second summit in Panama to initiate or speed negotiations with the United States. At the same time, the Millennium Operation prevented some narcotics traders from benefiting from the resocialization plan promoted by Vega. Being included in the Millennium list, for example, meant not being able to negotiate with American judges.

Ultimately, Operation Millennium created a dilemma. On the one hand, drug traffickers and paramilitaries did not know where to turn for protection in Colombia, but on the other hand, they knew that extradition to the United States was the worst outcome. As an agent of Vega pointed out, "the drug trafficking problem is with the American government, not with the Colombian government."[50]

Negotiations: Second Panama Summit, 1999

The secret negotiations that led to the second summit in Panama at the end of the century began to take shape shortly after the unsuccessful first summit. Baruch Vega, the key person in the whole process, was a Colombian photographer whom the CIA recruited in the Universidad Industrial de Santander to infiltrate the Venezuelan guerrillas.[51] In the 1980s he managed to meet with Rodriguez Gacha, as Gacha had been led to believe that Vega could clean his

---

49. Medina (1995).
50. Reyes (2007, p. 182).
51. See Téllez and Lesmes (2006); Reyes (2007).

record through a corrupt contact in the FBI. Vega was able to demonstrate his efficacy by having one of Gacha's friends freed from a prison in Los Angeles. The news about Vega's potential value spread, and he became very popular among drug lords. He held discussions with the leaders of the Medellín and Cali cartels and later with top second-generation narco-traffickers, including people close to the paramilitary leader Carlos Castaño. Castaño's resignation and subsequent murder was in part due to his active promotion of negotiations with the U.S. justice system and the split that it caused among his ranks.

For five days in October 1999 approximately thirty second-generation drug traffickers, who claimed to be responsible for 80 percent of Colombia's cocaine exports, met in Panama. The organizer was Baruch Vega, and the meeting—to begin direct dealings with U.S. justice—was with Drug Enforcement Agency officials, prosecutors, and half a dozen lawyers. A few years earlier, the U.S. Department of Justice had decided to try negotiating with Colombian drug traffickers rather than prosecuting, and with that goal in mind and the support of the prosecutor, U.S. Attorney General Janet Reno, they created a resocialization program for drug traffickers. The high-profile group, called the Blitz Committee, was established to coordinate the dozen agencies needed for the initiative, to devise strategies, and to guide the negotiations. Baruch Vega directly reported in writing to the committee about all of his meetings with drug dealers.

By 2006 nearly 300 Colombian drug traffickers had negotiated with the U.S. justice system. One of the first smugglers who came forward was Nicolas Bergonzoli, an Escobar lieutenant who had emerged as a major drugs exporter. Bergonzoli met the Castaño brothers early in his career, as well as paramilitary leaders and commanders of the AUC. Through him, Carlos Castaño had set out to convince the new drug lords—many of them paramilitaries—to initiate similar talks. Hernando Gómez, popularly known as Rasguño, attended the second summit in Panama and, on behalf of Castaño, expressed interest in starting direct negotiations with U.S. officials.[52] The mistrust generated by Castaño's proposal to negotiate between paramilitaries, along with the fear of betrayal, led to his replacement as AUC leader by Salvatore Mancuso, the promoter of the Pacto de Ralito.

Even though for Carlos Castaño it was better to negotiate with American courts, given that the deaths of an informant and three policemen were attributed to his group, the talks reached a halt. Not all *capos* wanted to forgo part of their fortunes and plead guilty before a U.S. judge. Instead, they preferred to consolidate the status quo and increase their political influence in the Colombian Congress. "Owners of large estates, the warlords managed to keep several

---

52. Téllez and Lesmes (2006).

government contracts, control oil royalties, sectors of the health system, and even the collection of taxes from gambling."[53] For these *neocapos*, Castaño's resignation and Mancuso's new leadership in the Pacto de Ralito was the better option.

Negotiations: From the Pact of Ralito, 2001, to Proceso 8000

In 2006 a major scandal erupted. This time it was over an agreement signed five years earlier in Ralito, a small village in northern Colombia, between lawmakers, public officials, and paramilitary leaders. Invitations to the meeting, made on behalf of the AUC, lacked any threats and were delivered by the governor of Bolivar, who was Mancuso's close friend. The document that came out of the meeting, known as the Pacto de Ralito, sought to "reestablish" the nation. As paramilitary leader and organizer of the meeting, Salvatore Mancuso characterized its purpose as consolidating the AUC's project. This case marks the consolidation of the economic and military power that, de facto, the paramilitaries exercised in the area, as well as the apogee of the *parapolitica*. Nearly thirty of the hundred attendees signed it.

With such a boost, the paramilitaries predicted that their candidates would win in the 2002 parliamentary elections. Some analysts argue that those elections changed Colombia's political history, as it was the first time that a group of senators and representatives befriended paramilitaries to the level that they were willing to defend their interests in Congress.[54] Specifically, the parapoliticians would represent them on issues related to their demobilization, for example, by taking extradition to the United States off the table. In their defense, some politicians claimed that the meeting had been an effort to reach peace with the illegal armed groups, while others argued that they had been forced to sign. Thus far, nearly a hundred parliamentarians have been prosecuted for having links to paramilitaries.

Both the Proceso 8000 and the parapolitics scandal of 2006 were more than public disgraces. The political and judicial discussions that ensued, as well as the hot debate in the media, immensely affected the administrations that presided during the turmoil and also Colombia's international relations. Interestingly, in both cases it was protagonists who leaked the information. Shortly after the political financing agreement, Proceso 8000, one of the candidates gave the government the recordings and other pieces of evidence that specified the use of drug money in political campaigns. Five years after the agreement, Mancuso himself purportedly leaked the document of the Pacto de Ralito.[55]

---

53. Reyes (2007, p. 215).
54. Valencia (2007, p. 26).
55. "La historia detrás" (2010).

Generally speaking, Proceso 8000 fits best the typical case of organized crime and political finance in exchange for legal benefits. The scheme was almost out of a textbook, as Colombians came to learn after listening to its every detail from the campaign treasurer.[56] As far as the paramilitary scandal is concerned, the impact was more mixed: some of it was classical campaign financing with drug dollars, but there were also direct threats to voters and even juries.[57] Even though these two financial deals with illegal armed groups have been the most widely publicized—and those that have had the most impact and been backed by the most evidence—they are unfortunately not unique in Colombia's history.

In particular, it is important to note that one cannot really speak of a stable recurrence of fraudulent deals in politics, financial or in kind. There does seem to be, however, a constant back and forth between agreements and confrontations. Arguably, such political finance arrangements have been a consequence, albeit indirectly, of previous battles. The first summit of Panama cannot be understood outside of the context of the war on drugs, which began with the murder of Lara Bonilla. The narco-terrorist war that ensued lay latent as a consequence of broken agreements between organized crime and political leaders. The second meeting in Panama, in which lawyers and federal agents participated, would probably not have been well attended without the Millennium Operation.

The cycle of confrontation and negotiations is also a consequence of the public repudiation of negotiations with drug dealers. Whenever talks to financial agreements have been made public, they have usually led to political scandals and judicial processes. Sudden repressive action against narco-traffickers, especially in the midst of a rapprochement period, increases uncertainty and creates a sense of betrayal, which intensifies the confrontation. The escalation of violence usually ends when the government eases back and makes people believe—as happened with the guerrillas—that it is time to negotiate again, at least privately. These are the most fertile periods for typical cases of organized crime and political finance. And the cycle begins again.

Mafia and Politics: Lessons from Colombia

Inherent in the issue of organized crime and political finance are two paradoxes. The first is the strange situation of illegal armed groups looking for protection when the essence of their business is precisely commercializing such services. Groups whose main activity is blackmail and extortion try to befriend politicians to avoid extradition and to prevent their property from being seized and

---

56. Medina (1995).
57. Beltrán and Salcedo (2007, p. 4).

their business destroyed. The second is the observation that the phenomenon of organized crime and political finance exemplifies the problem of a contract's not being legal and, therefore, not being enforceable through legal channels.

As we attempt to understand this dilemma in Colombia, hypotheses emerge that capture the idea that the link between politics and organized crime depends not only on the strength of government's institutions but also on the nature, structure, and level of development of the illegal business.

Two Hypotheses

One hypothesis posits that the source of income of the illegal armed group determines the way politicians and illicit groups collaborate and interact. If income is gained from highly lucrative activities, such as drug trafficking, the typical pattern of bribing politicians to gain political or legal concessions becomes likely. On the other hand, if resources come from coercive and less liquid activities, such as kidnapping and extortion, the prevalence of traditional schemes diminishes. The Colombian guerrillas are a case in point. Their electoral influence has always been based on intimidation rather than funding. The case of Pablo Escobar, with the Medellin cartel—which was second only to the FARC in kidnappings—also points to this relationship: Escobar's monetary resources were almost inexhaustible, but he obtained legal and political protection through threats rather than cash.

Another hypothesis posits that the size and the degree of vertical and horizontal integration of the illegal business play the crucial role in political financing. To illustrate this idea, it is useful to compare the relationship of organized crime and political finance with legitimate business lobbying. Conglomerates seem more prone to lobby and to finance political campaigns than highly specialized firms, and the reason is simple. Conglomerates are affected by a wide variety of legal reforms; therefore, investing in lobbying has a certain economy of scale. In Colombia, Bavaria, the flagship firm of the Santo Domingo Group, for decades managed not only to prevent unfavorable regulatory changes but also to thwart any attempt to raise taxes on beer. This conglomerate had an enormous team of lobbyists as well as important Congress members on their payroll. When the multinational company SABMiller acquired Bavaria, making the company liable to international rules against political funding, it became feasible to approve tax reform against the interests of this company.[58]

The case of the Rodriguez Orejuela brothers exemplifies the differing ways that large conglomerates and specialized businesses operate. The voluminous campaign financing associated with Proceso 8000 took place when it was already

---

58. "El senador 103 dejó de ser de Bavaria" (2010).

consolidated in various economic sectors and felt that its illegal business would be exposed. In contrast, the new, highly specialized criminal enterprises that are subcontracted at various stages of the export chain show less interest in political finance. Even among the narco-traffickers with a natural vocation for public life, such as Pablo Escobar, financial contributions to campaigns came when they did not know what to do with so much excess liquidity and felt like masters of the universe, controlling every detail of their business, starting at production and ending with money laundering.

Other Factors

With a few specific exceptions, such as asset forfeiture laws and sophisticated procedural issues that are handled by lawyers, in Colombia the main legal issue for organized crime is extradition. Preventing passage of extradition treaties is therefore of great interest to them, specifically, through influencing legislators.

The personality of those running illegal enterprises explains other levels of engagement in politics. In Colombia there are illegal armed actors with the profile of businessmen and there are others who are more politically inclined. It appears to be the case that those in the first category—and only under certain conditions—subcontract political services by supporting politicians with a shared ideology. The politically inclined, on the other hand, directly participate in public life. For them, the need to forge alliances with politicians arises when they expand geographically, as in the case of the paramilitaries. Within their territory, politicians tend to be long-standing allies, friends, or business partners of the underworld.

There are of course a myriad other factors, especially of a cultural or social nature, that may explain a criminal organization's political participation. A Colombian expert on the subject, for example, is currently trying to understand why the paramilitaries in Antioquia come from poorer socioeconomic backgrounds while those in coastal areas tend to be from the upper echelons of society.[59] As far as politicians are concerned, personal traits may also be very relevant. Some public figures have accepted financial support from illegal armed groups, while others have never done so—and observers have yet to discern why.

Today, one of the key puzzles in the literature has to do with whether or not political decentralization facilitates the infiltration of criminal organizations into government institutions. Latin American countries have undergone a process of decentralization in recent years, thereby making the question particularly relevant.[60] The Colombian experience over the past two decades suggests

---

59. Gustavo Duncan, personal communication.
60. Casas-Zamora and Zovatto (2010).

bad news: as Gustavo Duncan explains, the reforms to the political and administrative system embodied in the constitution of 1991 seemed to generate benefits for regional criminal organizations. While they were aimed at strengthening local democracy, the legal changes ended up favoring the warlords.

> The implementation of the electoral quotient law, the administrative decentralization, and the increased fiscal transfers made possible the emergence of independent politicians with a relatively small electoral base. The fragmentation of the professional political class facilitated the control of small-armed groups over regional party structures. It was much easier to intimidate and take control over small owners of votes than it had been to replace the hierarchical and influential machinery of the old *caciques*.[61]

The atomization of cartels that resulted from the war on drugs was accompanied by an atomization of politics, which in turn promoted a symbiotic relationship between neo-narco-traffickers and politicians.

Public Policy Implications

The Colombian experience suggests that efforts to change the legal framework that affects illicit activities may backfire. Through a combination of bribes, threats, and legal expertise, organized crime has managed to turn instances of reform into opportunities to strengthen its position. Such situations have been so common that they have a name, *narcomicos*, and they basically point to the fact that poor regulation can be worse than lack of regulation.[62]

Another lesson is that successful control of the relationship between organized crime and political finance must be preceded by efforts to prevent tax evasion and to ensure clean accounting practices. Any regulation of private funding sources has to ensure that the funds are visible to the regulator, something that is not possible with illegal or underground money. With regard to the underground nature of the funds for political finance, a survey in Colombia finds that, among legal businesses, only 56 percent report campaign contributions, and of those, only 51 percent verify that the recipient has duly recorded it. In other words, almost three-quarters of the legal funds that go to finance politics could be lying outside of official accounting records.[63]

The events leading up to Proceso 8000 show that limits on private funds to finance campaigns can be counterproductive. Part of the eagerness to accept

---

61. Duncan (2006, p. 273).
62. Casas-Zamora and Zovatto (2010, p. 11).
63. Transparencia Por Colombia (2009).

illegal money was precisely due to the fact that the campaigns had exceeded the caps set by law. This remark is not to be taken as an invitation to drop reforms. Rather, it is to promote an approach that is more long-term oriented. Needless to say, the general suggestions that follow require further empirical research and fine-tuning, especially to adapt them to local conditions.

Local Prevention

One of the basic concepts of contemporary criminology is that of the paths that lead to juvenile delinquency. Several studies in various countries show that young offenders almost never begin committing a serious crime but instead are progressively engaged in increasingly serious criminal conduct. Well-timed prevention tends to hold more promise than penalties delivered later, to a hardened criminal. This simple idea can be useful in the field of political finance—not in terms of prevention of youth violence or organized crime, which is a different field of public policy, but to identify and try to control political practices based on agreements with local violent actors.

In Latin American barrios, or poor neighborhoods and municipalities, gang members have de facto political control more often than commonly thought.[64] Informal taxes, illegal contributions to receive a business permit, tolls to public transportation, and direct threats to political and community leaders are the seeds of mafia interference in politics. Some incidents of political use of youth gangs in Central America are quite similar to partnerships, for electoral purposes or private justice enforcement, between politicians and paramilitary groups in Colombia. It is difficult to know whether or not such coercive practices are more widespread than vote buying or political financing. The Colombian experience suggests that they may exist simultaneously. The task of identifying such practices and alliances, and the specific policies to control them, cannot be theoretical but must be empirically documented on the ground.

Moral Persuasion

The tools available to control improper conduct are not limited to the legal realm. Especially in countries where law enforcement is weak and judges and officials are overloaded with work, it is useful to consider a wide range of social and moral sanctions.

Politicians and illegal armed actors are both sensitive to public opinion, although the former much more than the latter. The incident of the check trap from Porras that triggered the first major offensive against drugs in Colombia

---

64. Rubio (2007).

supports this observation. Colombian politicians went far to try to eliminate all traces of their contacts with criminal organizations, as they became national embarrassments. Pablo Escobar was very aware of politicians' Achilles heels, as they secretly visited him at his ranch, Nápoles. He took advantage of an occasion when several of them were gathered in a boat on a river and "laughing slyly, he asked a reporter from *El Tiempo* to take a photograph of them."[65] It is clear that in this field a timely picture can be worth a thousand legal words.

Global Coordination

In 1999 at the Maiquetia airport in Venezuela, a group of National Guard members carried the luggage of an Arab prince aboard his plane. Of the 150 bags, 92 contained a total of two tons of drugs that would leave for Paris. The cocaine had arrived from Medellin. Two Colombian neo-narco-traffickers associated with the prince and a Spanish financier in charge of laundering the money through Swiss banks had coordinated the operation. Interestingly, one of the obstacles that had to be overcome was the prince's distrust of the banker, whom he thought was an informer for the British intelligence services.[66]

A few years earlier, Medellin drug dealers associated with a chemical engineer from Bogotá had set up a synthetic cocaine factory in a huge barn located in Pristina, the capital of Kosovo. They had considered the possibility of installing the manufacturing in Madagascar, where one of them knew the prime minister. Yugoslav partners were responsible for the supply of raw materials and the transportation of the final product to Italy. Other investors would be in charge of the distribution in that country, and money was to be laundered by a Spaniard.[67]

There is no need to list more examples to illustrate that drug trafficking is a truly transnational business. It has been this way since the first generation of Colombian criminal organizations, which managed to establish contacts in, at least, Panama, Venezuela, Nicaragua, Mexico, Cuba, Haiti, the United States, and Spain. Needless to say, national laws are insufficient to tackle an international business of this scale. This observation is relevant to any aspect of the illicit business, including as it relates to organized crime and political finance. The coordination and cooperation required for drug seizures, and to control money laundering, are enormous and incredibly important.

In the fight against drugs, in efforts to dialogue with the guerrillas, and increasingly in criminal procedures against politicians, the role of foreign governments and nongovernmental organizations has been, and will continue to

---

65. Salazar (2001, p. 95).
66. Monti (2004).
67. Reyes (2007).

be, decisive. For these partnerships to bear fruit, governments need to enhance institutional coordination. Despite the fact that American influence in the war on drugs—and in the dealings with guerrilla and drug dealers—might have been excessive, it is still valid to recommend that the relationship between organized crime and political finance be addressed with a global perspective.

References

Archer, Ronald. 1990. "The Transition from Traditional to Broker Clientelism in Colombia: Political Stability and Social Unrest." Working Paper 140. Notre Dame: Kellogg Institute (http://kellogg.nd.edu/publications/workingpapers/WPS/140.pdf).

Beltrán, Isaac, and Eduardo Salcedo. 2007. "Narcotráfico y parapolítica en Colombia, 1980–2007: Evolución del Capital Social Perverso." Bogotá: Grup Método (www.grupometodo.org/metodo/workingp.html).

Bowden, Mark. 2001. *Matar a Pablo Escobar*. Barcelona: RBA Libros.

Casas-Zamora, Kevin, and Daniel Zovatto. 2010. "Para llegar a tiempo: Apuntes sobre la regulación del financiamiento político en América Latina." *Nueva Sociedad*, no. 225 (January-February).

Castillo, Fabio. 1987. *Los jinetes de la cocaína*. Bogotá: Editorial Documentos Periodísticos.

Castro Caycedo, Germán. 1996. *En Secreto*. Bogotá: Planeta.

Chaparro, Camilo. 2005. *Historia del Cartel de Cali*. Bogotá: Intermedio.

COPP (Corporación Observatorio para la Paz). 2002. *Las verdaderas intenciones de los paramilitares*. Bogotá: Intermedio.

"Cuco Vanoy, el 'señor' del Bajo Cauca." 2007. *La Semana*, May 7.

De la Calle, Humberto. 1998. "Financiación de partidos y campañas electorales." *Revista de Derecho Público*, no. 9 (http://derechopublico.uniandes.edu.co/pdfs/R9_A1.pdf).

Duncan, Gustavo. 2006. *Los Señores de la Guerra. De paramilitares, mafiosos y autodefensas en Colombia*. Bogotá: Planeta.

"El senador 103 dejó de ser de Bavaria." 2010. *La Silla Vacía*, June 25.

"Ex agente de CTI se consolidó en los últimos 5 años como uno de los narcos más importantes del país." 2010. *El Tiempo*, June 8.

"La historia detrás del 'Pacto de Ralito.'" 2010. *La Semana*, January 18.

Lee, Rensselaer. 1989. *The White Labyrinth: Cocaine and Political Power*. New Brunswick: Transaction.

Legarda, Astrid. 2005. *El Verdadero Pablo. Sangre, Traición y Muerte*. Bogotá: Ediciones Dipon.

Medina, Santiago. 1995. "Indagatoria de Santiago Medina ante la Fiscalía" (www.eltiempo.com/archivo/documento/MAM-380366).

Meisel, Adolfo. 2009. "Reseña. Contrabando en Colombia en el siglo XIX." *América Latina en la Historia Económica*, no. 32.

Monti, Fabrice. 2004. *La Coke Saoudienne. Au coeur d'une affaire d'état*. Paris: Flammarion Enquete.

Montoya, Nicolás, and Juan Navarrete. 2009. "El financiamiento electoral en Colombia." Bogotá: Misión Observación Electoral, Calidad de la Ciudadanía.

"Pacto con el Diablo." 2008. *Revista Semana*, February 16.

Payne, Mark, and Juan Cruz Perusia. 2007. "Reforming the Rules of the Game: Political Reform." In *The State of State Reform in Latin America*, edited by Eduardo Lora. Washington: World Bank.

Pizarro, Eduardo. 1998. "El Financiamiento de las Campañas Electorales en Colombia." *Revista de Derecho Público*, no. 9 (http://derechopublico.uniandes.edu.co/pdfs/R9_A2.pdf).

Posada-Carbó, Eduardo. 2008. "Democracy, Parties, and Political Finance in Latin America." Working Paper 346. Notre Dame: Kellogg Institute (http://kellogg.nd.edu/publications/workingpapers/WPS/346.pdf).

Reyes, Gerardo. 2007. *Nuestro hombre en la DEA*. Bogotá: Planeta.

Ronderos, Carlos. 2003. *Rebelión y Amnistía. La historia colombiana del siglo XX contada por sus protagonista*. Bogotá: Espasa.

Rubio, Mauricio. 2005. *Del rapto a la pesca milagrosa. Breve historia del secuestro en Colombia*. Bogotá: Universidad Externado de Colombia.

———. 2007. *De la pandilla a la Mara. Pobreza, educación, mujeres y violencia Juvenil*. Bogotá: Universidad Externado de Colombia.

Salazar, Alonso. 2001. *La Parábola de Pablo. Auge y caída de un gran capo del narcotráfico*. Bogotá: Planeta.

Salazar Pineda, Gustavo. 2006. *El confidente de la mafia se confiesa*. Bogotá: Nombrelatino.

Téllez, Édgar, and Jorge Lesmes. 2006. *Pacto en la Sombra. Los tratos secretos de Estados Unidos con el narcotráfico*. Bogotá: Planeta.

Transparencia por Colombia. 2009. "Encuesta sobre la financiación de las campañas electorales y la corrupción política en Colombia." Bogotá (www.transparenciacolombia.org.co).

Valencia, León. 2007. "Los Caminos de la Alianza entre los Paramilitares y los Políticos." In *Parapolítica. La Ruta de la Expansión Paramilitar y los Acuerdos Políticos*, edited by Mauricio Romero. Bogotá: Corporación Nuevo Arco Iris, Intermedio Editores.

Vallejo, Virginia. 2007. *Amando a Pablo. Odiando a Escobar*. Bogotá: Grijalbo.

Villar Borda, Carlos. 2004. *La Pasión del Periodismo*. Bogotá: Universidad Jorge Tadeo Lozano.

Zuñiga, Priscilla. 2007. "Ilegalidad, control local y paramilitares en el Magdalena." In *Parapolítica. La Ruta de la Expansión Paramilitar y los Acuerdos Políticos*, edited by Mauricio Romero. Bogotá: Corporación Nuevo Arco Iris, Intermedio Editores.

KEVIN CASAS-ZAMORA

5 Costa Rica: Four Decades of Campaign Finance Scandals

The growing role of money in politics has become one of the central issues in democratic debates throughout the world. Costa Rica, arguably the most consolidated democracy in the developing world, has not escaped this trend. In fact, the issue has been part of the national agenda, in different ways, for nearly sixty years. The enactment in August 2009 of a comprehensive overhaul of political finance regulations is merely the latest installment of changes. The discussions have centered on a generous public funding system and the recurring problem of questionable funding practices in the main political parties.

The 2009 reforms, which for the first time include political finance rules backed by stern sanctions, are a response to a series of scandals that reveal the vulnerability to corruption of a funding system largely reliant on public subsidies and fundraisers' self-control. They are also a result of concerns about the drug-trafficking maelstrom that has engulfed Costa Rica and the rest of Central America, dramatically transforming the political and security realities of the region.[1] The vast resources commanded by transnational crime syndicates in Latin America and the growing democratic competition in the region conspire to endanger the integrity of political institutions in an especially serious way. Unfortunately, some of these dangers have been borne out in Costa Rica.

Note: The author wishes to acknowledge Marta Acosta, Maureen Ballestero, Ronald Chacón, Leonel Núñez, and Milena Soto for their kind help in facilitating contacts and gathering primary information during a research trip to Costa Rica in June 2010. In the spirit of full disclosure, the author would like to state that he served as Costa Rica's second vice president and minister of national planning and economic policy during an administration of the National Liberation Party (PLN), under President Oscar Arias (2006–10). The relevance of this disclosure will become clear to anyone who reads the text.

1. According to the UN, nearly 90 percent of the cocaine destined for the U.S. market travels through the Central America/Mexico corridor (UNODC, 2008).

As shown below, the disturbing experience of the 1986 presidential election, in which drug-trafficking proceeds penetrated the coffers of the main parties, was a severe wake-up call that, to this day, shapes political funding discussions and practices in the country.

The following pages take stock of the experience of Costa Rica with regard to the funding of elections by organized crime syndicates and to the vulnerability of the country to this danger. To do so, the chapter starts by giving an overview of the Costa Rican regulatory framework of political finance and its evolution. This framework, particularly its long-held—but recently shunned—laxness toward the regulation of private political donations largely explains past episodes of political finance corruption, some of them involving the use of funds of questionable origin.

The next section of the chapter takes advantage of the remarkable wealth of public information on political finance practices—a result of six congressional probes held in the course of the past thirty-five years. In the brief description and analysis of the cases in which the use of crime-related money in campaigns has been documented, particular emphasis is paid to the allegations overshadowing the 1986 campaign. The chapter then looks at the evolution of campaign finance practices post-1986 and at the current situation, as described by practitioners across the political system. The final section teases out the main lessons of the Costa Rican experience and suggests some policy recommendations derived from them.

The story that emerges from these pages is slightly more hopeful than the author had expected. Despite the chronic political finance scandals of the past few decades, or perhaps because of them, there seems to be widespread awareness among the Costa Rican political elite of the significant risks faced by the country in the realm of political finance. These risks have activated social and institutional mechanisms of protection and the willingness to toughen transparency rules. While important challenges remain—including those derived from the opening up of new electoral arenas at the local level—Costa Rica today is, generally speaking, better prepared than in the past to withstand the assault of criminal rings on the integrity of its electoral process.

Some Background: The Regulation and Practice of Political Finance in Costa Rica

The regulation of political finance has a long history in Costa Rica.[2] In 1956 it became the second country in the world, after Uruguay, to enact direct public

---

2. See Casas-Zamora (2005, chap. 2).

subsidies for political parties.[3] Since its inception, the direct subsidy system became the pillar of the country's approach toward political finance, to the detriment of other aspects, such as the regulation of private donations, the control of electoral expenses, the imposition of financial transparency requirements, and the use of in-kind subventions. Indeed, the subsidies' evolving features as well as their remarkable generosity became the subject of acute political disputes, dominated by overestimations of the power of subsidies to determine political behavior and electoral outcomes.

The basic traits of the public funding system were laid out early on and incorporated in the constitution (article 96). The subvention was conceived as a reimbursement of the electoral expense incurred by parties rather than by individual candidates. The funds were to be proportionally allocated by votes received—but only among those parties that reached a certain electoral threshold. Moreover, to receive government funds, eligible parties had to submit a detailed and well-documented claim of their expenses to the state's accounting office. The amount of the subsidy was capped by the constitution at a level that was generous from the outset.

In the course of the next five decades these features would change in significant ways. To begin with, the eligibility threshold to receive the subsidy decreased gradually until it was fixed at 4 percent of the vote, or one seat in the Legislative Assembly, where it currently stands. More important, the purely postelectoral nature of the subsidy would be changed, contested, and changed again amid very acrimonious debates. In 1971 a constitutional amendment supported by the major parties introduced a preelectoral financing mechanism equivalent to 50 percent of the total subsidy. These resources would be allocated according to party performance in the previous election. Among bitter protestations from numerous critics who argued that the financing mechanism was a blatant attempt to lock in the party system, in 1991 the Constitutional Court struck down the 1971 amendment, returning the subsidy system to its postelection nature.[4] The reforms enacted in 2009, in turn, reversed this decision, reintroducing preelection disbursements equivalent to 15 percent of the total subsidy, distributed in equal shares among all registered parties. Last but not least, the generosity of the subsidy begot a decades-long political constituency dedicated to denouncing the apparent runaway growth of party subsidies.

---

3. Direct public subsidies means cash public subventions for parties. Indirect subsidies refer, generally speaking, to in-kind goods and services provided to the parties by the state.
4. SCCR (Sala Constitucional de la Corte Suprema de Justicia de Costa Rica [Constitutional Chamber of the Supreme Court of Justice of Costa Rica]), vote 980-91, May 24, 1991. On the controversies surrounding preelection financing in Costa Rica, see Casas-Zamora (2001).

Years of political haggling around the issue yielded a peculiar solution. The subsidy's amount is capped by the constitution at 0.19 percent of GDP, but the Assembly can legislate to fix it at a lower amount. For the 2010 election, it fixed the subvention at 0.14 percent of GDP, while introducing a crucial change: out of the overall sum, 0.03 percent of GDP would be earmarked for the election of mayors in the country's eighty-one counties, an election that has been separate from presidential and congressional elections since 2002. The December 2010 election of mayors put this amendment to the test for the first time.

The recurring denunciations of subsidy growth were at most half true. In real and per capita terms, the amount of the Costa Rican subsidy has experienced fluctuations, and until the large increase in 2010 it had generally been declining for some time. Even accounting for this downward trend, the subvention has remained lavish throughout (table 5-1).

The amount designated for the 2010 election cycle (including the presidential and legislative elections in February 2010, as well as the local election in December 2010) is equivalent to $30 million (1995 U.S. dollars) or $10.6 per voter.[5] This assistance compares very favorably to nearly all direct-funding systems in the Latin American context and to election-oriented subsidy systems worldwide.[6] The important point to bear in mind is that, ever since it was enacted, the Costa Rican system of direct party subsidies has been generous enough to become the dominant presence in the country's political finance landscape. Indeed, the most comprehensive study of political finance practices in Costa Rica concludes that during the 1978–98 period subsidies covered approximately two-thirds of the overall cost of presidential campaigns.[7]

As with many other democracies, Costa Rica pays much more attention to public funding than to the long-term lack of interest in regulating the parties' private income sources as well as their expenditures. While expenditures remain unregulated to this day, private contributions were bereft of any control until 1996, even though evidence of problems with this approach had been mounting since the 1970s. In 1996–97 major legal reforms obligated the parties to periodically report accepted contributions to the Supreme Elections Tribunal (TSE). Moreover, they explicitly banned foreign contributions and capped local donations at a sum roughly equivalent to $35,000 per donor and election cycle. Unfortunately, the reform failed to give electoral authorities a clear mandate to audit the parties' financial reports and to establish the locus of responsibility in case these rules were violated. The implications of both omissions would

---

5. In 2010 U.S. dollars, the equivalent sums are $42 million and $15.1 per voter.
6. See, for instance, Casas-Zamora and Zovatto (2011, table 1).
7. Casas-Zamora (2005).

Table 5-1. *State Funding to Parties in Costa Rica: Quantitative Evolution, 1953–2010*
Units as indicated

Election	Amount (in millions of 1995 US$)	Real growth (percent)	Subsidy per registered voter (in 1995 US$)	Real growth per registered voter (percent)
1953	6.1	...	20.7	...
1958	3.1	−49	8.7	−58
1962	3.9	26	8.1	−7
1966	5.5	41	9.9	22
1970	5.8	5	8.6	−13
1974	5.5	−5	6.3	−27
1978[a]	13.1	138	12.4	97
1982	4.9	−63	3.9	−69
1986[a]	12.2	149	8.2	110
1990	12.6	3	7.5	−9
1994	13.6	8	7.2	−4
1998	11.5	−15	5.6	−22
2002[b]	8.6	−25	3.8	−32
2006	11.1	29	4.4	16
2010[c]	30.0	170	10.6	141

Sources: Author, based on figures from Supreme Elections Tribunal and Banco Central de Costa Rica.

a. In 1978 and 1986 subsidy figures include preelection advances paid to parties that later failed to qualify for public reimbursement. Recipients were supposed to repay the funds but, in most cases, never did, adding to the state's net outlays. Excluding these funds, the subsidy amounts to US$9.7 million in 1978 and US$11.6 million in 1986.

b. Total electoral expenditure is significantly underestimated. There are no available data for the second-round runoff of April 2002. Also, given the decision by the Libertarian Movement Party (PML) to turn down public funding for that election, its expenditure figures are unknown.

c. Figures refer to allocated, rather than actually disbursed, funds. It includes local elections held in December 2010.

become evident during the 1998 and 2002 election cycles, as they were marred by allegations of financial misconduct by the main parties.

These scandals gave way to a major effort to revamp the controls over private funding, finally enacted in the run-up to the 2010 presidential election.[8] The new rules, informed by the goal of dramatically increasing the transparency of party finances, did away with donation ceilings yet banned all contributions

8. Law 8765, May 19, 2009.

from legal entities. As of today, only political donations from Costa Rican citizens are allowed, and they must be rigorously reported to the TSE. Moreover, for the first time the new rules define in very strict terms the responsibilities of donors, party treasurers, and candidates in the observance of political finance regulations, and they introduced stiff sanctions, including jail sentences, to punish breaches. Finally, the new guidelines grant the TSE extensive powers to monitor party finances, the perfect example of this being a specialized unit created for this purpose.

After the latest overhaul, the regulation of political finance in Costa Rica exhibits the traits summarized in table 5-2. The features of this system, and particularly those of the public funding scheme, have shaped political finance practices in Costa Rica in myriad ways. Dominant as the subsidy may be, its postelection nature burdens parties with the task of raising the funds they need during the campaign. The single most important assignment of a party treasurer in Costa Rica is to leverage the subsidy's eventual disbursement to raise cash in the short term. To do that, Costa Rican parties have long employed an intricate financial practice whereby they sell party-issued "bonds" to investors during the campaign. These financial instruments are redeemed when the state disburses the subsidies after the election. In other cases, those bonds are used as collateral to take up loans at financial institutions. The bonds embody the expectation of a future payment, which may or may not happen, depending on the issuing party's electoral result and its administrative ability to document its campaign expenses.

In most cases, the purchasers of these bonds are simple lenders expecting to make a profit. Sometimes, however, there is such a remote chance of recovering the loan—let alone making a profit— that in practice, purchasing a party bond is tantamount to making a political donation. As opposed to plain donors, the purchasers of these bonds remain anonymous.

Efforts to leverage public subsidies coexist in Costa Rica's main parties with a fairly stable set of practices to collect private donations.[9] For nearly fifty years the social democratic National Liberation Party (PLN) and its conservative opponents (a shifting set of actors that eventually merged into the Social Christian Unity Party, or PUSC, in the 1980s) deployed very similar methods to raise private funds within the small business elite. After all, despite a political cleavage born out of the country's 1948 civil war, both groupings shared a moderate probusiness platform that they took turns implementing while in office.

---

9. For a detailed study of fundraising practices in Costa Rica, see Casas-Zamora (2005, chap. 3). The following paragraphs rely heavily upon this text.

Table 5-2. *Key Features of Political Finance Regulation, Costa Rica, 2010*

Key feature	Details	Since
Public funding		
Direct subsidies	Recipient: Parties; primary elections not covered	1956
	Timing: Postelectoral reimbursement (but 15% of total distributed before the election)	1956 (2009)
	Threshold: 4% of the votes or 1 seat in the assembly (no threshold for preelection financing)	1997 (2009)
	Allocation: Proportional to votes (preelection financing allocated in equal parts)	1956 (2009)
	Amount definition procedure: capped by the constitution at 0.19% of GDP, but assembly can fix a lower sum by law (in 2010, 0.11% for national election plus 0.03% for local election)	2001
Indirect subsidies	Institutional support for parties in Congress	...
Controls over private contributions		
Anonymous	Banned	
Foreign	Banned, except for party research and training	1996
National	Unlimited for individuals; banned for legal entities of any kind (for example, corporations)	2009
Controls over expenditure		
General spending ceilings	No	...
Media advertising ceilings	No (however, only a limited amount of advertising is to be covered with public funds)	(1988)
Duration official campaign	Three-and-one-half months (October 1 to first Sunday of February, with an interruption between December 16 and January 1)	1988
Transparency rules		
Contributions	Parties report all contributions quarterly to the TSE and monthly during the official campaign	1996
	Presidential precandidates report all contributions to the party's treasurer	2001
Expenditures	Parties eligible for subsidy must document their expenditures to the TSE after the election	1950
Audit	TSE can order audits of the parties' finances	2009
Publicity	Parties must publish in a major newspaper an audited summary of their finances, including a list of donors	2009
Enforcement		
Sanctions	Up to six years in prison for a variety of political-finance-related offenses	2009
Liable parties	Donors, candidates, party treasurers, unauthorized fundraisers, party accountants	2009

Source: Constitution of Costa Rica; Electoral Code of Costa Rica; TSE.

In both cases, a respected businessman recruited by the party's presidential candidate among the country's traditional economic elite invariably coordinates the fundraising. While the details of this dynamic are beyond the scope of this chapter, it is worth noting the paramount role of reputation and connections within a close business elite for the fundraising operation to succeed. Campaign treasurers are able to raise money insofar as they know enough wealthy peers; donors, in turn, are willing to contribute money as long as they know the campaign treasurer, as long as the latter is not expected to line his or her pockets with donations, and of course, as long as the presidential candidate has a reasonable shot at winning the election. Regardless of legal controls, Costa Rican chief fundraisers have a status to protect. Many implications stem from this fact, including the fundraisers' willingness to exert self-control and their general wariness with regard to collecting donations abroad from unknown donors. Of course, such mindfulness is not simply the product of the social milieu. It is also a direct result of the generosity of public funding. To a certain extent, being selective is a luxury that Costa Rican fundraisers can afford.

The latter point has one important exception: presidential primaries, which to this day remain outside the scope of public funding. This gap leaves a very significant electoral arena entirely dependent on private contributions, not a minor issue in light of the costs associated with a presidential primary (estimated at around $1 million to $2 million for a main-party candidate).

In Costa Rica political donations tend to be rather small—rarely going beyond four digits—and are generally construed as a way to secure access to policymakers, rather than specific policy outcomes. In an environment in which neither the president nor members of Congress are allowed to run for consecutive reelection, donors tend to hedge their bets. Simply put, the institutional setup allows Costa Rican politicians to "take the money and run."

This is, to be sure, a broad-brush description of a complex process, which has seen numerous exceptions in the past and has undergone important changes recently. From the standpoint of the risks to political finance integrity, those transformations have been both good and bad. On the one hand, the emergence of the center-left Citizen Action Party (PAC) as the PLN's main opposition since 2006 has placed at the heart of the political system an actor defined by a strong anti-corruption platform and an instinctive distrust of private donors and, more generally, of traditional business elites.[10] On the other hand, the recent thrust toward political decentralization has opened up new

---

10. The results of the 2010 presidential election are PLN, 46.9 percent; PAC, 25.1 percent; PML, 20.9 percent; PUSC, 3.9 percent; others, 3.2 percent.

electoral arenas, most notably the direct election of mayors, with significant costs of their own.

Yet this general characterization of political finance in Costa Rica is accurate enough to put in context what follows. It is a picture in which a robust public-funding scheme and the reputational constraints that bind fundraisers were entrusted with the task of keeping the parties' financial practices honest. As is seen below, both mechanisms continue to play an important role in checking political finance abuses in Costa Rica. Alas, they offer an inherently fragile protection to fundraising integrity when coupled with very intense and increasingly expensive campaigns and, above all, with a lack of effective legal controls over private contributions. This was precisely the situation in which Costa Rican parties operated until very recently. Not surprisingly, these frail barriers broke down repeatedly over the past four decades. As the next section shows, in some cases the vulnerabilities of the system opened up the parties' coffers to the proceeds of organized crime, with major long-term consequences.

Organized Crime and Political Finance in Costa Rica: A Look at the Cases

Political financing scandals have been a recurring phenomenon in Costa Rica since the 1970s. Most of them concern the surfacing of foreign donations linked to a variety of shady characters, some connected to drug trafficking. More recently, the introduction of controls over private donations in 1996, however imperfect they may have been, has begotten a generation of scandals more linked to violation of the rules. The 1970 election marked the beginning of a path that would lead over the years to several congressional probes, electoral reforms, and lasting adjustments in fundraising practices in Costa Rica.

Indeed, during the 1970s it became known that EHG Enterprises, a Puerto Rico–based company, had bought $400,000 in PLN bonds during the run-up to the 1970 presidential election, which resulted in victory for José Figueres, the PLN's standard-bearer. Prominent among the firm's main shareholders was Clovis W. McAlpin, a controversial businessman indicted in the United States for his participation in various fund-diversion scams.[11] In the early 1970s McAlpin fled to Costa Rica, where he became a close associate of Figueres.[12]

The arrival of McAlpin was merely the prelude to a far more serious episode. In 1973 U.S. financier Robert L. Vesco, a former associate of McAlpin, arrived in

---

11. Block (1998, p. 139); Blum (1999, pp. 67–68).
12. *La Nación (LN)*, May 15, 1974; July 15, 1977.

the country fleeing prosecution in the United States, as Costa Rica was gearing up for the 1974 election.[13] Before his arrival, Vesco had embezzled more than $220 million—an enormous sum at the time—from the mutual fund investment firm International Overseas Services, Ltd. Moreover, according to U.S. Drug Enforcement Administration (DEA) informants, he was already involved in heroin trafficking. All the same, he soon became an irresistible magnet for Costa Rican politicians. He after all was no stranger to seeking political protection, having contributed generously to Richard Nixon's 1972 reelection campaign, as the Watergate investigation revealed.

Despite U.S. government and Costa Rican complaints, Vesco settled in the country under Figueres's protection. He cultivated friends across the political spectrum, lobbied to establish an international financial district, and poured millions of dollars into diverse business ventures in the country, including an unsecured loan of $2.1 million to Figueres's own family conglomerate, Sociedad Agrícola Industrial San Cristóbal S.A. For his efforts, Vesco was rewarded with a temporary Costa Rican passport and something invaluable for his purposes: a small legal reform to the country's extradition laws. In March 1974, a mere six weeks before the end of Figueres's term in office, the Legislative Assembly voted for a series of legal amendments that included a provision that gave the executive branch, rather than the judiciary, the power to approve or veto an extradition.[14] Given that Daniel Oduber, the standard-bearer of Figueres's PLN, had already been elected to succeed him in the presidency, the Vesco Law, as it came to be known, was a blatant attempt to thwart U.S. extradition requests.

Years later, Figueres would publicly accuse his own party, as well as others, of using Vesco's money to pay for a large part of their 1974 campaign.[15] Oduber was pointedly accused of receiving a $500,000 donation from Vesco, a charge he denied. The allegations prompted not only a public outcry but also the country's first legislative inquiry on party funding practices. Though it was suggestive of widespread foreign involvement in Costa Rican elections, the probe produced inconclusive results, having descended into party bickering in the run-up to the 1978 election. Vesco was expelled from Costa Rica in 1978. By then, the Legislative Assembly had repealed the amendments to the extradition rules. In the 1980s, after leading a peripatetic life that eventually took him to Havana,

---

13. On Vesco and his time in Costa Rica, see Hutchinson (1975); Suñol (1978); "A Last Vanishing Act" (2008); "Robert Vesco" (2008); "Vesco in Costa Rica" (1973); "Learning to Love Exile" (1976); Rosen (2008); *LN*, March 4, 1999.

14. Law 5497, March 21, 1974.

15. On the allegations see Bode (1977); *LN*, July 5–7, 1977; *La República (LR)*, May 11, 1977. On the inquiry, see Asamblea Legislativa de Costa Rica (ALCR [Legislative Assembly of Costa Rica]), Exp. Leg. 7898; *LN*, July 11, July 28, and July 30, 1977; *Excelsior*, August 14, 1977.

where he died in 2007, Vesco would be indicted twice by U.S. authorities on cocaine-trafficking charges linked to the operations of the Medellin drug cartel.

The Vesco ordeal had no consequences for political finance regulation in Costa Rica. Not surprisingly, the same phantoms returned with a vengeance a decade later. Between 1987 and 1992, a series of legislative inquiries into drug-trafficking activities in Costa Rica showed that, during the 1985-86 campaign and, to a lesser extent, the 1989–90 campaign, both main parties sought or accepted contributions from a number of donors later linked to organized crime.[16] In some cases, these criminals were even given fundraising responsibilities.

The probes show that Manuel Elizalde, a Philippine pensioner living in Costa Rica and allegedly linked to the white slave trade, had purchased nearly $100,000 in PUSC party bonds in the run-up to the 1986 election. The allegations against him led to his deportation from the country a year later.[17] A similar but more serious case involved Lloyd S. Rubin, a Panama-based financier. In the early days of the administration of President Rafael Angel Calderón-Fournier (1990–94), Rubin was appointed Costa Rica's commercial attaché in Panama, a post with diplomatic immunity. His appointment, preceded by nearly $140,000 in bond purchases during Calderón-Fournier's 1985–86 and 1989–90 presidential bids, was soon cancelled when it became known that Rubin was implicated in money-laundering activities.[18] While both these cases suggest problems in PUSC fundraising procedures, it was the PLN that was at the receiving end of the most compromising revelations made during the legislative investigations.

The inquiries established that Roberto Fionna, an Argentine restaurateur residing in Costa Rica and with a pending trial in France on drug-trafficking charges, had collaborated with high-ranking PLN politicians during the 1980s. Fionna admitted making a $5,000 contribution to the campaign of Carlos Manuel Castillo during the 1985 PLN presidential primary and having organized numerous fundraising dinners for the primary campaign of Rolando Araya, another PLN hopeful, in 1988. His political contacts stemmed from his association with Fernando Melo, a Cuban-born businessman who was well known in the PLN top circles. Since well before moving to Costa Rica in 1977, Melo had been the subject of U.S. investigations due to his presumed involvement in drug trafficking. His political contacts—notably with President Oduber—allowed Melo to become a Costa Rican citizen in 1978, hold low-ranking positions in the PLN administrations, participate successfully in procurement deals with the Costa Rican state, and even play an important mediating role between rival PLN

---

16. ALCR, Exp. Leg. 10200-10684-10934.
17. On Elizalde, see *LN,* January 21, 1992; ALCR, Exp. Leg. 10934, pp. 4849–98, 6992.
18. ALCR, Exp. Leg. 10934, pp. 4120–27, 4264–304, 4851–67, 4891–92, 6993; *LN,* January 21, 1992.

factions during the 1985 presidential primary. Oduber would later claim that Melo was an important fundraiser for the PLN and that he had contributed to the presidential bids of both Carlos Manuel Castillo and the eventual winner and future Costa Rican president, Oscar Arias (1986–90, 2006–10), in 1984–85. In 1988 Fionna was extradited to France. Melo's Costa Rican citizenship was cancelled after the revelations of the legislative probes became public.[19]

This incident was not the only uncomfortable finding involving former President Oduber. The congressional probes also evinced that, in the waning days of the 1986 campaign, Lionel James Casey, a U.S. pensioner living in Costa Rica, had donated $20,000 to the PLN campaign through Oduber. A few days before Casey made his contribution, a U.S. judge issued an arrest warrant against him for his involvement in a drug-trafficking ring. He was arrested in Costa Rica in 1988 and extradited to the United States five years later. As a result, the congressional committee that investigated the case strongly recommended Oduber's dismissal from all political responsibilities in his party.[20]

The embarrassing revelations did not stop there. Early in 1991 it became public that a $28,000 contribution from Ocean Hunter, a Miami-based company with large business operations in Costa Rica, was personally handed to the then presidential candidate Arias in 1985 and deposited in a PLN campaign account. Years later, the company was linked to drug trafficking by the U.S. government. Arias admitted to receiving the donation but claimed that its spurious origin was neither known nor could have been known at the time. Interestingly, the copy of the donation check only surfaced when the company's indicted owners expressed their displeasure at Arias's refusal to support the Nicaraguan *contras* or grant them business favors. Their attempt to "earn indulgences," to quote Ocean Hunter's own words, had proved a fiasco.[21]

The case of Ocean Hunter was, nonetheless, a small distraction for Arias compared to that of Ricardo Alem. Alem, a young Costa Rican entrepreneur and political newcomer, became a large contributor to the Arias campaign throughout 1984–85.[22] Though his contributions led to him being given an important campaign post, his name was conspicuously bypassed by Arias when appointing his cabinet after his 1986 electoral victory. Alem, who had clearly

---

19. On Fionna and Melo, see *LN*, January 19, June 1, and June 9, 1989; *La Prensa Libre (LPL)*, October 17, 1988; ALCR, Exp. Leg. A45-E8008, pp. 191–200.

20. On Casey, see *LN*, January 27, 1989; ALCR, Exp. Leg. A45-E8008, pp. 206–15.

21. On "Ocean Hunter," see *LN*, June 5, 1991, and January 31, 1992; ALCR, Exp. Leg. 10934, pp. 4976–5053, 6990–92.

22. His contribution to the Arias campaign was estimated at nearly $85,000 (ALCR, Exp. Leg. 10934, pp. 1680, 5033; ALCR, Exp. Leg. A45-E8008, p. 225). On Alem's case, see ALCR, Exp. Leg. A45-E8008, pp. 216–28; ALCR, Exp. Leg. 10934, pp. 1664–700, 4973–5053; *LN*, November 4 and 10, 1988; July 25, 1989; *Extra*, April 19, 1989.

hoped to land a key position in the administration, preferably the Ministry of Public Works and Transport, resorted to the PLN's newly elected legislative caucus, which lobbied in his favor before the president-elect. Though Arias eventually yielded to the pressure of his party, Alem's reward was meager: nearly one year into the administration he was appointed to an obscure diplomatic post, devoid of political power, from which he would be swiftly dismissed ten months later, when his suspicious financial activities became known to the president. A few months after his dismissal, Alem would be arrested on money-laundering charges, leading to a series of trials in Costa Rica and the United States and to his serving several years in a Florida jail for his involvement in international narcotics trafficking.[23] In the course of his trial in the United States, Alem claimed to have remained politically involved even after his arrest and to have contributed to the campaign of two PLN congressional candidates as late as 1993–94. The alleged recipients denied the accusations.

Serious as they were, these findings were not the main purpose of the investigations. The core of the allegations investigated by Congress concerned the purported donations received by both main parties in 1985 from General Manuel A. Noriega, neighboring Panama's strongman at the time.[24] When the accusations surfaced, in 1989, Noriega was already in the center of an international row over his own alleged drug-trafficking operations, which eventually led to his being ousted from power by a U.S. military intervention. Although the congressional probe confirmed that both major presidential candidates, Arias and Calderón-Fournier, had met Noriega during the campaign, his contributions were never unequivocally established. The only proven link in the story was a $60,000 contribution to the PLN from Panama's ruling Democratic Revolutionary Party (PRD), at the time controlled by Noriega. PLN officials indicated that this donation was part of a long tradition of collaboration among "sister" parties that was hardly suspicious in 1986.[25]

Although the probes failed to show that any party authority had knowingly accepted contributions from questionable sources, they did reveal a disturbing lack of selectivity on the part of fundraisers and the absence of mechanisms to filter out suspicious contributions.[26] In 1985–86 the economic strain of a close

23. Currently, Alem, who returned to Costa Rica after serving his sentence in the United States, is once again behind bars following a drug bust in Costa Rica in 2008. See *LN*, August 9, 2008, April 29, 2009.

24. *LN*, November 4 and 10, 1988; January 19, January 27, April 15, June 1, June 9, June 13, June 23, and July 25, 1989. *Extra*, April 15, April 19, July 21, July 27, 1989; *LPL*, October 17, 1988; *LR*, April 15, 1989.

25. ALCR, Exp. Leg. 10934, pp. 6987–89. Both the PLN and the PRD have long been members of the Socialist International.

26. ALCR, Exp. Leg. 10934, pp. 6996–97.

election, the parties' imperviousness to the threat of drug trafficking, and the lack of regulation proved a dangerous cocktail. Arias would later admit that, in 1985, "in a convulsed Central America, where drug traffickers wanted to infiltrate themselves to buy influence, . . . we simply did not notice that reality had changed and kept applying the traditions of the past: to accept contributions in good faith if we did not have any suspicion about the contributor's moral quality."[27] In the absence of a legal framework, money was "sought everywhere."[28] In terms of their legitimacy and the reputation of their leaders, Costa Rican parties paid dearly for their adherence to the "traditions of the past."

At this point it is worth pausing to consider some of the patterns common to these cases. The most obvious one is the prominent role of foreign donors in the narrative. The frequency with which foreign contributions lead to great political scandals may simply be a function of the particular distrust that they elicit—the tendency to harshly judge their underlying motives. But that's not the only reason. As the 1986 Costa Rican experience shows, the fundraisers' self-control mechanisms are peculiarly useless vis-à-vis foreign donors. There are more scandals stemming from foreign donations because in a very small country like Costa Rica, the odds that disreputable foreign contributors will go undetected are greater than is the case for national donors.[29] That is, contributions from nondomestic sources have less chance of being subject to the social and reputational filters that closely knit domestic business elites are subject to.[30]

The story's second remarkable element, directly related to the first one, is the foreign donor's quest of immunity from international prosecution by seeking either protection from extradition, Costa Rican citizenship, or a diplomatic appointment. This is most evident in the case of Vesco but is also present in those of Melo, Rubin, and probably Elizalde, Fionna, Casey, and the owners of Ocean Hunter. As opposed to the case of most political donors, who tend to court the good will of politicians, the expected payoff from foreign contributions appears to have been very specific in all these examples. It was access to top decisionmakers, but access with a definite purpose in mind. It is nothing short of remarkable, and probably a testament to the strength of Costa Rican institutions, that in all cases the bid for immunity ultimately met with failure.

Whatever the final outcome of these cases may have been, the 1986 experience proved a turning point for Costa Rican political parties, not least because of the immense embarrassment inflicted on high-ranking politicians—notably

27. ALCR, Exp. Leg. 10934, p. 5051. Similar remarks by several politicians from the PLN and the PUSC are frequent in this file (pp. 1686, 1873, 4294, 4852, 4996).
28. *LN*, June 23, 1989.
29. Costa Rica's population is approximately 4.5 million.
30. See Casas-Zamora (2005, pp. 131–33).

Presidents Arias and Calderón-Fournier—called to testify in a drug-trafficking probe.[31] A former PLN treasurer notes that the 1986 campaign "awoke our awareness that we couldn't hurry along with fundraising mechanisms."[32] As is seen below, the available evidence supports his words: private contributions to parties fell precipitously during the 1989–90 national campaign and have remained relatively low ever since. Moreover, the findings of the 1987–92 investigations also led to the revamping of political finance rules in 1996, which included a ban on foreign contributions, contribution ceilings, and the parties' obligation to periodically report their income sources.

As mentioned earlier, both the design and enforcement of these norms were defective. It soon became evident that neither the increased awareness of the risks nor the new statutes were enough to prevent fundraisers from engaging in troubling practices and cultivating inconvenient links. In May 1997 the press found out that PUSC presidential candidate and future president Miguel Angel Rodríguez (1998–02) and former president Calderón-Fournier had travelled to Toluca, Mexico, to visit Carlos Hank-González, a Mexican businessman and former cabinet member in the administrations of the Revolutionary Institutional Party (PRI).[33] A man of humble origins, Hank-González had long been a powerful and controversial figure in Mexico, where the source of his apparently immense fortune had been the subject of speculation for many years. In 1999 a U.S. National Drug Intelligence Center report accused Hank-González's family of using its businesses to move cocaine to the United States and also of laundering millions of dollars in drug money.[34]

Rodríguez's trip, clearly intended to remain secret, stirred up a scandal in Costa Rica, where the press and the PLN demanded to know whether Hank-González was bankrolling the PUSC campaign. The inevitable congressional probe was hampered by political disputes and, in the end, ended without any significant findings.[35] Rodríguez admitted to meeting Hank-González but denied any knowledge of the controversies surrounding his host or of him

---

31. Their testimonies before Congress were given prominent coverage in the press. The day after Arias's appearance, one of the newspapers ran the headline "Arias Survived His Bitter Hour" (1992).

32. Antonio Burgués, former PLN treasurer, interview by author, San José, November 11, 1999.

33. *LN*, May 24, 1997.

34. Dent (2002, pp. 156–58); Curzio (2000, p. 88); "Tons of Cocaine" (1995); "Prominent Mexican Family" (1999).

35. ALCR, Comisión Permanente Especial sobre Narcotráfico—Sobre los posibles vínculos, las actividades comerciales y las relaciones políticas del señor Carlos Hank González, sus hijos y su grupo empresarial en Costa Rica [Special Permanent Committee on Drug Trafficking—On the possible links, commercial activities and political relations of Mr. Carlos Hank González and his business conglomerate in Costa Rica]. *LN*, August 6, 1999; August 22, September 23, September 28, and September 29, 2000.

making any contribution to his campaign. To this day Hank-González's support for Rodríguez remains a matter of speculation.

Worse was to come four years later. In September 2002 it was divulged that fundraising irregularities had marred the presidential campaign of President Abel Pacheco (2002–06) of the PUSC.[36] The discovery of several donations that went unreported to the TSE, amounting to about $120,000, led to the discovery of a very complex financial operation managed by the president's entourage. The operation was at the margins of the party's formal organs and, presumably, was unknown to Pacheco. The parallel fundraising structure involved a number of bank accounts, some of them in Panama, which held more than $6 million in private contributions. In some cases the contributions came from foreign individuals and firms, openly violating the legal ban. Moreover, in at least four cases the contributions surpassed by a large margin the ceiling established by law. The two largest donations came from two Taiwan-based firms (Pacific Co. Ltd., $200,000; Sunshine Co. Ltd, $300,000) widely believed to belong to the Taiwanese government. At the time, Costa Rica was one of a handful of countries that granted diplomatic recognition to Taiwan.

Irregular fundraising practices, including concealment of donations under false names in party reports and acquisition of foreign donations, were also detected in the PLN and—to a lesser extent—the PAC campaigns.[37]

The unveiling of extensive political finance violations led to several relevant consequences. The PUSC's main fundraisers faced criminal charges, from which they were eventually acquitted due to the loopholes allowed by the rules enacted in 1996, thus revealing the urgency of reforming the latter.[38] In the meantime, the PLN's internal organs harshly punished the party's presidential candidate in 2002, Rolando Araya, as well as his chief fundraiser.[39] The affair led to yet another congressional probe on political finance (the sixth one in three decades!), this time a very comprehensive one.[40] It also led to a landmark decision by the Constitutional Court, lifting bank secrecy rules in all matters pertaining to political finance.[41] Most important of all, the scandal galvanized a new effort to reform campaign finance rules and their enforcement, which bore fruit in August 2009.

---

36. Casas-Zamora (2004, pp. 240–42). *LN,* September 20–25, September 30, October 9–10, October 14–19, and November 5, 2002; April 4, May 9, May 30, and June 7, 2003.

37. *LN,* January 29–30, February 12–15, March 24–26, September 21, September 24, September 26–27, 2002; September 5, October 8–10, October 31, November 7, 2003.

38. *LN,* September 25, November 12–13, 2002; August 3, 2007.

39. *LN,* March 7, 2003.

40. ALCR, Exp. Leg. 15002.

41. SCCR, vote 3489-03, May 2, 2003.

Notwithstanding the seriousness of the violations denounced after the 2002 election, an important factor was conspicuously absent from the scandal: organized crime. In 2002 Costa Rican fundraisers proved to be more than willing to violate a toothless law but not to drop their own internal mechanisms to filter out donations from compromising sources. This self-imposed boundary points to the lasting effects of the 1986 experience in the psyche of Costa Rica's top politicians and campaign managers. As is seen in the next section, fear of public association with drug traffickers among wealthy fundraisers continues to be a barrier against the penetration of dirty money, even in the absence of effective legal controls. This is, of course, a weak protection, but it is better than nothing.

New Controls versus New Risks: Political Finance in Costa Rica Today

The rules introduced in 2009 will likely have profound effects in the way Costa Rican political parties fund their activities. These effects add to the lingering consequences of all the scandals described in the previous section. At the national level—and this is an important qualification—Costa Rica is reasonably well equipped to fend off the threat of the penetration of crime syndicates through campaign finance. A simple repeat of the worst debacles of the past is, as of today, highly unlikely.

This assurance stands despite the fact that the cost of national elections in Costa Rica has gone up in the recent past (figure 5-1). Total expenditure in national elections tracks the availability of direct state funding very closely. The considerable spending leap in the 2010 election—when it reached almost $27 million[42]—was largely a function of the simultaneous increase in public funding. In other words, and crucially, the growth in campaign spending in Costa Rica appears to be supply driven rather than demand driven. This means that despite the growing cost of national elections, the urgency to collect private donations has remained in check.

In fact, the data suggest that the parties' overall reliance on subsidies reached 70 percent of total expenditure in 2006 and nearly 90 percent in 2010, well above the previous historic mean of 60–70 percent. The chief financial officer of the PLN's 2010 campaign, by far the biggest spender in the contest, estimated that 92 percent of the party's outlays ($12 million by his own reckoning) would end up being covered by public funding once the subsidies were disbursed.[43]

---

42. This figure excludes mayoral elections, held separately in December 2010.
43. Jorge Walter Bolaños, chief fundraiser for the 2010 PLN campaign, interview by author, San José, June 22, 2010.

Figure 5-1. *Election Expenditure and Direct State Funding in Costa Rica, 1978–2010*[a]

Millions of 1995 U.S. dollars

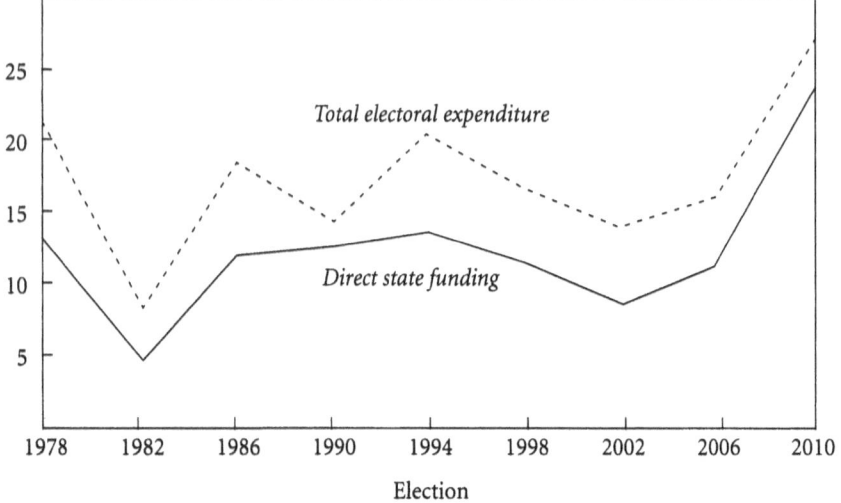

Source: Casas-Zamora (2005); TSE; Departamento de Financiamiento Político.
a. Expenditure data for 2002 exclude second-round run-off. Direct state funding for 2010 refers to allocated rather than actually disbursed subsidies.

For the PAC and the PUSC the proportion is even higher.[44] Among the party system's relevant actors only the Libertarian Movement Party (PML) deviated from this norm, partly out of conviction and partly because the party grossly overestimated its electoral prospects and the postelection subsidies it would collect. Even so, in all likelihood the PML will see nearly three-quarters of its spending covered by the state.[45]

As explained above, even though the bulk of the subsidies is not paid until after the election, the expectation of state disbursements is the single most important instrument for raising money during the campaign. The bulk of campaign resources comes from bank loans, using party bonds as collateral; in addition, goods and services are paid for using the same bonds as currency. As much as 80 percent of the PLN-issued bonds were used as collateral, as was the

---

44. Francisco Molina, PAC campaign manager in 2010, interview by author, San José, June 17, 2010. PUSC figures are author's own elaboration from TSE official public funding figures and party financial reports submitted to the TSE's Political Finance Department.
45. *LN*, June 18, 2010.

case with practically all those put in circulation by the PAC.[46] The rest are sold to private investors.

These financial operations raise many relevant issues, including the disturbing weight that opinion polls have in the banks' decision to accept the bonds as suitable loan guarantees. More fundamental from the standpoint of fundraising integrity, however, is the fact that while political parties must report each successive bond issue to the electoral authorities, bond purchasers remain anonymous. This leaves open a loophole amid the otherwise robust transparency rules that cover simple donations. Moreover, if party bonds are engineered in a way that makes their reimbursement contingent on unrealistic electoral expectations, they are turned de facto into plain, unlimited, anonymous contributions. Given the previous experiences with investors such as McAlpin, Elizalde, and Rubin, described above, the risks entailed by this loophole should be reasonably obvious. Correcting this weakness ranks very high among the priorities for future political finance reforms, according to the country's top electoral officer.[47]

Limited though their overall weight may be, parties continue to court private donors. The winning PLN campaign in 2010 collected approximately $1 million in private donations, a significant decrease from the $2.5 million raised by the party on the road to victory in 2006.[48] The chief fundraisers in both campaigns attribute the reduction largely to the recently introduced ban on corporate donations, which, coupled with more stringent transparency rules, made many business donors wary of openly contributing in 2010.[49] For the PAC, private donations were "almost nonexistent," in the words of its campaign manager.[50] According to available evidence, it is hard to argue with the assertion made by one of the PLN officials that over the past two election cycles in Costa Rica private funding has simply lost relevance.[51]

This is probably a piece of good news, but it is not the only one. All the party officials interviewed for this chapter confirmed that some of the better traits

---

46. Bolaños interview; Molina interview.
47. Antonio Sobrado, president of the TSE, interview by author, San José, June 21, 2010.
48. Author's calculation based on figures from the party financial reports submitted to the TSE's Political Finance Department.
49. Alfredo Ortuño, chief fundraiser for the 2006 PLN campaign, interview by author, San José, June 17, 2010.
50. Molina interview. He estimates them at less than $200,000, including bond purchases. This assertion does not run contrary to the fact that in 2010 the PAC submitted expense claims to the TSE for more than $8.3 million, which is nearly $1 million in excess of the subsidies to which it was entitled. While less severely than the PML, the PAC overestimated its electoral result and wound up indebted as a result.
51. Ortuño interview.

that usually define campaign fundraising in Costa Rica continue unchanged—and have in fact been further entrenched by the new regulations.

Thus private resources continue to be raised almost exclusively among business donors with whom the chief fundraiser and the presidential candidate are familiar or about whom they have direct and trustworthy references. Moreover, as one of the interviewees pointed out, in Costa Rica those donors are, by and large, the same in every election cycle.[52]

The sudden emergence of unknown characters offering to aid a campaign is met with immediate suspicion, particularly if the amount offered is large. And *large*, in the Costa Rican context, means, according to all sources, more than $10,000. One PLN fundraiser made the point very precisely: "The largest private contribution that we collected throughout the [2010] campaign was $50,000, and that was a purchase of bonds. In no case did pure donations go beyond $25,000."[53] He went on to describe his startled reaction when a Venezuelan donor referred by a local lawyer offered to buy $10 million in party bonds. The prospective contributor was put off with a curt, *Don't call me, I'll call you.* As one of the interviewees put it, "No one gives more than $50,000 out of pure conviction. People are not *that* generous. There is only one Mother Theresa."[54]

Besides the use of simple suspicion and hunches, fundraisers take other measures to protect themselves against the risks inherent in dealing with unfamiliar donors. One PLN fundraiser mentioned that in the very exceptional instances that he dealt with unfamiliar donors he submitted inquiries to World-check, a global screening system, and to the DEA, the result of which he saved in print.[55] Financial officers from different parties also agree on the critical importance of arranging a personal meeting with prospective donors. In one case this protection was taken further: the presidential candidate would never meet any donor on her own. As remarked by one of the interviewees, "Faceless donors are not game."[56]

Neither are contributions in cash. This is a basic security measure as much as a matter of convenience. While the image of a bagman carrying bundles of cash from the drug cartels features prominently in political finance debates in Latin America, the reality is far more complicated. In practice, in a modern country with adequate financial oversight, such as Costa Rica, cash is of rather limited use when running a campaign. As one of the party treasurers explained very convincingly to the author, among the most expensive campaign items—notably media

52. Bolaños interview.
53. Bolaños interview.
54. Ortuño interview.
55. Ortuño interview.
56. Molina interview.

expenditures, but also salaries, opinion polls, and transportation services—there is none that could be paid for in cash without raising the eyebrows of both service providers and financial authorities. In order to be useful, large cash donations must be formalized somehow, thus starting a paper trail. In the words of the treasurer of the PLN 2006 campaign: "Yes, cash is untraceable, but is also largely unusable."[57] While it is still possible to think of small-scale uses of cash in the context of a campaign, the interesting paradox of "futile cash" offers some kind of protection against the use of campaigns for money-laundering purposes.[58]

Far more important than all these measures, however, is the fact that Costa Rican fundraisers are acutely aware of the stringent legal controls that they are operating under and of the likelihood that the enforcement of political finance provisions will change dramatically as a result of the 2009 reform. This level of attention is a consequence of the unequivocal mandate given to the TSE, as well as of the unification of political finance enforcement under one roof, regardless of the funds' public or private origin. Before 2009 the TSE's mandate was not just unclear; it was also shared with the General Controller's Office, the body entrusted with the task of approving the parties' expense claims and, ultimately, the payment of state subsidies. With the legally ordered creation of the Department of Political Finance within the TSE, such division is now gone. This cohesion improves coordination and specialization.[59]

Fundraisers' caution is sharpest when they are seeking donations from foreign sources. The existing penalties, as well as the legacy of past political finance scandals—almost all of them linked to foreign donations—have made the quest for the latter a no-go area for most Costa Rican fundraisers. One of them remarked that "those campaigns in which it was said that *So-an-so had been sent to X country and had returned with a suitcase full of money* is something that I have never witnessed since I have been involved in this. That's not the way Costa Rican campaigns are funded these days."[60]

Both the experience of former president Arias with Ricardo Alem as well as that of Fernán Guardia, the hapless PUSC treasurer during the 2002 campaign, who spent years waging legal battles to avoid going to jail for abuses that were not entirely of his own making, were explicitly mentioned by PLN officials as dire warnings of what could happen to careless or risk-prone fundraisers. One

57. Ortuño interview.
58. The detection of a suitcase filled with $800,000 for the campaign of Argentina's president Cristina Fernández in 2007 confirms that these things do indeed happen, rare as they may be. See "Caso maletín" (2007); "Maletín" (2008); "Conviction in Spy Case" (2008).
59. Sobrado interview; Ronald Chacón, director of Department of Political Finance at the TSE, interview by author, San José, June 21, 2010.
60. Ortuño interview.

of them put it clearly: "The risk of seeing one's name associated with a drug trafficker is something one takes very seriously, not just for one's own sake but for the sake of the whole organization. That kind of thing is an indelible stain. The fact of the matter is that twenty-five years later we keep on talking about Alem."[61]

Underlying much of this wariness is fundraisers' realization of the role of the Costa Rican press, which has grown in assertiveness and credibility in the recent past. The press-driven scandals that led to the arrest and prosecution of former presidents Calderón-Fournier and Rodríguez on corruption charges in 2004 (unrelated to political finance) left behind an aggressive press corps for which party funding is an obvious target of investigation. The introduction of reporting rules in 1996, however imperfectly enforced, has endowed journalists with a frame for posing uncomfortable questions to candidates and fundraisers. That's exactly how the 2002 scandal came about: by the inquisitiveness of the press and with very little intervention from electoral authorities.

None of these safeguards are, of course, watertight. The risk with bond purchases has already been mentioned. The chief fundraiser for the current president, Laura Chinchilla, made known to the author his concern about the possible role of prominent law firms in the country acting as bundlers for contributions collected from some of their foreign clients.[62] Finally, the doubts raised by a series of cumbersome financial operations made by the right-wing PML during the 2010 campaign, amounting to nearly $700,000, had already raised the specter of renewed attempts to conceal donations from banned sources, either corporate or foreign.[63] While troubling, the allegations against the PML were widely aired by the media during the campaign, had consequences for the party at the polls, and quickly led to an investigation by the TSE that is still under way as of this writing.[64] Rather than a sign of systemic failure, these incidents are reminders that no amount of good legislation may be able to deter reckless fundraising practices in all cases.

While the danger of proceeds from organized crime making their way into campaign coffers has clearly receded at the national level, it remains a real concern at the subnational level. This is so despite the fact that election costs at this level remain relatively modest. A system in which the congressional election is held concurrently with the presidential election under closed party lists all

---

61. Ortuño interview.
62. Bolaños interview.
63. *LN*, December 24, 2009; January 8, January 12–14, January 20, 2010. Chacón interview.
64. Days after the election, Otto Guevara, the PML presidential candidate, admitted that the clouds around his party's funding practices cost him dearly at the polls (*LN*, February 9, 2010).

but guarantees that campaigns are run in a centralized fashion and that individual candidates are exempt from financial obligations. To be sure, in the PLN there is a fierce internal competition for the nomination to a slot on the party list, a competition that is ultimately settled by the presidential candidate.[65] This dynamic entails costs that in the worst cases are in the region of $50,000 per candidate.[66] In other parties, notably the PAC, those costs are between nonexistent and minimal.[67]

Equally modest are the costs of direct popular elections for mayors in the country's eighty-one municipalities, an innovation introduced in the past decade. In this case, however, the separation of the election from the presidential election means that the role of the parties' central offices is far more limited, and candidates are forced to develop their own campaign structures. A viable candidate at the local level typically spends $20,000 in a small rural municipality, about $50,000 in an urban jurisdiction, and in excess of $100,000 in the country's largest cities.[68]

Despite a decentralization process that seems to be gaining momentum, the powers of local governments and the attention paid to municipal elections continue to be very limited in Costa Rica.[69] Not surprisingly, costs at this level are low, and fundraising activities are hardly sophisticated, with the candidate, his family, and a few close associates bearing the brunt of campaign outlays. In many ways, these processes display the same features that define fundraising at the national level, only on a much smaller scale. By all accounts, the contributions raised at the municipal level are very small and only rarely come from donors with whom the candidate does not enjoy close personal links.[70] Unsolicited campaign contributions are almost unheard of. As a PLN mayoral candidate succinctly put it: "In this business nobody comes knocking on your door offering money. That's just not the way it is."[71]

---

65. See Casas-Zamora and Briceño-Fallas (1991).

66. Casas-Zamora (2005, p. 137); Ortuño interview.

67. Francisco Molina, a former PAC congressman, estimated at less than $4,000 the total cost of his nomination and eventual election to the Legislative Assembly. See Molina interview.

68. Feliciano Alvarez, mayor of Buenos Aires County—PLN, interview by author, San José, June 18, 2010; Jorge Rojas, mayor of Bagaces County—PLN, interview by author, San José, June 18, 2010; Fernando Trejos, mayor of Montes de Oca County—Costa Rican Renovation Party (PRC), interview by author, San José, June 18, 2010.

69. Municipal governments command only 2.3 percent of total public expenditure in Costa Rica, the lowest figure in Latin America. Absenteeism in the 2006 mayoral election was 77 percent (Letelier, 2007).

70. Alvarez interview; Rojas interview; Trejos interview.

71. Alvarez interview.

The real problem with subnational elections in Costa Rica is neither the cost nor the complexity of fundraising but rather the utter lack of financial controls as well as the very weak oversight exerted by the media and civil society groups. The fundraising structures developed by congressional or mayoral candidates are outside the oversight of both the TSE and the parties' central offices. With a certain degree of surprise, three mayoral candidates confided to the author that they are not required to file *any* reports on their finances to *any* authority, either internal or external.[72] Congressional candidates are not even expected to submit documents to back up the expenses made in their districts with the money transferred to them by the parties' central offices. As a result, electoral authorities, party officers, and even journalists know next to nothing about political finance realities at the subnational level.[73] When it comes to political finance in Costa Rica, laissez-faire rules at the subnational level.

In a context of total deregulation, the limited cost of subnational elections has an ambiguous effect. While it keeps risk-prone fundraising behavior in check, it also makes sure that a very little sum of money can get the candidate very far. In other words, gaining access and influence is a very inexpensive endeavor at the local level. Not only that: low expenses also dissolve most of the problems created by the use of cash in campaigns. Disbursing cash to pay for small-scale goods and services is considered normal, particularly in rural areas.

The inexpensive and free-flowing nature of local campaigns is likely to become a pressing concern if the powers of local governments, notably their police prerogatives, grow stronger. So far there have not been any public allegations about the use of money from spurious sources in mayoral elections, although some of those interviewed in the course of this research expressed concern about the situation in Limón, the country's main port on the Caribbean, where drug trafficking thrives.[74] One of the senior fundraisers interviewed summed up the risks: "If the corruption of organized crime is to filter through campaigns in Costa Rica, it would happen at the local level."[75]

While it failed to introduce political finance controls at the subnational level, the 2009 reform did make a crucial change in earmarking almost $9 million in public subsidies for the December 2010 election of mayors. Given the limited electoral outlays, the availability of these resources (subject to the same rules as the subsidy for national elections) is likely to ease the candidates' financial pressures and temptations. But if history is any guide, it will not be enough to protect the system in the long run.

72. Alvarez interview; Rojas interview; Trejos interview.
73. Bolaños interview; Ortuño interview; Molina interview; Sobrado interview; Chacón interview.
74. See Porth (2011).
75. Ortuño interview.

A Final Reflection on Lessons and Policy Recommendations

The last passage of the previous section points to one of the crucial lessons of the Costa Rican experience on the role of organized crime in funding political activities. The sheer availability of public funding, no matter how generous, is a blunt instrument to protect political finance integrity in the absence of other tightly enforced regulations. The robust public funding scheme may have helped the selectivity of fundraisers on the margins, but it did not immunize the system against egregious abuses and reckless fundraising practices. The scandals kept bubbling up with disturbing regularity. And it should be remembered that this happened in a small country where the social dynamics that surround fundraising, with their heavy premium on reputation, offer some protection against the penetration of organized crime. Quite simply, for the dangers of organized crime to be fended off there are no substitutes for strong transparency rules and well-enforced controls over the parties' finances.

The adoption of a comprehensive and well-designed political finance reform package in 2009 is a very good sign that the risks that beset political finance activities in Costa Rica have finally sunk in. As seen above, the scandals that tainted the 1986 campaign were a turning point and modified political finance practices in important ways, even before the government adopted legal controls. The Costa Rican experience is that of a process of social learning in which the total lack of regulation over fundraising activities was replaced by weak controls and, eventually, by much stronger measures. As it has been shown time and again all over the world, political finance scandals were the driving force behind this process. The adoption of political finance regulations is almost always a reactive process, rather than a preemptive one.

Along the way, even very imperfect regulations may help. The introduction of poorly enforced norms in 1996 was certainly a source of grief in subsequent campaigns. However, it also helped entrench the notion that political finance transparency is necessary and that reporting to the authorities the state of their finances should be a normal part of the workings of parties in a democracy. At this point, the reporting task has been accepted as part and parcel of the role of any party treasurer in Costa Rica, at least at the national level. Moreover, and crucially, even in the absence of effective auditing by the authorities, party reports endowed other social controls with hard data to start asking questions. If the parties were lying about their finances, now they were doing so in writing. This paper trail proved critical for the media's role in uncovering the abuses of the 2002 campaign. There is a lesson here for would-be political finance reformers: aim at the perfect but settle for the good or even the less than good. In many cases, poorly designed and enforced political finance regulations may be better in the long run than no regulation at all.

When examining the Costa Rican case it is hard to avoid the conclusion that foreign donations demand special attention if the political finance system is to be protected against organized crime. Foreign donations of spurious origin are simply more likely to slip through the cracks of the social controls that inform fundraising practices in Costa Rica. Besides other kinds of risks, the use of political donations to seek immunity from international prosecution is a possibility that must be taken seriously in a country that, sadly, has developed a troubling reputation as a haven for all sorts of shady characters.[76] Fortunately, it is with regard to coveting foreign donations that Costa Rican fundraising practices seem to have improved the most in recent years, not just out of fear of the existing regulations but also out of the genuine conviction of most fundraisers about the inconvenience of these contributions.

Generally speaking, today the Costa Rican political finance system is much better prepared to deal with the threat of organized crime than a generation ago. Yet it is essential that the current regulation be subject to permanent revision and adjustment. Bolstered by their success in getting the 2009 reforms through Congress, the electoral authorities appear ready to engage in a second round of political finance reforms. Some of the critical assignments are about bringing down campaign costs, which to this day remain unregulated. This requires, as seen above, controlling the increase in public subsidies. In Costa Rica, subsidies drive election spending and are, in essence, linked to the country's economic growth, as measured by the GDP. Replacing the current subsidy rules with a system that fixes a subvention amount per vote and then indexes it according to inflation would be a welcome change. Equally important is the banning of paid television advertising during campaigns, to be replaced with free media allowances distributed equally among parties. This public service has long been the standard in most Western European countries as well as a few Latin American ones, such as Mexico, Brazil, and Chile. Today, according to senior party officials in Costa Rica, television advertising comprises at least 50 percent of total expenditures in national campaigns.[77]

Other important reforms concern the increase of preelection subsidies and the regulation of party bonds to preclude the anonymity of their holders. This would go a long way in closing a weakness in the current transparency rules.

The most urgent reform, however, is about reining in fundraising activities at the subnational level, which today are the weakest link in the chain to forestall the threat of organized crime to political finance integrity. Introducing the

---

76. See *LN*, October 26, 1997.

77. Bolaños interview; Ortuño interview; Molina interview. Casas-Zamora (2005) reports a much lower proportion until 1998, based upon the documents submitted by the parties to the authorities in order to claim public subsidies.

simple obligation of mayoral candidates to report their funding sources to the TSE would be a significant improvement to the status quo. Yet it is worth giving consideration to the adoption of the British electoral agent, as a prerequisite to run a candidacy at the local level.[78]

The adoption of these changes would turn Costa Rica into a remarkable exception: a country that reforms its political finance rules to preempt a foretold disaster. For an unsavory episode may happen again. Diminished as it is, the threat of organized crime to Costa Rican elections is nonetheless real and will continue to loom large over campaigns for many years to come.

References

"A Last Vanishing Act for Robert Vesco, Fugitive." 2008. *New York Times*, March 5.
Asamblea Legislativa de Costa Rica (ALCR). Comisión Permanente Especial sobre Narcotráfico (Special Permanent Committee on Drug Trafficking). Sobre los posibles vínculos, las actividades comerciales y las relaciones políticas del señor Carlos Hank González, sus hijos y su grupo empresarial en Costa Rica.
_____. Expediente Ley No. 2036.
_____. Exp. Ley No. 2667.
_____. Exp. Ley No. 4765.
_____. Exp. Ley No. 7094.
_____. Exp. Legislativo A45-E8008.
_____. Exp. Leg. 7898.
_____. Exp. Leg. 10200.
_____. Exp. Leg. 10684.
_____. Exp. Leg. 10934.
_____. Exp. Leg. 15002.
Blackburn, Robert. 1995. *The Electoral System in Britain*. London: Macmillan.
Block, Alan. 1998. *Masters of Paradise: Organized Crime and the Internal Revenue Service the Bahamas*. New Brunswick, N.J.: Transaction.
Blum, Jack. 1999. "Offshore Money." In *Transnational Crime in the Americas*, edited by Tom Farer. New York: Routledge/Inter American Dialogue.
Bode, Ken. 1977. "Don Pepe." *The New Republic*, April 23.
Casas-Zamora, Kevin. 2001. "Contribución estatal a los partidos políticos en Costa Rica: Apuntes sobre sus efectos en la dinámica del sistema de partidos." In *La Democracia de Costa Rica ante el Siglo XXI*, edited by Jorge Rovira. San José: Editorial Universidad de Costa Rica/Fundación Friedrich Ebert.

---

78. The election agent is an innovation introduced in Britain in 1883, aimed at centralizing the control of and responsibility for the financial activities of candidates. Candidates must appoint a financial manager for their campaign. All electoral contributions and expenditures must be channeled through the electoral agent, who is legally responsible for the campaign's compliance with political finance laws (Blackburn, 1995, pp. 270–71).

———.2003. "Financiamiento de campañas en Centroamérica y Panamá." *Cuadernos de CAPEL*, No. 48. San José.

———.2004. "Regulando el financiamiento político en Costa Rica: Algunas reflexiones prácticas." In *Modernización del Estado Costarricense*, edited by Mimi Prado. San José: Centro Internacional para el Desarrollo Humano/Fundación Konrad Adenauer.

———. 2005. *Paying for Democracy: Political Finance and State Funding for Parties*. Colchester: European Consortium for Political Research.

Casas-Zamora, Kevin, and Olman Briceño-Fallas. 1991. *¿Democracia Representativa en Costa Rica? Análisis del Sistema de Elección de Diputados y sus Perspectivas de Cambio*. San José: Tesis de Grado, Universidad de Costa Rica.

Casas-Zamora, Kevin, and Daniel Zovatto. 2011. "Para llegar a tiempo: Apuntes sobre la regulación del financiamiento político en América Latina." In *Financiamento de los Partidos en América Latina*, edited by Pablo Gutiérrez and Daniel Zovatto. México, D.F.: UNAM/IDEA/OAS.

"Caso maletín: cuatro detenidos en EE.UU." 2007. *BBC mundo.com*, December 13.

"Conviction in Spy Case over Cash-Filled Suitcase." 2008. *New York Times*, November 3.

Curzio, Leonardo. 2000. "Organized crime and political campaign finance in Mexico." In *Organized Crime and Democratic Governability*, edited by John Bailey and Roy Godson. University of Pittsburgh Press.

Dent, David. 2002. *Encyclopedia of Modern Mexico*. Lanham, Md.: Scarecrow.

Excelsior (EXC). San José, various years.

Extra (EXT). San José, various years.

Hutchinson, Robert. 1975. *Vesco*. New York: Praeger.

La Nación (LN). San José, various years.

La Prensa Libre (LPL). San José, various years.

La República (LR). San José, various years.

"Learning to Love Exile." 1976. *Time*, February 9.

Letelier, Leonardo. 2007. *El Gasto Municipal en Centroamérica y la República Dominicana*. Washington: Inter-American Development Bank.

"Maletín: apuntan al gobierno venezolano." 2008. *BBC mundo.com*, October 17.

Porth, Michael. 2011. "Costa Rica in the Crosshairs." *Insight Crime: Organized Crime in the Americas* (www.insightcrime.org/costa-rica-in-the-cross-hairs-part-i).

"Prominent Mexican Family Viewed as Threat to the U.S." 1999. *Washington Post*, June 2.

"Robert Vesco." 2008. *The Times* (London), May 12.

Rosen, James. 2008. "Rogue on the Run." *Portfolio* magazine, February.

Sala Constitucional de la Corte Suprema de Justicia, Costa Rica (SCCR). Vote No. 980-91, May 24, 1991.

———.Vote No. 3489-03, May 2, 2003.

Suñol, Julio. 1978. *Robert Vesco Compra una República*. San José: Imprenta Trejos.

"Tons of Cocaine Reaching Mexico in Old Jets." 1995. *New York Times*, January 10.

UNODC (United Nations Office on Drugs and Crime). 2008. *World Drugs Report*.

"Vesco in Costa Rica." 1973. *Time*, May 21.

Interviews Conducted by the Author

Feliciano Alvarez, mayor of Buenos Aires County—PLN: San José, June 18, 2010.
Jorge Walter Bolaños, chief fundraiser 2010 campaign—PLN: San José, June 22, 2010.
Antonio Burgués, former party treasurer—PLN: San José, November 11, 1999.
Ronald Chacón, director of Department of Political Finance, Supreme Elections Tribunal: San José, June 21, 2010.
Francisco Molina, campaign manager 2010—PAC: San José, June 17, 2010.
Alfredo Ortuño, chief fundraiser 2006 campaign—PLN: San José, June 17, 2010.
Jorge Rojas, mayor of Bagaces County—PLN: San José, June 18, 2010.
Antonio Sobrado, president of the Supreme Elections Tribunal: San José, June 21, 2010.
Fernando Trejos, mayor of Montes de Oca County—Union for Change Party: San José, June 18, 2010.

LEONARDO CURZIO

6 Mexico: Organized Crime and Elections

Managing money in politics has been a challenge for democracies since the time of ancient Greece. Even though the dilemmas associated with political financing vary across time and space, the central concern remains the same: preserving the autonomy of the political system and keeping the influence of money—and the agenda of those who provide it—at bay.[1] As we know all too well, the consequences of unbridled funds in politics are dire, as the voice of a select group takes over that of the general public, and the priorities and preferences of oligarchic circles override the national interest. Mexico is, in many ways, a typical case of a democracy gone astray, given the influence of powerful—legitimate and illegitimate—economic interest groups.[2]

This chapter traces the destructive effects of drug money on Mexican institutions and captures the evolution of the relationship between illicit money and politics in the country, culminating with the Felipe Calderón administration as it faced ever-growing and stronger criminal organizations. The aim is to determine whether dirty money—particularly from drug cartels—became a threat to the functioning of Mexican democracy. Intuitively, the answer is yes. But it is important to establish the exact ways in which the institutional system has developed to counter this undesirable penetration. It is worth noting that the chapter does not cover all dimensions of drug trafficking; the aim is more modest and is limited to studying the new interactions between the criminal world and the party system, with particular emphasis on electoral campaign financing.

Following in the footsteps of other nations afflicted with similar ills, the Mexican government's chief response has been to pass campaign finance legislation

---

1. This topic has been dealt with in depth by Fisichella (2002).
2. The distinction between legitimate and illegitimate economic interests is not determined by moral or normative criteria; rather, it is simply a legal distinction. By *illegitimate* I mean those that operate and profit from illegal activities such as drug trafficking.

and to provide public financing to political parties. For decades, however, Mexico had targeted these measures at legitimate businesses, such as banks, oil and insurance companies, and the military-industrial complex, in order to curb their undue influence in politics. The reform process was void of discussions about the threat posed by criminal organizations, as the government deemed them relatively benign when it came to having access to decisionmakers.

But data published by *Forbes* magazine, revealing the list of the world's wealthiest people, burst the belief that illicit economies cannot garner enough influence to merit political attention. In 2010 *Forbes* ranked Mexican drug kingpin Joaquín "El Chapo" Guzmán 701th on its list of magnates with a fortune of $1 billion, suggesting that criminal organizations' economic muscle, like any other, has to be carefully monitored to see what kinds of links it establishes with the democratic political system.

Mexico in a Regional Context

Mexico is a mosaic of relatively weak institutions: a rather uninstitutionalized system of political parties, a civic culture with high social tolerance for corruption and very powerful criminal groups, and a government too small for the size of the country. These particularities taken separately are, of course, not unique to Mexico, but it would be difficult to find them reproduced in the same way and to the same degree somewhere else. The eight factors (outlined below) make the problem of drug money in politics particularly intractable in Mexico.

For one, the proximity to the United States makes Mexico—especially the border states in the north—strategic for introducing narcotics into the world's largest market.[3] As long as the demand exists and the business remains extraordinarily profitable, the border is destined to be the main battleground in Mexico.

Second, Mexican criminal organizations have highly trained armed wings—the most notorious of which is the Zetas—that are able to contest the state's monopoly over the use of force. In some regions of the country, these armed groups possess complete territorial control, which facilitates their taking part in other lucrative activities, such as contraband of gasoline and human smuggling.

The web of businesses in which these organizations become involved lead to the third complicating factor: their vast wealth and economic power.

Fourth, criminal organizations have become ever more consolidated and sophisticated, which translates into increasing aspirations and needs beyond

---

3. The Mexico-U.S. border stretches almost 2,000 miles. On the Mexican side are the states of Baja California, Sonora, Chihuahua, Coahuila, Nuevo León, and Tamaulipas. Some of these states are home base for the most important criminal organizations.

physical protection from their forces. In fact, there are indications that their desire to penetrate politics is not limited to Mexico and has reached countries as far away as Argentina. There is credible evidence that the Juarez cartel contributed funds to Eduarte Duhalde's 1999 presidential campaign.

Fifth, the widespread practice of corruption in political affairs flourishes in Mexico as a consequence of a civic culture that turns a blind eye to the corrosive practice. Double bookkeeping, cash payments for crooked services, and illegal commissions are rampant.

Sixth, with the advent of democracy and decentralization, the president's power has decreased. The federal system operates as a redistributor of competencies and power, but at the same time it fragments state action and weakens its response to criminal organizations. Criminals thus more easily penetrate local governments. As Moisés Naím explains, the weakening of state governments implies a relative increase in the power of criminal organizations seeking to use money as a modus vivendi with the established powers, and one of the ways of achieving this goal is through the financing of parties and candidates' political activities.[4]

The seventh factor is an extension of the sixth. Given that local authorities are not subject to the same monitoring mechanisms as federal authorities, Mexican public institutions are more vulnerable today than before the decentralization process.

Last, political parties are highly adept at organizing and mobilizing their base and patronage system, but they are theoretically and ideologically weak. Therefore, their candidate selection process is more likely to be influenced by the public figure's fundraising skills rather than by the ability to lead and represent certain values. Their platform is likely to constitute a list of disjointed demands aimed to please the mood of society, and the party is certain to be a catch-all of priorities. Given this, elections are largely won through an exchange of favors, which serves as an incentive for seeking extralegal sources of funding. Party loyalty is not maintained through philosophical affinity but rather through provision of services, which makes resources even more indispensable.

Even though this list is by no means exhaustive, it allows us to position Mexico within the larger context of Latin America. A quick balance sheet, such as the one drawn by the United Nations Development Program, suggests that (setting each country's historical, political, and cultural particularities aside) the Latin American democratic electoral system is characterized by three main traits: extensive patronage, expensive electoral campaigns, and diffuse state power.[5] Corporatism, vote buying, cronyism, and pork-barrel politics are widespread.

4. Naím (2006).
5. PNUD (2004).

These long-standing practices go along with the use of massive amounts of public and private funds, kept secret through double bookkeeping. As a consequence, prosecutors have a very difficult time proving any wrongdoing.

The political education of the electorate, which is arguably the most important form of political action, has been replaced by two great trends. The first is the survival of the forms of control mentioned above. The second is the growing use of the media to promote candidates and government officials. Both contribute to the eclipse of ideology as the basis for mobilization. The weakening of what the theorist Angelo Panebianco calls "collective incentives" (that is, the ideology or defense of a cause) and the pervasiveness of "selective incentives" (that is, tangible, concrete privileges and status) makes political negotiations look more like a commercial transaction than a political negotiation in the canonical sense.[6]

While the commercialization of politics is continentwide, there are differences across countries. In Brazil the electoral system favors the proliferation of parties motivated more by specific interests rather than by the representation of a system of ideas. In Mexico the party-as-business model has flowered; this model is a version of the rent-seeking model through the public system of party funding.

These impure forms of democracy veer the machinery of political parties toward decisions based mostly on money considerations. In addition, the intensive use of the mass media also contributes to making political campaigns exceedingly money focused. Indeed, access to television and other forms of communication substantially increases the cost of elections. In short, the kind of competitive democracy that has developed in the region requires enormous sums of money for the operation of parties and the staging of elections.

If these trends continue, public financing of campaigns and political parties will become ineffective and unsustainable. Despite electoral organisms with more oversight and new rules on public funding, it has become common to identify corruption in the financing of political activities. Some of these cases of corruption verge on illegality. Examples of crooked schemes that Latin America has seen in the recent past are the funneling of public servants and services to party work instead of their stipulated jobs; buying votes or signatures, or "renting" people to show muscle at a rally; different forms of bribery, such as paying money to receive some undue or illicit privilege in the future or to secure a government contract or to access privileged information; inflating invoices for services rendered to defraud public coffers; and trafficking in drugs, arms, or people.

Within this regional profile, Mexico has certain particularities that are worth outlining, including the seventy-year rule of the Partido Revolucionario Institucional (PRI) and the unique electoral reform process that it has undergone.

6. Panebianco (1993).

Mexico transitioned from a hegemonic party system—which kept operating until 1996 with a few variations as time progressed and some rather important schisms—to a competitive democratic system. One of the least documented aspects of the authoritarian system's modus operandi, perhaps because it was an open secret, was the way in which the official party was financed. The fact is that the symbiosis between party and government guaranteed the PRI funds for its political campaigns and other activities. Taxpayers financed the official party, while a residual amount was earmarked for opposition parties, which legitimized the less-than-democratic system.

Mexico's electoral system today is the product of a series of reforms that began in the late 1970s and culminated in 1996. The most recent reform effort expanded the system's competitiveness by making generous public funds available to political parties, considered by the constitution as entities of public interest. The system privileges public financing but, in a restricted manner, allows parties to accept contributions from their membership base and private donors. Article 41 of the constitution establishes that the total amount of private contributions shall not surpass the equivalent of 10 percent of the cost of the previous presidential campaign. There are also ceilings to private contributions: articles 77 and 78 of the COFIPE (Federal Code of Electoral Institutions and Procedures) specify that churches, enterprises, firms, and especially foreigners are not allowed to raise funds for political purposes. Due to these provisions, the opposition (against the PRI) had enough money to carry out their activities for the first time in history during the 1997 federal congressional elections (table 6-1).

When the president was no longer in control of Congress, a new era began of divided government and authentic separation of powers. The most immediate and direct consequence of the new power-sharing arrangement could be seen in the passing of the federal budget. Appropriations made it more difficult for the PRI to access its traditional sources of funding—the public coffers—and thanks to the monitoring of federal government relief programs, the use of public money for electoral purposes was further mitigated. It is important to point out that parliamentary checks and balances were strengthened by the approval—in the first years of the twenty-first century—of a law guaranteeing public access to information and ensuring that all information handled by the government was made public.

Nevertheless, the PRI's political operating model did not disappear with the arrival of the new system. The corporatist fiber of the union world, just to cite one example, continued alive and well, and the three main parties (PRI, Partido de Acción Nacional [PAN], and Partido de la Revolución Democrática [PRD]) operated to a greater or lesser extent by feeding unions millions in kickbacks and grafts in exchange for the electoral support of their base. The difference was that

Table 6-1. *Public Funding of Federal Congressional Elections, 1997–2009*

Year	Nominal amounts (Mexican pesos)	Indexed amounts (Mexican pesos of 2009)	US$ equivalent
1997	4,559,760,000	2,111,493,862	379,916,666
2000	4,565,360,000	3,064,092,232	380,416,660
2003	6,221,670,000	4,823,580,695	518,416,660
2006	4,755,050,475	4,171,096,908	396,254,206
2009	3,631,639,027	3,631,639,027	302,583,000

Source: Instituto Federal Electoral.

the system was no longer dominated by a single party but worked as a kind of condominium managed by the three major parties. In this way, direct support through cash transfers of goods and services delivered to the population was a perfectly functional model of political control. Elections are won to a great extent because of campaigns' budgets and the graft they can spread around. These kinds of transactions are seldom reported to electoral authorities.

To target urban areas, the middle class, and other segments of society that do not benefit from the clientelism just described, campaigns invest heavily in marketing through various media. During the twelve years between 1997 and 2009, the cost of electoral campaigns in Mexico grew exponentially, and the item on the budget that grew the most is publicity in the media. If we look at the figures the parties themselves reported to the electoral authorities (Federal Institute of Elections, or IFE) for the 2006 presidential elections, 95 percent of campaign spending was used for the media.[7] This transfer of public funds to the private TV networks has created indignation among citizens.

The 2007 electoral reform reversed this upward trend in media spending. This legislation stipulates that political campaigns and party ads in the broadcast media would be aired during official time slots reserved for the government. As a consequence, the exorbitant budgets of the past were not needed for the 2009 midterm elections. The leaders of the three main caucuses in the Senate—Manlio Fabio Beltrones of the PRI, Santiago Creel of the PAN, and Carlos Navarrete of the PRD—drove the reform process with the goal of making

---

7. Party reports can be viewed at www.ife.gob.mx. In 1997, 1.09 billion pesos was spent on political ads; three years later the figure was 1.31 billion; in 2006 it was 1.68 billion, an increase in nine years of almost 600 million (around US$60 million). This upward trend was due to the formula used to earmark public funds, something that theoretically was corrected with the 2007 reform.

campaigns less expensive for the government.[8] Legislators assumed that, with these provisions limiting the cost of campaigns and with public funding, federal campaigns would be proof against illicit contributions.

There were, however, two major loopholes in the regulatory system. The first was the possibility of creating secret agreements between the media and politicians through press office budgets, in order to publish partisan stories disguised as unbiased information. The second was the lack of measures to control corrupt campaign activities that fuel the need for money. Further complicating federal reforms is the fact that each state organizes its own local elections and supervises party spending. In practice, this decentralization means that even if the most elemental measures are in place at the local level, the institutional capacity to enforce them is very weak. Cronyism at the local level is rampant, as is mismanagement of public monies.

The transition to democracy has not spread uniformly throughout the country. Not all the states have undergone a thorough process of opening. In practice the use of public funds for partisan ends has not been eliminated in many local elections. Each state has the power to organize its own elections and establish its own control mechanisms, but they do not all have independent bodies to detect violations. Although they have signed cooperation agreements with the IFE to better control the monies used in campaigns, regional disparities are enormous.

In fact, a large number of the complaints brought by political parties before the federal judiciary's electoral tribunal (TEPJF) include charges of the inappropriate use of public funds to favor a specific candidate or to finance party activities.[9] Significantly, as of this writing, no complaint has been brought before the

---

8. The 2007 reform came from a negotiation unprecedented in Mexico. The heads of the three main party caucuses agreed to work together very discretely and with limited participation from the federal government. Among other things, they made a pact to remove the IFE's president councilor and withdraw millions of pesos that were transferred to television networks every three years. The work of Jorge Alcocer (1993) and Arturo Núñez Jimenez (1997) was decisive for the success of this process.

9. TEPJF president María del Carmen Alanís, interview by author, Mexico City, May 2010. "If we look at it generally, it could certainly be said that the complaints alleging 'inappropriate use of resources' are a large part of the cases that come before the Federal Judiciary's Electoral Tribunal, because a series of controversies touching on multiple issues are brought before us. Among them are the following: 1. Complaints involving the review of reports presented by political parties on their income and spending, either as part of their day-to-day functioning or during election campaigns (annual reports and campaign spending reports). These kinds of complaints can refer to federal or state law. 2. Complaints involving decisions by electoral authorities regarding monitoring party and political groups' resources. This can also be federal or local. 3. Complaints involving decisions or omissions by electoral authorities about administrative norms alleging the use of public funds by public servants to favor a political party or candidate. This can also refer to federal or local bodies. 4. Complaints involving decisions or omissions by electoral authorities about administration norms alleging a political party or coalition's misuse of public funds. This may refer to federal

tribunal by any party or candidate alleging that another party or candidate has used money from drug traffickers.[10]

There have been some important corrections made to the political financing regulatory system, particularly when it comes to the monitoring of resources during elections. The understanding that there was a need for revisions did not come about randomly. The 2000 campaigns of Vicente Fox (PAN) and Francisco Labastida (PRI) suffered from financial irregularities. In Fox's case, double bookkeeping—hiding corporate campaign contributions to an organization called Friends of Fox—was discovered. The coalition PAN/PVEM got a historic fine of 545 million pesos (US$50 million) for mismanagement. In the case of the PRI, it was proved that cash from Mexico's oil giant Petróleos Mexicanos (PEMEX, the state-owned oil company) had been channeled to Labastida's campaign. The electoral authority imposed the maximum fine, the first ever imposed on a political party.[11] The amount was 1 billion pesos (US$94 million).

According to the former IFE council member Alonso Lujambio, the number of reviews, fines, and audits of political parties has increased over the years in an attempt to dissuade them from exceeding their campaign spending limits and acquiring illegal funding.[12] Considerable advances have been made, but problems remain because some sources are very difficult to monitor. There are also limits on private and public funds channeled through city, state, and federal governments, both in money and in kind, which continue to be opportunities for breaking the law.

In order to improve the ability to review party finances, legislators in 2007 introduced an amendment to article 41, chapter 5, of the constitution that creates an autonomous technical unit for monitoring political parties.[13] Parties cannot hide behind the right to banking or fiduciary secrets if this unit calls for them to be examined. In addition, the unit can ask for proof of activities and even assign a monetary value to donations in kind, including the

---

or local bodies. 5. Complaints relating to the validity of the elections, proposing they be invalidated because of the use of forbidden financing (such as public funds that do not come from the electoral authority in question) for the winning candidate or the party that ran him/her. This kind of allegation can be made about any federal, state, or municipal election."

10. Del Carmen Alanís interview: "When the use of money from, for example, drug trafficking, has been mentioned, it has been to justify the form of funding of political parties, which are only allowed to receive income from the sources permitted by Mexico's constitution and the federal or state electoral law in question. Examples of these kinds of references can be found in decisions SUP-RAP-158/2008 and its joint findings, and SUP-RAP-163/2008."

11. Córdova and Murayama (2006, p. 282).

12. Lujambio (2003, p. 382).

13. The members of this body are appointed by a two-thirds vote of the IFE General Council.

spontaneous appearance of a candidate on a sports or entertainment program. It has the authority to review campaign and precampaign reports, order audits and inspection visits, and require necessary information from individuals and public or private companies. In theory, the unit has clout, which it can use not only to impose financial sanctions on parties and candidates but also to restrict registration and to declare candidates ineligible.[14] The new regulatory system also requires expeditious proof of expenditures: requests for information need to be answered within thirty days.

These new supervisory mechanisms cannot be underestimated: they have closed loopholes, given parties an incentive to keep a tight control over their finances, and discouraged collusion with illicit entities. But the growing capability—particularly on the economic front—of criminal organizations cannot be underestimated either. Their financial muscle makes them a threat, as they take advantage of cracks in the armor of regulations to boost their protection networks.

Crime and the Mexican Government

Organized crime is not new in Mexico. Criminal organizations centering on contraband and drug trafficking have existed for decades. It is deeply rooted in national life, and some authors such as Luis Astorga argue that the illicit drug trade developed in tandem with the construction of the political apparatus that came out of the 1910 revolution.[15] In the 1980s criminal groups began to emerge from the underground and to reach government officials and have more autonomy in the spaces where they operate, sparking well-known incidents with the United States, such as the murder of Drug Enforcement Agency agent Enrique Camarena. This event tarnished the Mexican government's image in U.S. political circles and the media. In the 1990s criminal organizations gained strength and began to operate in areas where although they did not necessarily supplant local government, they could demand its noninterference. It is difficult to imagine complex criminal transactions occurring without at least the tacit approval of the police. When local public forces turn a blind eye to illicit activities and federal authorities are kept at a distance, drug traffickers are able to operate unhindered and even to expand. The goal of criminal organizations, then, is to

---

14. The penalties include a public reprimand, a fine equivalent to 10,000 days' pay at the minimum wage, a fine of an amount equal to the amount of excess spending, doubling the fine for repeat offenders, a 50 percent reduction in financing, cancelation of party registration, and loss of the right to register as a candidate.

15. For more on Luis Astorga's hypothesis that drug trafficking grew on a par with the political system, see Astorga (2005).

operate stealthily, to keep regional balances intact, and to avoid compromising the Mexican government vis-à-vis the United States.[16]

In spite of this aim, however, in 1993 drug traffickers assassinated a Catholic cardinal in the Guadalajara airport. The official investigation determined that Cardinal Juan Jesús Posadas Ocampo had been mistaken for drug kingpin Joaquín "El Chapo" Guzmán by gunmen from a rival cartel. With this episode, the Salinas de Gortari administration seemed to lose control, as drug traffickers spread their sphere of influence and economic clout throughout Sinaloa, Baja California, Tamaulipas, and Michoacán.

Given the complex forms and degrees of collaboration that can exist between governments and criminal organizations, it is useful to base the analysis on two established typologies. The goal is for this classification to help illuminate the following two questions in the case of Mexico: What is the relationship between the economic power of criminal organizations and the political system? And how have institutions tried to curtail this influence? According to Peter Lupsha, the political system and organized crime relate in three ways. These three relationships are not necessarily consecutive but can coexist in different regions of a single country.[17]

One is the predatory relationship. This relationship is usually associated with the one that street gangs establish with local police. Authorities may be intimidated in neighborhoods where these groups are strong. Gang members may also work as thugs on the payroll of a political party or candidate. They may hire snitches inside security and jail systems to give them timely information about operations and other tactical tips. But the gangs have not developed to the point that they require institutional protection, and the political system is not usually compromised.

Second is the parasitical relationship. Here the implications are more profound, as criminals systematically corrupt the security structure, especially the police. Authorities start tolerating illegal activities, and large-scale contraband is made possible. In some cases this form of corruption becomes so ubiquitous that it generates an irregular culture with distorted notions of right and wrong, where people see these problems as relatively benign and inevitable.

Third is the symbiotic relationship, which takes shape when criminal organizations and the government forge a mutually beneficial relationship. This level of complicity can take the form of criminal control over specific government services, such as construction and garbage collection, and can lead to the effective control of whole regions. This extreme scenario is unlikely to occur in

16. See Toro (1997, 1998).
17. Lupsha (1996).

countries with complex institutional structures, such as Mexico. However, it is possible to imagine a symbiotic relationship forming between criminal organizations and specific state institutions like customs, the police, and the city attorney's office. Territorial control by criminal organizations could lead them to have power over municipal or state officials, a more likely outcome in countries with a federal system.

It is useful to complement Lupsha's relationships with the more precise five-level typology developed by Edgardo Buscaglia and Samuel González Ruiz.[18] The first level of association consists of sporadic acts of corruption, such as bribing the police to buy impunity. The second level is a systematic effort by criminal groups to put police officers and low-level officials on their payroll to guarantee that their operations will continue unhindered. These arrangements are especially common in transnational crime, as the frequent crossing of borders requires more stable relationships with authorities. The third level is criminal infiltration of the ranks of midlevel officials of the executive and judicial branches. At this level of complicity, criminals expect to regularly receive reports about government plans, strategies, and capacities. The fourth level of infiltration happens when criminal groups control police chiefs or the heads of law enforcement agencies. In the fifth and highest level of collusion criminal groups design or direct public policy, legislation, and even judiciary decisions. It is in this phase that drug traffickers finance electoral campaigns or forge economic agreements with the state apparatus.

The power of drug traffickers in Mexico is enormous, though difficult to pin down precisely. Nonetheless, a few figures shed light on the magnitude of the problem. According to the United Nations, the U.S. illegal drug market is valued at about $82 billion a year.[19] How it is that a financial system can process this amount of money without causing suspicion remains a mystery, but what is increasingly evident is that criminals are finding ways to launder the cash and to use it to protect and expand their business. In 2010 Mexico's Ministry of Finance reported an annual surplus of $12 billion in the financial system without a traceable origin. Worse, this amount does not even include illicit transactions in Mexican pesos or other currencies. While some of those funds come from political corruption, tax evasion, and other non-drug-related factors, the main suspects are criminal organizations and particularly drug traffickers. Finally, the number of cargo airplanes involved in drug trafficking is also indicative of the extent of their operations: between 2007 and 2009, the government confiscated 377 planes.[20]

18. Buscaglia, González Ruiz, and Ratliff (2005).
19. UNODC (2009).
20. For more information on the topic, see "Resultados de la Política Mexicana contra la Delincuencia Organizada" (www.pgr.gob.mx).

Within this context, it is useful to characterize Mexico's problem of drug money in politics today by using the typology described above. Two things become clear through this classification. One, there are important subnational differences in the degree of drug-trafficking infiltration into politics and, specifically, into political financing. Two, Mexico as a whole has a serious and worsening problem of drug money influencing public affairs.

Some areas of the country, such as Tabasco and Colima, are at levels one and two of the Buscaglia-González scale, in which drug traffickers have the protection of the local police and have even put a few low-level officials on their payroll. In other areas, organized crime groups—and their exorbitant profits—have managed to deeply corrode state institutions. This reality puts states such as Nuevo León, Chihuahua, Veracruz, and Tamaulipas at the fifth level of the Buscaglia-González typology, a level that represents the most serious threat to the state. Many accusations have been made about mayors of border cities like Nuevo Laredo, Ciudad Juárez, and Tijuana receiving financial support from organized crime to finance their election campaigns. Criminal organizations have caused such mayhem in these cities that direct federal intervention has been necessary.

What ought to give us pause is that along the northern border drug money has crept into public institutions beyond the municipal level and even into some of the most prosperous and quiet areas of Mexico. The city of Monterrey is Mexico's economic and innovation center, but in recent years insecurity has skyrocketed, drug trafficking has increased, and criminal infiltration in politics has become commonplace.

The question remains: Has level five become so endemic and destructive that Mexico could become a failed state? The Failed States Index is an analytical tool that takes into account several factors, such as demographic pressure, the presence of a vengeance-seeking group, inequality, violations of human rights and the rule of law, and factionalized elites. The index classifies countries into the following four categories, according to how close to failing they are: alert, warning, moderate, and sustainable, with *alert* being the most dire category.[21] In both 2010 and 2011 the Fund for Peace placed Mexico in the *warning* category. So, in spite of the assessment of some analysts and government officials, Mexico is not in imminent danger of becoming a failed state.[22] That said, the reality is far from rosy: there are what Juan Gabriel Tokatlián calls regional narcocracies.[23]

Regional narcocracies are spaces controlled by drug kingpins over which the state has no effective control and within which public services are provided by

21. "Failed States Index" (2010).
22. Tokatlián (1995).
23. Tokatlián (1995).

criminal organizations. These are areas with great economic weight because of the booming illicit businesses; they are also areas where a culture of violence and fear reigns.[24] Whether these criminal organizations operate out in the open or in secret, they usually have implicit agreements with the local government or the acquiescence of officials. Eight of the thirty-one states in Mexico may already be regional narcocracies: Tamaulipas, Chihuahua, Sinaloa, Nuevo León, Baja California, Michoacán, Guerrero, and Quintana Roo.

Even though the situation in each of these states is unique, drug trafficking has a sweeping presence in the lives of the inhabitants and in the state institutions. Jorge Tello argues that it is impossible to arrive at a general interpretation of what is happening in all these states, as the political will to face the threat is different from one governor to another and from one governing party to another.[25] Being surrounded by drug traffickers does not necessarily mean that the authorities or the political system as a whole are subservient to them: the ways in which criminal organizations achieve their aims vary. In some cases, threats are their tactic of choice, which may be cheaper and more effective than financing political campaigns. These groups also launch violent and even terrorist attacks to destabilize the state and instill fear in the public. In other cases, criminals finance politicians and elections to make sure that politicians turn a blind eye to illicit activities, often in exchange for lessening violent crimes against civilians. This is the pact that the PRI government sustained for decades.

The degree to which a political party, while in office, resists and is able to remain impermeable to crime has a direct impact on the way in which criminals attempt to penetrate the electoral system. State governments can be divided into four types, according to their control over crime. In one, electoral institutions do a decent job of supervising public finances and effectively close most avenues to criminal infiltration of the political system. Once in office, these administrations fight crime head on and coordinate with federal authorities to decrease vulnerabilities. It is not easy for criminals to penetrate a system like this; therefore, the line separating the underworld, on the one hand, and society and its institutions, on the other, is clearly demarcated. The capital of Mexico, Mexico City's Federal District, is the clearest example.

In the second type of state government response, organized crime has not achieved sufficient power to corrupt the institutional system but is able to channel massive sums to the police in the form of bribes. These governments thus deal with local criminals and avoid confrontations with cartels, which usually

---

24. Tokatlián (1995).

25. Jorge Tello is a presidential adviser on security issues and professor of strategic intelligence at the Monterrey Technological Institute of Higher Learning.

use these territories for transit or safe havens where their families can live in relative tranquility. States like Jalisco and Aguascalientes fit this profile.

In the third category, society and government coexist with organized crime. In these states drug traffickers have social and economic roots, and as a consequence, political parties and local governments face a structural problem that they learn to live with. Politicians may have family ties to criminals and may be impacted by pressure groups, but they make an effort to avoid bloodletting and violent confrontations among rival gangs. For these public officials, tranquility is their main value. This is the case of Sinaloa, Tijuana, and a few other border cities where it is very difficult to establish a clear dividing line between legal and illegal spheres.

The fourth category is that in which drug traffickers and others involved in illicit activities impose territorial and population control. The public pressures its representatives to confront the problem, sometimes leading to direct confrontations between criminals and police. In this category, criminals try to buy off politicians who can influence government responses. Nuevo León, Tamaulipas, and Quintana Roo fit into this category.

The Situation in Quintana Roo and Tamaulipas

What follows is a longer exposition of the situation in Quintana Roo, especially Cancún, and Tamaulipas. In these states official information provided by federal agencies gives us relatively solid ground to explore deeper the link between politics and criminal organizations' money. To shed light on these sorts of challenges at the national level, I summarize a few scandals that have involved Mexican presidents.

Quintana Roo borders Belize and has a long coastline on the Caribbean. Cancún is the state's biggest city and one of the country's main drug distribution centers. The link between politics and drugs is systemic in Quintana Roo and has involved two political parties, the PRI and the PRD. Although it has not been possible to document the allegation that the former Quintana Roo governor Mario Villanueva (PRI), who was in office from 1993 to 1999, received money from criminal organizations during his electoral campaign, one thing is clear: he did not attend the inauguration of his colleague Joaquín Hendrix because he was running from the authorities, accused of working with drug traffickers. When Villanueva was elected to office in 1992–93, the PRI still had complete hegemony in Mexico, which made his victory—with or without accepting drug money—extremely likely.

It is equally plausible that in his previous post as mayor of Cancún, Villanueva established important relationships with the drug cartels. When he took office as governor, it is likely that he took hefty bribes to allow drug shipments through the territory—a crime for which he was finally charged. It is important to underline that Villanueva was a high-ranking politician who had been under indictment for drug-related offenses and who, in 2010, was extradited to the United States to face charges for links with organized crime and money laundering.[26] The presence of drug traffickers in the state's political life had been a kind of open secret, but during the gubernatorial campaigns of 2010 the disgraceful symbiotic relationship between crime and politics was in the limelight.

A decade after the fall of Mario Villanueva another Cancún mayor and gubernatorial candidate, running on the ticket of a coalition of left parties, was arrested by federal authorities at the height of his campaign.[27] Gregorio Sánchez Martínez, alias El Greg, was born in Guerrero into a poor and large family (fourteen children). He moved to Cancún and after working as a musician and church pastor, he emerged in public life with a small fortune and growing political clout. He ran for the Senate in 2006 with the Broad Progressive Front (FAP) and then for mayor in 2008.[28] The elections were challenged, but the Electoral Tribunal confirmed Sánchez's victory, and he took office as the mayor of Cancún. A PEMEX contractor, Steven Santander, said he had given Sánchez $10 million, an amount that he said would be returned to him upon Sánchez taking office.[29]

Two major scandals marred Sánchez's administration. The first had to do with the administration of the municipal jail by Nicolás Mollinedo, the person in charge of logistics for Andrés Manuel López Obrador. The second incident surrounded the murder of General Tello Quiñones in February 2010. Tello considered himself a public security adviser to the mayor, but after a meeting with Sánchez's security team he was assassinated. Among those arrested in relation to this case are a former Cuban military man who worked as an adviser to Sánchez named Boris del Valle Alonso; Francisco Velasco Delgado, the head of the municipal police; and Marco Antonio Mejía, the person in charge of the municipal jail. Finally, the third scandal erupted with the discovery of a shadowy espionage team run by Manuel Vera Salinas, a lieutenant in the Mexican navy.

Gregorio Sánchez Martínez's detention provoked a scandal because of the nature of the charges and the popularity of the accused.[30] After reading the

26. Callejo Anzures (2002).
27. The Partido Revolucionario de los Trabajadores (PRT), the Partido del Trabajo (PT), and the Convergence Party ran him on the ticket of a coalition named Everyone for Quintana Roo.
28. The FAP ran Andrés Manuel López Obrador that same year for the presidency.
29. Chapa (2010).
30. This ill-fated candidate alleged that the state PRI apparatus had used an illegal process to try to oust him from the campaign by amending electoral statutes to require gubernatorial candidates to prove twenty years of residence in the state, a maneuver openly aimed at Sánchez. The Supreme Court finally declared this reform unconstitutional. The PRI operation turned out marvelously for Sánchez, because he gained support and empathy due to the persecution. But the second blow

court record of the proceedings, a judge from the state of Nayarit issued an arrest warrant.[31] The charges against the candidate were mainly related to his links to two cartels, the Beltrán Leyva and the Zetas, to which he allegedly gave information and offered protection.[32] The government also accused Sánchez of carrying out financial transactions with illicit parties, in an amount exceeding 11 million pesos (US$900,000).

A few days after Sánchez's arrest, the municipal treasurer, Carlos Trigos Perdomo, disappeared, after being summoned to appear before the city council to explain a deficit in the treasury of 150 million pesos (US$12 million). The attorney general's office issued a communiqué stating that "on February 11, 2010, the unit of financial investigation received allegations from the Ministry of Finance that Sánchez had moved large sums of money that made it possible to suppose that he handled resources that did not jibe with his income."[33] When Sánchez's arrest became public, the federal government stated that it had notified the PRD in January that the party's candidate was the object of a federal investigation for the crimes that he was directly charged with in May.[34] Amid the hubbub caused by Sánchez's arrest, PRD leader Jesús Ortega denied having been notified.

Even though this is the most important criminal investigation a PRD member has been involved in, it should be noted that it is not the first. One of the party's deputies-elect for the 2009–12 federal Congress, Julio César Godoy, could not take office at the beginning of his term because federal authorities had issued an arrest warrant for him on charges of being involved in organized crime and offenses against health (the term used for drug-related crimes in Mexico). By maneuvering the system, Godoy managed to take the oath of office and thus gain the immunity given to members of Congress. Godoy must now be tried by his fellow members of Congress before he can be handed over to the attorney general's office for prosecution. The accusations against him are particularly serious since the Ministry of Public Security identifies him as the liaison with Servando Gómez (La Tuta), the leader of La Familia criminal organization, "in charge of institutional protection networks for operations in the

---

came from the attorney general's office in the hands of the PAN government. In contrast to what was happening in states such as Durango, Sinaloa, and Oaxaca—where the PAN had established alliances with the left to run joint candidates—in the case of Quintana Roo, despite Sánchez's popularity, the PAN preferred to run its own candidate, Alicia Ricalde Magaña, because of Sánchez's murky past.

31. Criminal case 122/2010-IV.
32. PGR Boletín 622/10, May 25, 2010.
33. PGR Boletín 622/10A, May 26, 2010.
34. Secretaría de Gobernación Communiqué 202/10, May 26, 2010.

region of Lázaro Cárdenas, Arteaga, and Nueva Italia."[35] Michoacán is the state where the army and federal forces deployment strategy was first launched to recover territory controlled by criminals.

Although Quintana Roo and Michoacán are in very grave straits, in Tamaulipas drug cartels are even more solidly entrenched, particularly the Gulf cartel and the Zetas. The indicators are evident and ominous. For the 2010 elections, the two main opposition parties did not nominate candidates because of the risk that their internal structures could be controlled by drug traffickers. The PRD had already had direct experience with this sort of infiltration. In 2009 it was made public that the PRD leader in that state, Miguel Ángel Almaraz, worked with a network operated by the Zetas to sell stolen fuel. Almaraz was arrested and tried, but the incident brought his party's vulnerability to light. The next year, the PRD national leader Jesús Ortega acknowledged that his party was unable to nominate candidates in at least six municipalities of Tamaulipas because of the hegemony of the drug traffickers.[36]

The PRD is not the only party under this kind of pressure. In May 2010 the PAN mayoral candidate in Valle Hermoso, Mario Guajardo, was murdered in cold blood, and thus far the police investigation has been unable to explain the assassination except the pressure that criminals have brought to bear on the electoral system. The strength of the drug traffickers in Tamaulipas makes even the national ruling party tremble. It decided not to consult with its rank and file to pick a candidate for governor to avoid interference from outside interests, particularly organized crime. The PAN decided that its National Executive Committee would make the nomination directly.[37] This candidate was not very popular, and after a tragedy (explained further on), the PRI won the elections hands down.[38] Alarmingly, a direct effect of the overwhelming presence of drug traffickers in the state has been a weakening in electoral competitiveness and a breakdown of the popular democratic process. Something similar happened in Chihuahua in the 2010 elections, although in that state there has been alternation of parties in the governor's seat.

It is important to point out that in Tamaulipas no party but the PRI has ever sat in the governor's chair, and despite declining performance in all the parameters measuring governance and state effectiveness, the PRI candidate Rodolfo Torre Cantú was ahead in the polls. There is, without a doubt, harassment of

---

35. Ministry of Public Security (2009).
36. Jesús Ortega, interview by author, May 8, 2010 (www.enfoquenoticias.com.mx).
37. *Milenio*, Mexico City edition, February 2, 2010.
38. Of 1.1 million votes cast, the PRI received almost 700,000. See these data and the election results for local deputies and city councils at www.ietam.gob.mx.

opposition parties and meddling in their activities in some parts of the state. There has also been systematic intimidation of the media to the point that many of them have stopped reporting on the criminal groups and, therefore, on any connections they might have with the political system. The pressure on the media has even extended to Televisa, the country's biggest corporate media outlet.[39] The silencing and restricting of journalists in this manner have undermined the right to information, a cornerstone of democracy.

The hardest blow against the PRI in Tamaulipas occurred amid this atmosphere of silence and fear. Their gubernatorial candidate and his bodyguards were assassinated on June 28, 2010, a week before the elections. The facts surrounding the murder have disturbed Mexicans immensely: it is apparent that the execution was premeditated and calculated and that it happened because of information leaked by his own security team. Why he was assassinated remains a mystery, but the fingerprints of the drug traffickers are all over the case. The fact that federal authorities took over the case left no room for doubt that the crime was presumed to be traceable to organized crime.[40]

At the national level, three major scandals have shaken Mexico, the most important one involving General Gutiérrez Rebollo in 1997. During the administration of President Zedillo (1994–2000), the war on drugs became a priority. Some innovations in cooperation with the United States included the creation of the High-level Contact Group, with the participation of both countries' attorneys general and the heads of their anti-organized-crime law enforcement agencies. Zedillo created the National Institute to Fight Drug Trafficking and appointed José de Jesús Gutiérrez Rebollo as the head. The press promptly dubbed Gutiérrez the drug czar.

Within months Gutiérrez Rebollo began to gain the trust of certain sectors of the public in both Mexico and the United States. However, in February 1997 he was arrested and accused of having ties to the Ciudad Juárez cartel, headed by the legendary Amado Carrillo Fuentes, nicknamed Lord of the Heavens. Gutiérrez Rebollo's protection of Carrillo Fuentes allowed the latter to exploit the strategic position of Ciudad Juárez as the main route to smuggle drugs, arms, and persons to and from the United States.

---

39. A car bomb blew up in front of Televisa's local station in Ciudad Victoria, and its repeater towers in Matamoros have been attacked with grenades.

40. The attorney general's office initiated an investigation (PGR/DGCAP/ZC/-IV/093/2010) into the violation of the Federal Law on Weapons and Explosives. Simultaneously, the local city attorney's office in Ciudad Victoria, Tamaulipas, began its own investigation (323/2010) into the June 28 attacks that led to the deaths of Rodolfo Torre Cantú, Enrique Blackmore Smer, Luis Gerardo Soltero Zubiate, Rubén López Zúñiga, and Francisco David López Catache and to the injury of several others (www.pgr.gob.mx).

Even though they detained Gutiérrez Rebollo in a maximum-security prison, the Mexican government's ability to prevent the penetration of criminals into high government circles was now questioned. In fact, Luis Astorga's explanation of the success of drug trafficking in Mexico seems to be borne out: he argues that, from the beginning of the twentieth century, drug trafficking in Mexico had been under the control of powerful regional political groups.[41] That characterization is important for understanding the relationship that the authoritarian Mexican government has had with organized crime and the problems that have become even worse with alternation in office.

The Mexican Response

Given the gravity of these cases at the federal and state levels, it is pertinent to ask what Mexico's response has been to the infiltration of drug-trafficking money into politics. As is apparent from the discussion that follows, the Mexican government has no coherent strategy but has proposed institutional changes in tandem, undertaken efforts to allocate federal resources to fight local battles, brought some of the guilty politicians to justice, and improved international cooperation—particularly with the United States—recognizing that drug trafficking is a transnational phenomenon that requires the participation of other countries.

Former presidents Ernesto Zedillo and Felipe Calderón, at different moments in history but with the same sense of urgency, made statements warning the public about the extent to which criminal organizations were infiltrating the government. In 2009 President Calderón offered a diagnosis of the risks to the political system: "The challenge continues to be to find a system of financing that contributes to giving parties and candidates the greatest possible autonomy vis-à-vis private interests, and particularly keeping illicit money out of political campaigns at any level."[42] In Calderón's analysis, drug cartels have gone from maintaining a low profile aimed at controlling drug routes to a much more aggressive strategy of territorial control and of co-opting government officials. One way that "the criminals experimented with was financing campaigns," he says. "Once an economic link is established between criminals and the candidate, it is practically impossible to dissolve that link," he continues. "What are monitored are the books, and these operations are in cash. . . . This implies making an additional effort on a local level to monitor party and candidates' spending, not just what's on the books, but what is clearly apparent."[43]

The president's concern over organized crime's destructive progression was not just theoretical. During his administration, Calderón saw how organized

---

41. Astorga (2007).
42. Calderón (2009).
43. Calderón (2009).

crime was capable of striking back. In June 2010—after a criminal group assassinated the PRI gubernatorial candidate in Tamaulipas, Rodolfo Torre Cantú, only a few days before the elections he was predicted to win—President Calderón called upon political stakeholders to work together to prevent organized crime from intervening in electoral processes. Reflecting on the gravity of the incident, the president in 2009 did not mince words: "We cannot, we must not allow criminals to impose their will and their perverse rules, as they now are attempting to intervene in the decisions of the citizens and the electoral processes."[44] These warnings stemmed not only from the top echelons of the executive branch but also from the Chamber of Deputies. Before the elections of November 2008, PAN and PRD leaders had sent a letter to the president of the IFE expressing concern over "the risk of organized crime [gaining influence] on political-democratic processes" and asked the IFE to say what "actions it would take . . . to guarantee the citizens that their will would not be changed by the criminals."[45]

The petition also gave the IFE the responsibility of safeguarding the electoral process, ignoring the fact that political organizations themselves had control over their own institutions. Rather reticently, political parties have incorporated internal checks and balances, and electoral authorities confirm that these reforms have indeed been put into effect. The supervisory bodies that the seven political parties have formed are as follows:

—PAN: Watchdog Commission
—PRI: Auditor General
—PRD: Auditor's Commission
—PT: National Comptroller's and Supervisory Commission
—PVEM: (No title given)
—Convergence: National Financing Commission
—New Alliance: Comptroller

The existence of an internal body in each party resolves the formal aspect and provides an incentive for certain kinds of behavior, but it is important to ask if the parties have developed a method of identifying the origin of the resources they or their candidates receive. The head of the IFE unit responded in the following way:

> We can say that it is our perception that the political parties have concerned themselves with fulfilling their responsibilities in managing the resources they get. So, the parties consult the authorities and go to the sessions they are entitled to for checking the data when the Unit detects errors and omissions in the annual reports on campaign and pre-campaign

44. Calderón (2009).
45. IFE (2009).

spending. The parties have become more professional and their internal central, state, and district financial bodies have become more structured; this has given them experience for setting rules for pre-verifying documentation, support, and amounts of financing, among other things.[46]

These institutional transformations have taken place in spite of enormous doubt about the integrity of politicians. At the beginning of the 2009 campaign, the Social Democratic Party (PSD) proposed that all candidates for deputy be certified by the national security agency (CISEN) to ensure that they had no connections to drug traffickers. The proposal was not accepted, but it did echo public opinion, as drug-related corruption in the political system became increasingly well known. The growing number of articles in the media exposing associations between organized crime and politics most likely contributed to this perception.[47]

The threat of narco-politics has been a constant theme in local and federal elections at least since 1994, when an American journalist affirmed that money from the Colombian cartels was being filtered into the PRI presidential campaign.[48] In some parts of the country, scandals over irregular financing (like the case of the PRI gubernatorial candidate in the state of Tabasco, Roberto Madrazo) influenced the president's decision to support the public financing model in 1996.[49]

As noted above, the system for financing political parties approved in 1996 put the emphasis on public, as opposed to private, funding. The reason behind this decision was to avoid the political parties raiding public monies or taking money from private interests, particularly organized crime. The main defender of this model was the last president to come out of the PRI, Ernesto Zedillo, who had to separate the official party from the government apparatus and guarantee its financial autonomy. More recently, in June 2010 the federal government put forward a series of rules for cash transactions in the financial system, one of the favorite venues for money laundering. In August 2010 it restricted cash purchases of vehicles, real estate, boats, and planes.

---

46. IFE (2010).

47. The *Proceso* weekly newsmagazine, no stranger to scandal, has published many reports on the topic. It also put out a summary in book form of its work in this area: see Castañeda (2009). Another article in this weekly reports that twenty-one members of the Chamber of Deputies from the main parties (thirteen from the PRI, six from the PAN, and two from the PRD) have been mentioned in different official Mexican and U.S. documents relating to the politics-drug-trafficking link. The documents are of different kinds, ranging from affidavits by protected witnesses to circumstantial snapshots. In any case, the magazine reflects a kind of unproven presumption that narco-politics is a very widespread reality in contemporary Mexico. See Cervantes and Rodríguez (2010); Ronquillo (2010).

48. This issue is developed in Curzio (2000a).

49. I cover this in depth in Curzio (2000b).

In addition to public rhetoric and institutional reforms, since 2006 the federal police, the military, and even naval officers have participated in state programs to prevent drug traffickers from controlling more territory and penetrating state institutions. The armed offensive has led to very violent reactions on the part of drug cartels, most conspicuously in Nuevo León and Chihuahua, where there have even been acts of narco-terrorism, like the use of car bombs and attacks on U.S. consulates and their staffs.[50] Recently, organized crime is responsible for the murder of three mayors in Durango and another three in Chihuahua. Two mayors in Guerrero and two in Michoacán have suffered the same fate, as well as one in Tamaulipas, in Nuevo León, and in the State of Mexico. This adds up to thirteen sitting mayors assassinated by organized crime.

Given the real threat that drug trafficking poses to the Mexican democracy and the state's capacity to maintain the monopoly over the legitimate use of force, the international community has an increasing role to play. The most important player so far has been the United States and its major avenue, the Mérida Initiative. The spirit behind the Mérida Initiative is to shore up the state's capacity to deal with criminal organizations' power through coresponsibility.[51]

Mexico's Achilles' Heel

Mexico, for all its history of being the center of organized crime in Latin America, lacks an official appraisal of the system.[52] Although there is information in the media and also presidential warnings, there have been no rigorous and systematic investigations that spell out the nature of drug money in politics. Reports by federal authorities in charge of supervising party finances or by congressional commissions would be especially welcome.

Mexico and its missing piece of the puzzle stand in contrast to some other Latin American countries, where parliamentary and judicial commissions have revealed the mechanisms used by organized crime to penetrate the political system. No investigation by Mexican congressional or judicial commissions has produced anything similar to the revelations by Colombia's Investigation 8000 about the Cali cartel's $6 million contribution to Ernesto Samper's presidential campaign. In Costa Rica several commissions of this kind have been set up. And

50. In October 2008 there was an attack on the consulate in Monterrey, later attributed to the Zetas, concretely to a group headed by Sigfrido Nájera Talamantes, jailed since 2009. In March 2010 they assassinated two U.S. citizens and the wife of a Mexican citizen who worked at the U.S. consulate.
51. Rico (2008).
52. In an op-ed piece about the biggest problems the country is facing, one of Mexico's most prestigious political scientists, Luis F. Aguilar, includes among the questions that must be answered, "How can we assure that the electoral institutions are not taken over by the drug traffickers and the incentive for holding elections is not dampened by their acts of intimidation." Aguilar (2010).

Brazil has established a commission to determine whether President Luiz Inácio Lula da Silva received illegal funding in 2002.

In Baja California, Sinaloa, and Chihuahua, states where drug traffickers have been ensconced for several decades, the local press routinely publishes information about the symbiotic relationship between drug traffickers and public institutions. Increasingly, however, this valuable source of stories is receding. In August 2010 United Nations and Organization of American States special rapporteurs for freedom of expression—Frank La Rue and Catalina Botero, respectively—visited Mexico and concluded that freedom of expression was under threat. The murder of journalists, many investigating criminal cases, threatens a democratic society's right to objective information. Of course, illicit activities fare better in the dark.

The real Achilles' heel of Mexico's electoral system is the focus on what happens at the national level, rather than at the local level. Thus any progress in driving organized crime out of political campaigns has been at the federal level. The control and auditing mechanisms explained above have inhibited political parties from taking funds from criminal organizations. In addition, radio, newspapers, and television report on national politics, as opposed to small towns and rural areas.

Regulatory frameworks for monitoring, controlling, and sanctioning—combined at a national level with high-quality media coverage—can reverse what some call "autopsies of the illicit," or opening investigations only after the fact and not beforehand.[53] Many of these scandals have had no real impact on electoral results; other scandals have been missed altogether.

We know little about the accounting practices of political parties involved in local elections, as their electoral mechanisms lack the technical means, and in many cases the political will, to ask for help from the federal supervisory body. Legislation approved in 2007 allows local electoral institutions to establish agreements with the IFE's technical supervisory body to audit party spending. The supervisory unit does not have the authority to review state and municipal elections, however. This task falls to state electoral institutes and councils. In the case of appeals, the local electoral tribunal and the federal judiciary's electoral tribunal intervene, and if there are suspected crimes, the special investigator's Office for Electoral Offenses takes on the case. Local electoral authorities can access bank, fiduciary, and fiscal documents through the supervisory unit if they have an agreement to do so.[54]

---

53. Zovatto (2003, p. 93).

54. These agreements are regulated by article 79, number 4, and article 81, number 1, parts of the Electoral Code. They have been signed by nineteen states: Aguascalientes, Baja California, Campeche, Chiapas, Chihuahua, Coahuila, Durango, Jalisco, Michoacán, Nuevo León, Querétaro, Quintana Roo, San Luís Potosí, Sinaloa, Tabasco, Tamaulipas, Veracruz, Yucatán, and Zacatecas.

These mechanisms for cooperating with federal authorities consist of information exchange, so that the resources that political parties receive are thoroughly monitored without banking and tax limitations or fiduciary secrets. Authorities are able to follow the money without hindrance, at least in theory, as well as to verify whether funds were legally obtained. Evaluation of the reports resulting from these agreements remains a vital pending task.

Conclusions and Recommendations

Given the level of penetration by organized crime into the Mexican electoral system, it is appropriate to offer practical recommendations that could prevent the further deterioration of democracy in that country—and ideally even to reverse the damage.

First and foremost, it is essential for the Mexican government to gather systematic data from public institutions to construct a consistent narrative of the problem and thus avoid guiding policy by sporadic expressions of concern from the highest echelons of the state. The problem of organized crime and politics is not relegated to a low rank on the Mexican public agenda, as is demonstrated here. Yet thus far there has been no detailed official report specifying the capability of drug traffickers to penetrate the political system. Reports that estimate their economic strength do exist, as well as others that calculate the volume of the illicit business and the number of people directly or indirectly working in these activities. But Mexico lacks an accurate profile of the phenomenon and its dynamic and a well-documented plan for moving forward to a resolution of the problem.

IFE, for example, has published an enormous number of worthwhile documents about how the political system works and has even fostered an ambitious publishing program on topics ranging from political culture to procedural guides. But IFE has failed to emphasize the issue of organized crime in political campaigns. The same can be said of the Specialized Investigator's Office for Electoral Offenses.[55]

Congress is also guilty of not paying particular attention to the issue, especially to the extent that legislatures have done in other Latin American countries. Unfortunately, Mexico's legislative branch simply reacts to scandals; it has not been proactive in forming parliamentary commissions to deal with all the dimensions of the problem. Neither has the judicial branch. It is debatable whether the Supreme Court could make up for the lack of information, but it is worth considering. Given a particularity in the Mexican constitution, the Supreme Court

---

55. See www.pgr.gob.mx/fepade/.

has the right to carry out investigations into issues of great importance to the national agenda.[56] It might be feasible for the court to step up and map out the situation to compensate for the passiveness of other public institutions. Having institutionally sanctioned information on the link between politics and organized crime is fundamental for devising and implementing measures to protect the political system from such subordination to criminal interests.

In contrast to the silence of public institutions is the role played by the media in denouncing the connection between drug money and politics. A large part of what we know is thanks to investigative reporting and leaks from whistleblowers. The problem is that the national media rarely delve into local politics to uncover these stories. Disturbingly, many local media outlets no longer investigate—much less publish—the arrangements that they perceive between government structures and criminal networks. The Fundación Prensa y Democracia (Press and Democracy Foundation) has systematically studied the problem, and in general terms, we can say that the local media in some states have stopped fulfilling their role for three fundamental reasons. The first is the direct threat to journalists and editors who dare to expose in detail how local authorities collude with drug barons. The second is the general climate of terror created by these criminal groups, which leads many journalists and media owners to exercise self-censorship. The third reason is that some journalists themselves establish mutually beneficial relationships to organized crime.[57]

Whether out of fear or complicity, the result is equally pernicious to Mexican democracy because the space par excellence for public deliberation offered by the media stops being a front in the fight against illegality. The nexus between criminals and politicians requires silence to survive, so the media's contribution to developing a culture of transparency, free information, and legality is of utmost importance. Leoluca Orlando, an Italian politician known for his opposition to the Sicilian mafia, spells out the importance of the media in an emotional statement:

> The media were our most subtle, and at the same time, most profound difficulty.... The conspiracy of silence about the Mafia and its attack on

---

56. The constitution of the United States of Mexico, article 97, paragraph 2, reads, "The Supreme Court can appoint one or several of its members or a District or Circuit Judge or designate one or several special appointees, when it considers it pertinent or when the Federal Executive or any of the Chambers of Congress or the Governor of a State, solely for the purpose of investigating a fact or facts that constitute a grave violation of any individual guarantee. It can also request that the Council of the Federal Judiciary investigate the conduct of any federal judge or magistrate" (www.diputados.gob.mx/LeyesBiblio/pdf/1.pdf).

57. The organization's article 19 and Cencos (the National Center for Social Communication), with support from the British embassy, published a detailed report about attacks on journalists in Mexico. See INFORME 2009 (2010).

Sicilian life was so successful that it created a kind of parallel universe. ... Our local newspapers were divided between their duty to provide truthful information and the fear that doing it would worsen Sicily's image. ... When I familiarized myself with the dilemmas our city faced, I saw that I would never be free of Mafia domination until we had an aggressive free press.[58]

Knowing more about the situation, whether through official channels or journalists' revelations, will make it possible to develop appropriate legislation and more precise control mechanisms. But intuitively we can say that reducing the sheer costs of political campaigns would also be a step in the right direction, as less expenditure would make it unnecessary for parties and candidates to risk receiving dubious funds. Theoretically, the 2007 electoral reform reduces party funds, but the amounts earmarked continue to be very high, and reforms are still pending to reduce the possibility for using public resources.[59] The head of the IFE points to this as a huge legal vacuum:

The 2007 reform introduced a ban on using money from state and municipal public coffers to finance political and promotional campaigns in article 134 of the constitution. The last paragraph stipulates that complaints and lawsuits will be conducted according to regulations that legislators still have not passed. The IFE is competent to hear any complaint linked to illegally utilized public funding, as are the state electoral institutes, but there is no regulatory legislation to force the municipal, state, and federal governments to provide access to their accounts so an investigation can verify that public monies are not being used. What we have here is a very serious legislative loophole.[60]

Reducing the cost of electoral campaigns is also a heartfelt demand of Mexican society. Public participation in the entire candidate selection process is crucial for reducing the gap between the government and the governed, thus reversing the very worrying trend of the Mexican party system coming under the "thumb of the oligarchy." The widely held view is that Congress does not have the

---

58. Orlando (2004, p. 188). Orlando was the mayor of Palermo who led one of the most studied experiences of recovering a city from mafia power.

59. In theory, public spending on this budget item has dropped. In 2009, 3.73 billion pesos was earmarked for public funding of political parties, while in 2003 the item came to 6.835 billion pesos. In 2010 the amount was slightly over 3 billion. It should be mentioned that, until the 2007 reform, in an electoral year the parties received an amount similar to the one they usually got for regular operations. The new law stipulates that they will now receive 50 percent of that amount for general election campaigns and 30 percent for midterm election campaigns.

60. Leonardo Valdés, interview by author, Mexico City, July 2, 2010 (www.enfoquenoticias.com.mx).

public interest at heart when it drafts legislation. In fact, only one out of every ten people surveyed think that legislators take people's interests into account, while half think that the determining factor for drafting laws is self-interest.[61]

It is essential for political parties to shore up their internal controls and to convince themselves that the best way to keep drug traffickers at bay is for the party system to improve the quality of representation, reflect private interests less, and offer a broader program of national aspirations. Candidates should make public commitments to transparency, starting with their own holdings and campaign donations.

Public opinion matters when it comes to the fight against dirty money funds in politics. For example, people thought that ties to organized crime marred the electoral process in Guerrero in 2011. Even though this perception seemed misguided by the time of the elections in January, a survey shows that 47 percent of people thought that there was drug money involved in the campaign, while 43 percent did not know or did not answer, and only 10 percent said that they did not think illicit businesses had meddled. Regardless of whether or not there is sufficient proof of corruption, people's opinion is that the problem is pervasive. Interestingly, when the survey asked individuals which party they thought most of the organized crime financing went to, 34 percent answered all of them, 30 percent answered the PRI, and 7 percent answered the PRD.[62]

At the party level, several avenues can be pursued to resolve the problem of criminal money. Parties should not allow their candidates to receive cash contributions at all. Parties' internal auditing and monitoring structures need to be reinforced. Parties should ban cash donations. Parties need to be monitored by the authorities and also increase their own transparency.

Local politics, however, often has its own logic and dynamic, in which subordination to de facto powers or a patronage system that uses lots of resources can often develop, even when this is minimal at the national level. Candidates' independence cannot be interpreted as license to avoid monitoring. The story of Gregorio Sánchez Martínez is a case in point. Many other practices could reduce the risk of illicit funds getting channeled into politics and should not represent major problems for implementation.

Alfredo Cristalinas Kaulitz, the head of the IFE's watchdog unit explains:

> In principle, what is needed is for political stakeholders to take on board the importance of competing in a framework of equity, transparency, and within a culture of legality. On the other hand, it is also necessary to

---

61. This can be seen in "Survey on Political Culture" (2008).
62. Survey conducted by *El Universal* newspaper, Mexico, January 13, 2011.

strengthen the collaboration with other federal and state authorities so that operations can be implemented in their jurisdictions to review risk areas during the electoral process. The faculties of the monitoring unit should also be broadened out in two ways. First, freezing bank accounts in the names of third parties with whom the political parties carried out operations in the periods reviewed and who did not respond to the authorities' request for information. This measure allows the monitoring authority to confirm information presented by a political party or determine if there have been omissions. Secondly, carrying out verification procedures on Election Day in order to detect possible cash flows, donations, or unreported expenditures [is important].[63]

In conclusion, generating information fosters the participation of society, increases political parties' responsibility, and reduces campaign costs. But this entire undertaking—closing the door of the electoral system on organized crime—must happen simultaneously with reducing impunity in Mexico. In a sense, the most serious problem in Mexico is not the quality of regulations and not even the absence of monitoring and controlling bodies. The issue of crucial importance is broad sectors of society breaking laws and the state's weakness in enforcing them.

References

Aguilar, Luis F. 2010. "Hacernos preguntas." *Reforma*, May 19, p. 14.
Alcocer, Jorge, ed. 1993. *Dinero y Partidos*. Mexico City: CEPNA/Fundación Ebert.
Astorga, Luis. 2005. *El siglo de las drogas*. Mexico City: Plaza y Janés.
———. 2007. *Seguridad, Traficantes y militares*. Mexico City: Tusquets.
Buscaglia, Edgardo, Samuel González Ruiz, and William Ratliff. 2005. "Undermining the Foundations of Organized Crime and Public Sector Corruption." Essays in Public Policy 114. Hoover Institution.
Calderón, Felipe. 2009. "Closing remarks." Conference organized by IDEA, the IFE, and the Ministry of the Interior. December 2 (www.presidencia.gob.mx/movil/index.php?contenido=51047).
Callejo Anzures, José. 2002. *De Cancún a Almoloya: el imperio de Mario Villanueva*. Mexico City: Océano.
Castañeda, Rodríguez. 2009. *El México narco*. Mexico City: Planeta.
Cervantes, Jesusa, and Arturo Rodríguez. 2010. "El narco en el Congreso." *Proceso*, June 12.
Chapa, Granados. 2010. "PGR política, candidate equívoco." *Reforma*, May 27.
Córdova, Lorenzo, and Ciro Murayama. 2006. *Elecciones, dinero y corrupción*. México: Cal y Arena.

63. Alfredo Cristalinas Kaulitz, interview by author, Mexico City, April 2010.

Curzio, Leonardo. 2000a. "Crimen organizado y financiamiento de campañas políticas en México." In *Crimen Organizado y gobernabilidad democrática*, edited by John Bailey and Roy Godson. Mexico City: Grijalbo

———. 2000b. *Gobernabilidad, democracia y video política en Tabasco 1994–1999*. Mexico City: Plaza y Valdés.

"Failed States Index." 2010. *Foreign Policy* (July/August).

Fisichella, Domenico. 2002. *Dinero y democracia. De la antigua Grecia a la economía global*. Barcelona: Tusquets.

IFE (Instituto Federal Electoral). 2009. *Manual de Transparencia para partidos políticos*. México: IFE.

———. 2010. See www.ife.gob.mx.

INFORME 2009. 2010. *Entre la violencia y la indiferencia*. Mexico City.

Lujambio, Alonso. 2003. "México." In *Dinero y contienda político-electoral*, edited by Manuel Carrillo, Alonso Lujambio, Carlos Navarro, Daniel Zovatto. Mexico City: FCE.

Lupsha, Peter, A. 1996. "Transnational Organized Crime versus the Nation-State." *Transnational Organized Crime* 2, no. 1.

Ministry of Public Security. 2009. Press release 302, July 14 (www.ssp.gob.mx).

Naím, Moisés. 2006. *Ilícito*. Mexico City: Debate.

Núñez Jimenez, Arturo. 1997. "Las reformas constitucionales de 1996 en materia político electoral." In *Senado de la República e IIJ/UNAM LVI Legislatura: 80 Aniversario de la Constitución* (www.biblio.jurídicas.unam.mx/libros/1/165/14.pdf).

Orlando, Leoluca. 2004. *Hacia una cultura de la legalidad*. Mexico City.

PNUD. 2004. "La democracia en América Latina: Hacia una democracia de ciudadanas y ciudadanos" (www.gobernabilidademocrática/pnud.org).

Panebianco, Angelo. 1993. *Modelos de Partido*. Madrid: Alianza.

Rico, Carlos. 2008. "La iniciativa Mérida y el combate nacional al crimen organizado." *Foreign Affairs* (in Spanish) January–March.

Ronquillo. 2010. "Violencia, narcotráfico, pobreza: elecciones amenazadas." *Revista Mileni*, April 7.

"Survey on Political Culture and Civic Practices." 2008 (www.encup.gob.mx).

Tokatlián, Juan Gabriel. 1995. *Drogas, dilemas y dogmas*. Bogotá: TM Editores.

Toro, Celia. 1997. «Narcotráfico: lo que la interdependencia no nos explicó." In *La política exterior de México, enfoques para su análisis*. México: Colegio de México.

———. 1998. «La política mexicana contra el narcotráfico: un instrumento de política exterior." In *Nueva Agenda bilateral en la agenda México Estados Unidos*, edited by Rafael Fernandez de Castro, Mónica Verea, and Sydney Weintraub. México City: ITAM-FCE.

UNODC (United Nations Office on Drugs and Crime). 2009. *World Drug Report*.

Zovatto, Daniel, ed. 2003. *Dinero y contienda político-electoral*. Mexico City: FCE.

DANIEL SMILOV

7 Bulgaria: Perception and Reality

Organized crime is highly context dependent.[1] The Bulgarian type is different in important respects from the Italian Mafia, from Mexican and Colombian drug lords, and from other criminal networks. By extension, there are also variations in the impact that organized crime has on the political process, including political finance.

At a sufficiently abstract level, one could of course discuss organized crime as a single phenomenon with global dimensions. Standardization of meaning comes at the expense of important embedded local understandings and perceptions, however. This chapter argues that perceptions, at least in certain societies, are crucial to understanding the problems associated with organized crime as well as to elaborating successful policies to fight it.

In terms of public opinion—both within and outside the country—Bulgaria stands out as a polity seriously affected by organized crime. This view emerges from domestic sociological surveys and from external monitoring exercises conducted and published by the European Commission.[2] Bulgarian society and external observers are convinced that the fight against organized crime and corruption constitutes the gravest challenge for the country. Yet Bulgaria does not face quite the same level of problems as countries like Italy, Mexico, and Colombia. For one, there are no extensive, socially based criminal networks exercising open control over whole regions. Second, the economic output of

---

1. The use of the concept of *organized crime* to describe a global phenomenon, essentially removing each case from their specific national contexts, has become commonplace, but it is a theoretically and practically problematic exercise. For a critical assessment of the globalization of the usage of organized crime terminology, see Beare (2003), especially the chapter by Woodiwiss (Woodiwiss 2003).

2. For an analysis of the monitoring exercised by the EC in the justice and home affairs area (which covers corruption and organized crime), see the publications of the EUMAP project (EUMAP, 2001, 2002). See also Smilov (2006).

criminal groups, although impressive, is not of a magnitude that would allow these groups to seriously challenge the state. Finally, and possibly most important, the interpenetration of state officials and alleged criminals takes on a very unique form, which has given grounds for Misha Glenny to suggest that while there is mafia in many states, in Bulgaria the mafia has a state.[3]

This is a gross exaggeration, of course, but it reflects what many people in Bulgaria think and the way in which they conceptualize the problem of organized crime. Taking a clue from these widespread perceptions, one could argue the following. *Organized crime* is an umbrella term, which covers a broad array of other problems. The narrow meaning of the term refers to the activities of organized criminal groups, such as drug dealing, smuggling, extortion, and prostitution. The broader meaning is more popular in Bulgaria, and it refers to the spread of corruption among the political elite, its distancing from the people, and the continuing political influence of former members of the now defunct communist secret services. The narrow and broad meanings of the term are not usually analytically distinguished in their public usage, which in part explains the perceived elevated status of the problem of organized crime in Bulgaria.

In terms of the link between organized crime and political finance, one should distinguish between the narrow and the broad concepts in order to better capture the problem. Following the narrow definition, the fact is that there is a dearth of hard evidence pointing to criminal funds being channeled into politics. Allegations abound, but almost none of them have been substantiated. There are good reasons to believe that during the revolutionary reforms of the 1990s the flow of dirty money into politics faced few obstacles. Since the 2000s, however, regulations have been tightened, political parties and state institutions are generally stronger, and state subsidies for political parties have been introduced. Consequently, the incentive to resort to funds of suspicious origins should have decreased. At present, the alleged links between organized crime and politicians are not so much related to campaign or party donations as to sophisticated and ingenious links between the political establishment and the criminal world. These links are implicit in the broader meaning of the concept of organized crime.

The typical scenarios that fall under the second meaning are the following:

—The political protection of shady businesses in return for financial support and other resources

—Kickbacks to political parties and politicians for specific favors, especially during the privatization process of the postcommunist era

---

3. Glenny (2008).

—The setting up of political parties by members of the criminal underworld or with their help
—The control of politically relevant media of people allegedly associated with organized crime.

In none of these scenarios have the allegations been proven. This uncertainty leads to a situation where myths abound and start to substitute for reality. The hard evidence—as is argued below—does not substantiate fears that organized crime has penetrated deeply into the political system, deprived it of autonomy, and captured it. This divergence between perception and reality produces a dangerous situation, whose results are, broadly, the following:

—Delegitimized mainstream political actors: traditional parties increasingly seen as corrupt and linked with organized crime, understood in the broader meaning of the concept
—Ascendancy of new populist players whose main policy goal is to fight organized crime and corruption
—Instability of the party system and volatility of the political process
—Very low trust in traditional politics and representative institutions
—A shift in the political focus from socioeconomic issues to topics such as personal integrity and commitment to fighting organized crime and corruption
—Increasing influence of money and financial resources for electioneering and political mobilization: the falling value of party loyalty and ideology compensated by media presence, public relations, and sometimes even vote buying, which all require considerable resources.

The widespread perception of organized crime as a phenomenon in the broad sense of the concept explains an apparent paradox: Bulgaria entered the European Union (along with Romania) as the poorest member. But instead of focusing on the problems of underfunding and inefficiency in the health care and education systems, the country turned its attention primarily to the fight against organized crime and corruption, specifically to the police, the judiciary, and special services.

The Bulgarian Penal Code description of an "organized criminal group" states that the activities of gangster groups are not only manifested in the accumulation of grave crimes but also constitute a collective act of individuals who continuously coordinate their actions and whose relationships are well structured and hierarchical. Generally, organized crime is the formation of criminal networks, the creation of illegal quasi-institutions. Hence it is a criminal competitor to the government in the areas of enforcing rule and order. This competition is most evident with the monopoly on violence and the monopoly on collecting taxes, duties, and levies. Whatever it is, however, as the Bulgarian political scientist Ivan Krastev put it (in an informal discussion with the author), organized crime appears to be the country's most organized structure, especially in comparison to public authorities.

Political Context

Bulgaria has undergone a tremendous metamorphosis over the last twenty years. The country went from being one of the closest satellites of the Soviet Union, known for its ideological orthodoxy and intolerance of dissent, to becoming a member of the European Union and NATO. Bulgarian democracy has consolidated, albeit at relatively low levels of quality, and now has a vigorous civil society, free media, and improved conditions for minorities. The Turkish ethnic minority, comprising around 10 percent of the population, was subject to repression during the last years of the communist regime, but it is today well represented in the political process through a party of its own.[4]

In terms of living standards and economic growth, the worst period of the transition was the financial crisis of the mid-1990s, as the severe hyperinflation that came along with it wiped out people's savings. The crisis was homegrown by the then unreformed ex-communist party, the Bulgarian Socialist Party, which was slowing down or blocking necessary reforms for privatization, restitution of property, and market liberalization. To this policy failure one should add the effects of the Yugoslav embargo from the early 1990s. Blocking Bulgaria's main trading routes to Europe created ample opportunities for smuggling fuels and other goods.[5] Since 1997, however, Bulgaria has had a series of economically successful governments that have managed to partially compensate for the economic slump of the previous period. These more recent sound policies helped Bulgaria on its road to European Union membership in 2007. The 2008 global economic crisis proved the resilience of the new Bulgarian economy: in 2011 the country still had significant fiscal reserves, although it suffered from a contraction in economic activities due to meager foreign investment and shrinking international markets.

Bulgaria transformed itself with the help of a very dynamic political process. Contrary to some transitologist dicta, the country fragmented its party system *and* consolidated its democracy in the sense that democracy had become the "only game in town."[6] The political parties are numerous and ever changing,

---

4. For a more detailed analysis of the transition period in Bulgaria, see Smilov (2010).

5. For an analysis of the importance of the Yugoslav embargo and the financial crisis of the mid-1990s in the development of Bulgarian organized crime, see Nikolov (1997, pp. 80–85).

6. See http://pewglobal.org/reports/pdf/267.pdf. In 2009 Bulgarians, together with Hungarians, were the most convinced among Eastern Europeans in the value of such democratic principles as freedom of speech, free elections, and freedom of religion (60 percent of Bulgarians, in

however. Parliamentary elections on July 5, 2009, confirmed that the electoral strength and appeal of traditional parties were already in decline, regardless of whether it was the center-left Bulgarian Socialist Party (BSP) or the successor of the once-mighty center-right Union of Democratic Forces (UDF). These two major parties dominated the political scene during the most decisive years of the Bulgarian transition. But as of March 2011 these traditional parties enjoyed the combined support of less than 20 percent of the population. Most of the remaining 80 percent expressed a preference for new political players, who campaigned mainly on the fight against corruption and that against nationalism. Since 2001 the new players have proven increasingly successful.

In line with this trend, in July 2009 the clear winner of the parliamentary elections was Citizens for European Development of Bulgaria (GERB), which was the political party of the charismatic mayor of Sofia, Boiko Borissov. The party took 117 of the 240 seats in the Bulgarian National Assembly. In second place came the incumbent BSP, with 40 seats, which was less than half of what it won in the 2005 elections. The Movement for Rights and Freedoms (DPS)—the regional party representing mostly Bulgarian Turks—was the only party of the triple ruling coalition of 2005–09 (the two others are the BSP and the NDSV, or the National Movement for Stability and Progress) that was able to stabilize and even slightly increase its performance in comparison with 2005. In contrast, the NDSV (the party of the former tsar, Simeon II) failed to get the 4 percent electoral threshold to qualify for seats in parliament—a dramatic development given its 40 percent win in 2001. Of particular importance is the fact that most of the remaining votes went to populist and nationalist parties such as Ataka, Order, Law and Justice (RZS), and Lider. The first two met the 4 percent electoral threshold and were able to have seats in parliament.

The number and percentages of votes the parties received are as follows:
—GERB: 1,678,641 (40 percent)
—BSP: 748,147 (18 percent)
—DPS: 610,521 (14 percent)
—Ataka Party: 395,733 (9 percent)
—Blue Coalition: 285,662 (7 percent)
—RZS: 174,582 (4 percent)
—Lider Party: 137,795 (3 percent)

---

comparison to around 40 percent and less of Slovaks, Lithuanians, and Russians, for instance). Yet again, together with Hungarians, Bulgarians are most dissatisfied with the actual workings of their democracy (76 percent). In this sense, the Bulgarian democracy could be considered consolidated (no alternative) but frustrated and, to an extent, angry. As far as Europeanization goes, Bulgarians are still among the most enthusiastic about EU integration, and they take extremely seriously advice and criticism coming from Brussels.

These electoral results point to the seemingly everlasting capacity of the Bulgarian party system to disintegrate and transform. The dominant parties of the 1990s (BSP and UDF) and the dominant party of the early 2000s (NDSV) are losing strength and becoming marginalized: the NDSV did not make it into parliament in the most recent elections, and the successors of the UDF are dangerously close to the electoral threshold. Meanwhile, there are rising new players, but they lack well-formulated programs, an ideological foundation, party structure, and organization. It is as if these political groups emerge from the virtual world of electronic media, materialize during elections, and then disappear within a few years.

Organized Crime in Political Context

The fight against organized crime and corruption became a top political priority in Bulgaria toward the end of the 1990s. It could be argued that the prioritization of this issue coincided with—and was helped by—the preaccession negotiations with the EU. In every regular report—the main admissions monitoring instrument of the European Commission—it was stressed that Bulgaria needed to make a better effort to fight corruption and organized crime.[7] The last document of its kind, published in 2006, even stated that Bulgaria had regressed on these two crucial dimensions and fell behind Romania, the traditional straggler in this regard. This insistence on the issue of organized crime continued, as a monitoring tool, after Bulgaria was welcomed into the EU.[8] It was not until 2010 that the EC indicated that there was the "political will" in Bulgaria in its fight against corruption, although the results were considered still partly unsatisfactory.

In short, Bulgaria entered the EU with the reputation of the most corrupt member state and with the most severe problem of organized crime. Subsequently, a number of structural funds and other forms of EU subsidies were either blocked or delayed, and Brussels has successfully used financial leverage to get the Bulgarian government to institute reforms. The list of said reforms is too long for this chapter; suffice it to say that they range from constitutional amendments, structural laws regarding the judicial system, reforms of the penal and the procedural codes, to the joint monitoring—by Bulgarian institutions and EU observers—of cases deemed to be of "specific public interest."

---

7. For the regular reports of the EC for the period 1998—2005, see http://ec.europa.eu/enlargement/archives/key_documents/reports_2005_en.htm.

8. For the so-called reports on the progress of Bulgaria and Romania within the framework of the Cooperation and Verification Mechanism of the EC, see http://ec.europa.eu/dgs/secretariat_general/cvm/progress_reports_en.htm.

Given the numbers, it is hard to conclude that Bulgaria is somehow exceptional in the EU when it comes to organized crime. It is true that, as far as corruption indexes and rankings go, the country is not faring particularly well, as it is grouped with Romania, Latvia, and Poland.[9] Domestic measurements of transactional corruption remain steady and at arguably high levels. There are hardly any reliable comparative analyses on levels of organized crime, however.

Three main sources of information can help us get at the scope and spread of organized crime in Bulgaria. First, there are research papers produced by civil society organizations (think tanks, primarily), such as the Center for the Study of Democracy, RiskMonitor, Transparency International Bulgaria, and the Center for Liberal Strategies.[10] Unfortunately, although these reports provide useful information, they are rarely methodologically rigorous enough to be a reliable basis for comparison. Yet interesting findings do exist.

Consider the claim by the Standing Group on Organized Crime that Bulgarian criminal organizations have taken over a significant portion of the sex market in Western Europe.[11] Between 8,000 and 12,000 Bulgarian women are being sexually exploited outside the country. These women generate around EUR 1 billion for Bulgarian organized crime. Despite that, Bulgarian law enforcement institutions often treat human trafficking as a crime done by individuals, not by organizations. As a result, they do not follow the route of the generated income and so do not restrict the crime.

The second main source of information is reports by investigative journalists. The group of such professionals working on the issue in the country are led by Slavi Angelov (of *24 Chasa* newspaper) and Yovo Nikolov (of *Capital* weekly). The basic story of the origin of Bulgarian criminal networks is known, as is the profile of the most notorious members, thanks to the findings of these journalists. But the popular press has generally become increasingly unreliable. Among the best reports is Misha Glenny's chapter on Bulgaria in *McMafia: Crime without Frontiers,* which is a superb synopsis of some of the most prominent journalistic accounts of organized crime.[12] At the lower end of the spectrum we find the tabloid press, which discovered that it could make money out of organized crime stories. Thus there are now pages in many editions (and definitely in the most popular ones) allotted to the trials and tribulations of alleged organized

  9. For 2010, according to the CPI of Transparency International, Bulgaria is right after Romania in the rating but before other EU countries, like Greece, for instance. See www.transparency.org/policy_research/surveys_indices/cpi/2010/results.
  10. The institute RiskMonitor specializes in research on organized crime. For its reports, see Petrunov (2010a, 2010b); Smedovska (2010); also www.riskmonitor.bg.
  11. Petrunov (2010c).
  12. Glenny (2008).

crime members, presented in the form of soap opera. Prominent journalists who initiated this reporting subsequently published a series of books on the life of organized crime's popular heroes. In a macabre turn of events, two of these authors were killed (one of them rather demonstratively), in what the public probably interprets as proof of the veracity of their stories.

Contract killings, in general, are probably the most important area where myth and reality concerning Bulgarian organized crime publicly meet. In terms of hard data, these are the most significant for assessing the impact of organized crime on the Bulgarian political process.[13] The truth is that criminal organizations systematically resort to (or at least used to until a few years ago) violence when resolving internal disputes, and in this aspect, Bulgaria stands out in comparison with countries like Romania. While general crime and homicide levels in Bulgaria are relatively moderate, the number of unresolved contract killings is alarmingly high—a fact made clear by official statistics, which is the third most important source of information about OC.

According to a report from the government's prosecutor's office, during the period from 1992 to 2005, 173 contract killings were documented.[14] It is important to stress that, with possibly two exceptions, none of these contract killings could be termed political. The assassination that comes closest to being of a political nature is that of former prime minister Andrei Lukanov in the mid-1990s.[15] He was still an active political figure with the capability to mobilize support within his party, the Bulgarian Socialist Party, and indeed some allege that the killing was aimed at preventing Lukanov from taking over the BSP. The second case of arguable political assassination was the killing of Iliya Pavlov in 2003. Pavlov was the richest man in the country, was a sponsor of most of the established parties, and had close links to the political elite. The cases remain

---

13. Of course, in terms of hard data, other statistical information (like number of investigations and convictions in more ordinary cases) could be used as well. However, these data are scarce, and generally they underreport the phenomenon. The European Commission in its Cooperation and Verification Mechanism reports follows closely these statistics, especially the development of high-profile cases. This is a typical observation from these reports. See www.europe.bg/upload/docs/com_2010_112_en.pdf. Since mid-2009, Bulgaria carried out a number of arrests and launched investigations in connection with organized crime groups. During the same period, two indictments in high-profile cases were filed, one for murder and for setting up an organized crime group and another for tax evasion. Substantial assets were frozen in the second case. A possible witness in a high-profile organized crime case was killed in Sofia on January 5, 2010. Organized crime cases in court have generally shown little development since mid-2009. The most significant success in terms of convictions were the sentences against a group involved in kidnapping in the post-2009 period.

14. Prosecutorial Office (2005).

15. Lukanov was killed in 1996. See Nikolov (2000).

unresolved. The rest of the contract killings could hardly be interpreted in political terms, although there have been cases of organized crime sponsoring political parties, presidential advisers, and other officials.

To these more or less traditional sources one should add a certain postmodern phenomenon: information from Wikileaks. In the beginning of 2011, cables sent by a former U.S. ambassador to Bulgaria were leaked and widely reported in the press.[16] In these cables, the ambassador reviews the organized crime world in Bulgaria as of 2005. Several of his statements are of particular significance to the present study.

He argues that organized crime's immunity from the law was the most serious problem in Bulgaria and that such immunity underlay corruption, the ineffectiveness of the legal system, and the country's poor economic development. Organized crime, says the ambassador, was particularly involved in international money laundering, drug trafficking, and counterfeiting. According to the National Service for Combating Organized Crime of the Bulgarian Ministry of Interior, an estimated 118 organized crime groups were operating in Bulgaria at the end of 2004. Organized crime continues to be pervasive in many spheres of Bulgarian life, despite domestic and international efforts to combat it. To date, not a single major crime figure has been punished by the Bulgarian legal system, despite the continuing assassinations.

Other statements by the ambassador have to do with the link between organized crime and political parties:

> In an attempt to maintain their influence regardless of who is in power, organized crime figures donate to all the major political parties. As these figures have expanded into legitimate businesses, they have attempted—with some success—to buy their way into the corridors of power. During the 2001 general elections, a number of influential "businessmen," including Vasil Bozhkov and Emil Kyulev, heavily financed and otherwise supported the NMSS (NDSV) campaign. At the beginning of his term in office in 2001, Prime Minister Simeon Saxe-Coburg Gotha held a high-profile meeting with members of Vuzrazhdane in which he invited Iliya Pavlov, Vasil Bozhkov, et al., to become part of a "business consultative council" advising the government. Later that year, Kyulev helped finance the successful presidential campaign of BSP leader Georgi Purvanov.

The ambassador also claims that "Ahmed Dogan, the leader of the government's junior coalition partner, attended Iliya Pavlov's funeral in 2003" and

---

16. The full report was originally published at www.balkanleaks.eu/bgoc.html.

made "no attempt to conceal his close relationship with the slain Multigrup chairman." Further, "during the 2005 election campaign, business interests with connections to organized crime (including Lukoil and Sasho Donchev's Overgas), Bozhkov, Kyulev, and others spread their support and money across the political spectrum, focusing primarily on the NMSS and the BSP." The cable continues, "Below the level of the national government and the leadership of the major political parties, organized crime 'owns' a number of municipalities and individual members of parliament. This direct participation in politics—as opposed to bribery—is a relatively new development for Bulgarian organized crime. Interests were protected whatever the outcome of the vote."

Finally, the cable provides a detailed analysis of who is who in Bulgarian organized crime, providing descriptions of many business groups in the country. The main argument is that a new group, the regional Varna-based TIM, started to dominate the landscape after the killing of Iliya Pavlov.[17]

It is problematic to rely on this source, of course. At first impression it looks like a synthesis of journalistic publications in the Bulgarian press supported by interviews with state officials and politicians. But there is the problem of the reliability and legitimacy of Wikileaks.

After 2005 the government launched criminal investigations against most of the people mentioned in the cable, but some of these criminal proceedings still linger on. There have been no proceedings, for example, against TIM. All in all, the leaking of this cable does not resolve the main problem of sources: allegations of widespread organized crime abound, while the hard data substantiated by judicial verdicts remain scarce.

Causes and Origins of Organized Crime

There is consensus among scholars and analysts in Bulgaria that the origins of organized crime in the country are linked to the dismantling of the repressive apparatus of the communist state, which began in the early 1990s. In a sense, the origins of organized crime are top down rather than bottom up. With the fall of the regime in 1989 came a vacuum in many of the spaces once occupied by communist security services. These spaces range from the smuggling routes of arms and drugs and prostitution to ordinary law enforcement. This change overlapped with the dismantling of some police services as well, such as the laying off of "professionals" who gradually "privatized" the activities and became "violent entrepreneurs"—this last term coined by Vadim Volkov.[18]

---

17. The description of TIM is in appendix A.
18. Volkov (2002). Also see Holmes (1997); Coulloudon (1997).

Since this process is well studied in the Bulgarian context, what follows is a synthesis of the major features of organized crime produced by this top-down, semiadministrative transformation.[19]

—Important figures becoming organized crime members, including former athletes, former police officers, and the nomenklatura[20]
—Significant political/administrative protection for organized crime projects
—Infiltration of law enforcement by former or future members of organized crime
—Close links of organized crime to politicians.

Consider the following case as an example. Currently, the most high-profile investigation in Bulgaria is against Alexey Petrov, the alleged organizer of a grand criminal "octopus," as it is popularly referred to in the media. Petrov started his career under communism as a sportsman with a police relationship: he practiced karate, a martial art that the police planned to use in the future. Bear in mind that this was standard procedure under communism, as the police and the secret services closely monitored certain sports. In the beginning of the 1990s Petrov started his own business, and predictably, it was a private law enforcement agency. The company gradually grew into an insurance company dealing primarily with automobile insurance. Then toward the end of the 1990s, he was recruited as an informer by the state security services of the emerging democracy. In 2008 his career peaked when he became a senior officer at the State Agency for National Security (SANS), the Bulgarian state security agency. He was in charge of the fight against organized crime. In the autumn of 2009 he was indicted on organized crime charges, specifically for being the leader of a criminal group.

Petrov was eventually released from pretrial detention and was put under house arrest. In the beginning of 2011, the court lifted this restriction and substituted a requirement to regularly report to authorities. Subsequently, Petrov gave numerous interviews in the media, attended public events, and even participated—in his capacity as a leader of an employers association—in a meeting with the deputy prime minister. Further, while in custody, he started publishing a newspaper, *Galeria*, which published constant allegations of corruption against the current GERB government. Also in 2011 *Galeria* managed to stir a major scandal affecting the minister of the interior and exposing widespread instances of wiretapping by the government in the fight against corruption and organized crime. The case against Petrov is still in its judicial phase at the

---

19. See the publication of the Center for the Study of Democracy (http://unpan1.un.org/intradoc/groups/public/documents/UNTC/UNPAN017117.pdf).
20. Nikolov (1997) makes this argument.

moment of this writing; thus it remains to be seen whether the prosecutors will manage to substantiate their allegations against him.

It is interesting that Petrov has been able to befriend a number of different governments and maintained contacts with many government officials, including the former prosecutor general. During the 1990s he had a business relationship with Boiko Borissov. During the parliamentary campaign of 2009, SANS, with Petrov among its top ranks, became unusually politically active. The agency leaked sensitive information and specifically accepted corruption leads from a new party, called Order, Law, and Justice. To many observers, this insistence looked like political engineering aimed at strengthening the electoral prospect of the then ruling party (BSP) and weakening the chance of the opposition (GERB). Reportedly, Petrov's brother was member of this new party.

This case illustrates the intricate interrelation between alleged organized crime members and the political establishment in Bulgaria. It is also a good example of the utility of using the broad meaning of organized crime in the Bulgarian context. Organized crime in Bulgaria is in fact constituted of a political elite that is closely connected to members of the former communist secret services and the police. These groups took over as the institutions of communist Bulgaria disintegrated. What the majority of people understand by organized crime is the prevalence of such links during the better part of the Bulgarian transition to democracy and a market economy. Whether this is the case or not, Petrov is held in the public imagination as the personification of the largely illegitimate origin of contemporary political elites.

The Petrov example also shows the lack of analytical clarity in defining both organized crime and political networks. This confusion is apparent in the public discourse: the media generally portray politicians as corrupt. In fact, for the public, politicians come in two models—those who are corrupted and those who fight corruption. For the past ten years this portrayal has become the main cleavage in the Bulgarian party system, overshadowing socioeconomic issues and other traditional dividing lines.

Organized Crime and Political Finance

The discussion thus far stresses the importance of distinguishing between the narrow sense of organized crime (criminal networks dedicated to smuggling, drugs, and prostitution) and the broader sense of the concept, which gets at the interconnectedness between the political elite and such groups. The Petrov case illustrates the dominance of the broader sense in the Bulgarian context. The distinction, as becomes apparent below, is also telling of the relationship between organized crime and political finance.

If we stick to the narrow conceptualization of organized crime, we should look for financial or resource exchanges between criminal networks and political parties or candidates, primarily through campaign and party donations or via the provision of services during elections. As mentioned above, there have been such instances in Bulgaria, especially in the 1990s, when criminal groups like VIS and SIK reportedly contributed funds to the two main parties of the period, the center-right UDF and the center-left BSP. There are no hard data on these incidents, however, as starting in the mid-1990s—when these links flourished—the severe financial crisis that hit Bulgaria hampered the ability of the state to conduct basic monitoring and control. As a consequence, from 1996 to 1998 political parties did not file reports, the state did not provide funds for elections, and there were no supervisory bodies. Political parties were left to their own devices, and the only concession to them was the lack of financial regulation. Considering that this free rein took place immediately after the Yugoslav war and the embargo, which encouraged smuggling on a massive scale, it is by no means far-fetched to suggest that parties easily resorted to shady funds.

The repercussions can still be felt in Bulgaria. For example, the practice of returning donations from potentially illegitimate sources has not been established. A revealing case happened in 2009–10, when the court tried two high-profile political donors to President Georgi Parvanov—Mario Nikolov and Ludmil Stoykov—for fraud with EU funds. Both were ultimately acquitted, which was curious since their partners were convicted in Germany for participation in the same business transaction. It is interesting, however, that throughout the process the president never returned the donated funds, nor did he publicly dissociate himself from the two individuals on trial. That the president would get away with that behavior points to the high level of tolerance of politicians' relations with (alleged) criminals. Widespread perceptions of such links, and perhaps even their inevitability, reinforce public cynicism about politics in general.

The broader definition of organized crime brings out a different aspect of the link between organized crime and political finance. Instead of candidates receiving the occasional illicit donation from criminal networks, there is a systematic interaction between these networks and the political elites. These structured ties are forged by criminal networks when they capture political institutions or by the political elite when it becomes one and the same as criminal organizations. This definition is far more salient in Bulgaria as the narrow definition. As argued above, Bulgarian organized crime is generally a top-down phenomenon, created by the disintegrating communist state and its repressive apparatus.

Different countries are affected to varying degrees by the four types of link between political finance and organized crime (table 7-1). Arguably, type 4 is

Table 7-1. *Four Types of Link between Political Finance and Organized Crime*

	Top-down origin of links	Bottom-up origin of links
Narrow sense of organized criminal networks in the field of smuggling, drugs, prostitution	Type 1. Politicians seek resources for campaigns: criminals extort them in exchange for desired funds; occasionally, politicians use criminal groups to put pressure on opponents; and criminals extract concessions when giving in-kind support (cars, communications, offices, personnel).	Type 2. Organized crime seeks political influence to protect its business: criminals donate to parties or candidates in exchange for political concessions; criminals conduct vote-buying campaigns for political parties and candidates who they deem to be on their side; criminals threaten opponents; criminals buy advertisements and coverage in the media of political activities by criminal groups; criminals give occasional in-kind support to political parties.
Broad sense of systemic relationships between criminal networks and members of the political elite (parties and candidates)	Type 3. Extensive political patronage and favoritism results in client groups immune to criminal prosecution: creation of political "umbrellas" or "roofs" for specific actors, which are de facto above the law; gradual marginalization of the political opposition; government circles steadily take over major sectors of civil society (media, business, NGOs) and stifle political competition.	Type 4. Capture of parties and candidates by powerful criminal networks: organized crime colonizes the political elite and dictates its agenda; territorial control (including de facto control) by organized crime in parts of the country.

more appropriate to countries like Colombia, Mexico, and Italy.[21] Type 3 applies to countries like Russia, where authoritarian tendencies overlap with the disintegration of the repressive bodies of the state, and the line between the criminal world and the political establishment blurs. Types 1 and 2 are more widespread; examples of them could possibly be found in most countries.

To the best of my knowledge, Bulgaria has been mostly impacted by type 1 and to a lesser extent by type 2. This is what can be deduced from the hard data

---

21. Consider the Tommaso Buscetta statement that "the Cosa Nostra figure maintains a sort of monopoly on that politician." See della Porta and Vannucci (1999, p. 221).

available—statistics, court reports, journalistic investigations, and government reports—as well as from the general development of the country, especially the progress associated with EU and NATO memberships. Since organized crime in Bulgaria has primarily top-down origins, officials have occasionally interacted with criminal groups, especially in the 1990s, when state institutions were weak. Governments have attempted political patronage and favoritism, but due to the dynamic political process, these relationships have not become entrenched enough to merit being labeled type 3.

In the minds of most Bulgarians, however, the government's relationship with organized crime is best described by type 3 rather than by type 1. This mismatch between reality and perception damages the political process by delegitimizing its actors and by changing societal priorities.

Party Finance Regulation

Setting the discussion on organized crime aside for the time being, this section focuses more specifically on political finance in order to prepare the ground for a more detailed analysis of the link between the two in Bulgaria. The primary function of political funding regulation is to ensure a stable and viable democratic process of representation. Political parties and electoral candidates need to have sufficient resources in order to function and be successful. It is therefore no surprise that political financing regulations are tailored to the institutional and ideological specificity of the given democratic system.[22]

Institutional Specificity

Varying separation of powers structures and electoral systems explain the existence of different political finance models. The institutional choices that most directly account for this variety are, on the one hand, the choice between a presidential and a parliamentary system and, on the other, the choice between majoritarian and proportional representation. Presidential regimes, especially in combination with majoritarian electoral systems, tend to weaken political parties and boost the influence of individual candidates. These effects are illustrated by the U.S. example, where individual candidates are the central players in (electoral) politics and in campaign finance in particular. Accordingly, the U.S. model may be called the candidate-centered model of political finance (table 7-2).

In Europe, and in Eastern Europe in particular, candidate-centered models are not common, but some federal countries with large populations, such as Russia and Ukraine (especially in the 1990s), have come close to this archetype

---

22. The analysis in this section is based on Smilov and Toplak (2007).

Table 7-2. *Four Models of Political Finance Based on Ideology and Institutional Specifics*

Ideology	Candidate centered	Party centered
Libertarian	Libertarian-presidential: United States	Libertarian-parliamentary: United Kingdom before the 2000 reform
Egalitarian	Egalitarian-presidential: Russia (especially in the 1990s)	Egalitarian-parliamentary: Bulgaria, Europe in general

Source: Smilov (2008).

in certain respects. The most important feature of these models is that, at least at the federal level, political parties focus on the individual contest for funds and on that carried out by ad hoc electoral associations. In the region, candidate-centered models tend to go with presidential (or superpresidential) systems, as political parties are, as a rule, weaker than parties in parliamentary systems. This is so because in such systems governments are appointed by powerful presidents and need not rely on the support of the legislative majority for their existence. Since political parties are most powerful and necessary when they participate in the formation of a majority government, the propresidential and antiparliamentary biases in the constitutional structures of both Russia and Ukraine weaken political parties, obliging them to compete for influence with clans, oligarchies, and ad hoc formations of representatives seeking to obtain presidential favors.

In contrast to the candidate-centered model of political finance is the party-centered model. As a rule, this system emerges in tandem with the parliamentary system, in which legislative majorities are based on strong, cohesive parties needed to support the government. Proportional representation tends to favor the party-centered model, although this model can exist even in countries with majoritarian electoral systems, as the example of the United Kingdom demonstrates. The parliamentary systems of continental Europe and Scandinavia constitute the quintessential example of the party-centered model. Most of the countries of East-Central Europe, including Bulgaria, fit this type. Its defining feature is that political parties are the major players in political finance: they carry the major burden with respect to raising funds, are responsible for the bulk of the expenditure, and are the main beneficiaries of state aid. The propparty constitutional bias is reflected in the regulation of political finance as well. State aid mainly benefits established parties with parliamentary representation. Numerous regulations impose burdens on individual candidates and ad hoc electoral groups in terms of registration and fundraising. Distribution of in-kind state aid, such as free airtime, is also done through the major parties.

Ideological Specificity

The second major dividing line between political finance models concerns the ideological difference between egalitarian and libertarian political views. Libertarians generally believe that the government should uphold the status quo by not attempting to alter the playing field in any direction. If a particular actor has superior financial resources that were legitimately acquired, he or she can bring those resources to bear in political competition. In the United States, this libertarian idea is constitutionally entrenched in the principle that "money is speech," which allows for unlimited financial contributions under the First Amendment because they are considered a form of political expression. Therefore, there are no limits to campaign expenditure or to private contributions unless they serve anticorruption purposes.

In contrast to the libertarian model is the egalitarian model. Egalitarian ideology is based on the principle that the government has the responsibility to help level the playing field, thus enabling it to change the status quo in the face of differences of wealth and financial resources. These manifestations of egalitarianism translate into specific policies vis-à-vis political competition. Bridging the wealth gap can be done through a variety of instruments in political finance, and they fall into two major categories: state aid to help equalize the resources of the major political actors, on the one hand, and on the other, limitations on expenditures and contributions designed to decrease the influence of wealthy political donors.

The German model of political finance relies mainly on generous funds from the state; the U.K. model, after the reforms of 2000, relies on spending limits with the same equalizing aim. Most Western European models could be described as egalitarian, although to different degrees, insofar as a particular intervention is considered legitimate. Eastern European states, Bulgaria among them, generally follow this pan-European trend of egalitarian regulations. This ideological bias should come as no surprise, bearing in mind the legacy of communism, which placed heavy emphasis on social equality and state intervention.

Political Finance

Bulgaria fits the egalitarian-parliamentary model rather well. The country has introduced restrictions on political expenditures and, more recently, significant state aid for parties—the main player in political finance. Bulgaria uses a proportional representation system for general elections (with 4 percent rationalizing threshold), which—together with the parliamentary form of government—augments the leverage of political parties. The central statute regulating this area at the moment is the Law on Political Parties, adopted in 2005 and amended in 2008–09.[23] The sources of funding of political parties in Bulgaria are membership fees, donations and contributions, revenue from economic activities (limited to publishing of party materials and a few other initiatives), and subsidies from the state budget. Anonymous donations have been banned since 2005. The two most important sources are private donations and, increasingly, state subsidies. At the present moment, state subsidies account for most of the income of political parties in Bulgaria.

Donations

Toward the beginning of the transition, the reorganized Communist Party obviously prioritized preventing foreign financial aid to the opposition. With this aim, the Political Parties Act (or, Law of Political Parties) of 1990 prohibited political donations from foreign states and organizations.[24] Donations from foreign citizens were capped at $500 for individuals and $2,000 for groups of individuals. Since there is not a large or politically influential Bulgarian diaspora, the entities most significantly affected by this reform were foreign political organizations, especially foundations and institutes.

As the first law regulating political parties was being drafted, the Communist Party was still connected to the political and economic structures of the country. The leaders, the members of these structures, and their organizations as a whole were potential donors to the Bulgarian Socialist Party. Under pressure from the opposition, along with the new elections and the adoption of a new constitution, a simultaneous process of privatization of the BSP had to take place. First, the law prohibited the establishment of party organizations in enterprises, institutions, or other organizations as well as any interference with the governing of these bodies.[25] Second, any existing organizations of political parties within enterprises had to be dissolved a month after the promulgation of the law.[26] Thus the reorganized Communist Party (BSP) was deprived of a very powerful source of preelectoral propaganda and fundraising. Third, public institutions (departments), enterprises, and organizations were not allowed to channel funds to political parties.[27]

The most significant recent development, as far as donations are concerned, is the ban on corporate donations that was introduced in 2009. Under the influence of the French model (as presented by French experts), the triple coalition

---

23. For a detailed analysis of the legal framework, see www.ucp.pt/site/resources/documents/Docente%20-%20Palbu/Greco%20Eval%20III%20Rep%20_2009_%207E%20Final%20Bulgaria%20PF%20CONF.pdf.
24. Article 17 (2).
25. Article 12 (1).
26. Article 13 (5).
27. Article 17 (3).

government of BSP, NDSV, and DPS introduced the ban, arguing that it was an efficient anticorruption measure.

Public Funding

The first law addressing party financing stipulates that the state, through budget appropriations, may finance the regular operations of political parties and their electoral campaigns. State subsidies for these two purposes are among the central tenets of the egalitarian-parliamentary model. However, subsequent legislation has limited public funds to elections. The government introduced direct subsidies for political parties only after 2001. In 2009 the state subsidy was raised significantly. Today, due to this increase, state subsidies account for the biggest share of a political party's resources.

The first statute also afforded tax privileges to political parties, which is another feature consistent with the egalitarian-parliamentary model. In the first place, they were allowed to carry out business activities in order to ensure their maintenance. "In accordance with their founding goals and program," the income from their activity was to be granted certain tax benefits and exemptions pursuant to a procedure established by the Council of Ministers.[28] The implementation of this provision caused a major controversy, however. In the period 1991–92 the Council of Ministers introduced an import duty exemption for party firms and companies. The exemption unleashed energetic competition among party firms in reaction to the importing of various goods, mainly cigarettes and alcohol. This brought huge profits that verged on the criminal.

There was no transparency in the process aimed at addressing the controversy. It was hard to convince anyone that imports of tobacco products and alcohol are "in accordance with the founding goals and program" of political parties. The Council of Ministers was forced, within a year, to revoke the exemption, given that a number of embarrassing scandals surfaced. Probably the most infamous, but by no means the only, case involved a foundation called Sapio, which allegedly was close to the finance minister, Ivan Kostov. The investigation into this scandal was terminated and reopened several times without a formal indictment or at least a revelation of irregularities. Among political scientists and observers in the country there is almost unanimous consensus that there have been serious irregularities and probably crimes related to the regulation of duty exemptions. Therefore, there has been no other duty or tax exemption for political parties since 1992.

By the standards of the country, the subsidy is quite sizable (table 7-3). Parties that obtain more than 1 percent of the vote in the general elections qualify

28. Article 20 (2, 3).

Table 7-3. *State Subsidies, Political Parties, 2010 and 2011*
Leva

Party	2010	2011
GERB	17,819,548	20,954,736
BSP	6,673,195	7,847,283
DPS	6,156,485	7,250,246
Ataka	4,102,108	4,823,837
SDS	1,657,427	1,949,036
RZS	1,474,731	1,734,197
DSB	990,221	1,164,441
Lider	1,428,397	1,679,711
NDSV	1,321,163	1,553,610
United Agrarians	193,928	228,048
Bulgarian Social-Democrats	180,355	212,087
Total subsidies to all parties	42,944,333	50,500,000

Source: State Audit Office.

for it. As of now they receive 12 leva per vote (1 lev = EUR 0.5, approximately). These 12 leva represent 5 percent of the minimum wage (in 2009 the subsidy was raised from 3 percent to 5 percent of the minimum wage, a significant boost).

Transparency

In the first years of the democratic transition in Bulgaria, parties were not obliged to maintain accounting records and reports. This practice became mandatory in 1996. Regulations that covered reporting, also missing from the 1990 Law on Political Parties, required parties to present (to a committee of Parliament) annual reports on the size and sources of income and expenditure. The first election laws also carried this obligation. The 1990 Law on Political Parties was rather naïve and contained regulations that were neither binding nor feasible. Finally, there was a 1991 provision stipulating that parties report their revenue and expenses during campaigns.

The Bulgarian government introduced relatively effective regulatory systems for the transparency of parties only in 2001, when the State Audit Office (SAO) was empowered to review annual reports of the political parties. Gradually, the powers of the SAO were expanded to cover reports of electoral expenditure as well. As of 2009, the SAO has the right to do extensive audits and financial revisions to monitor political parties. Another major improvement of the SAO's work is the practice of publishing financial reports of the parties and campaigns on its website. Now all of those documents are available, along with some analyses of violations encountered by the SAO. Online registration for private donations to political parties was introduced for the 2013 parliamentary elections; the SAO is to oversee this enterprise, which further promotes transparency.

Despite successes, the model has weaknesses. First is that the SAO does not specialize in political parties and elections. It is primarily composed of accountants and lawyers doing ex post facto checks of receipts and documents. There is no coordination between election monitoring bodies, electoral commissions, the prosecution, and the SAO. Thus de facto control is generally weak. Indeed, matching documents with real activities still remains a problem. Nevertheless, the improvement in comparison with the 1990s is immense.

Organized Crime and Political Finance: Evidence from Bulgaria

The Bulgarian case elucidates certain vulnerabilities in the egalitarian-parliamentary model vis-à-vis organized crime, but it also demonstrates that the safeguards that are built into the system may serve to alleviate problems and gradually reduce illegitimate flows of cash into the political process.

First, the 1990s were very favorable years for criminals who wanted to influence the political process. Parties were forced to rely primarily on private and corporate donations, various legal restrictions were placed both on fundraising and expenditure, which led to unavoidable violations of the law even by bona fide participants, and control and transparency were virtually missing. This combination of factors encouraged the parties to fundraise recklessly, thereby creating a culture of impunity. Even in such circumstances, however, it would be far-fetched to say that illegitimate interests privatized political parties. There might have been smaller parties that fit this label, but the two main parties of the 1990s—BSP and SDS—were too powerful to be captured by organized crime. They might have occasionally resorted to organized crime funding, they might have even had relationships with certain organized crime groups, but by and large the autonomy of the main parties vis-à-vis such interests seems to me undisputable.[29]

---

29. It is especially revealing that the already cited GRECO report—the most recent and authoritative assessment of the political finance of Bulgaria—does not single out organized crime concerns as central for the system. In fact, such concerns are hardly present in the report at all. Of course, the recommendations mention that much is to be desired in many fields that may have to do with organized crime—money laundering for instance. But even when pointing out that improvements must be introduced in such areas (as in the use exclusively of bank transactions and the banning of cash donations), the report states that auditors in Bulgaria are subject to the requirements of national anti-money-laundering legislation, which implies customer due diligence procedures and the reporting of suspicions of money laundering to the financial intelligence unit of Bulgaria. "The same obligations are applicable to political parties. . . . This can be explained by the fact that the financing of political parties and election campaigns is actually exposed to risks of money laundering."

If we returned to the four types in table 7-1, the Bulgarian case of the 1990s could be categorized mostly as type 1, with elements of type 2. The strength of the political parties, thanks in part to the parliamentary mode of government, the electoral system, and the very high level of ideological confrontation in Bulgarian society (which reinforces loyalty to the main parties), preserved the autonomy of the these important groups. Curiously, the political system by and large preserved its integrity and avoided colonization by illegitimate or illegal interests despite the lack of safeguards in terms of political finance. Of course, problems did exist, but again, these problems should be put in the larger context—a context of a relatively successful institutionalization of political parties after half a century of communism.

The end of the 1990s spelled the end of the "first" Bulgarian party system: the two-party confrontation of the ex-communist BSP and the proreform Union of Democratic Forces (SDS). Since 2001 there have been, as already stated, successive waves of new, populist players in Bulgarian politics, like the NDSV, GERB, Ataka, and others.[30] As a result, the party system became much less stable, and both in 2001 and 2009 extraparliamentary parties did manage to win parliamentary elections. Thus the stability and autonomy of political parties granted by the parliamentary form of government have worked less well over the last ten years in comparison to the 1990s.

In terms of political finance regulations there have been major improvements, such as the introduction of significant state subsidies, tightened control and transparency measures, and a ban on anonymous and corporate donations. The legal measures safeguarding the integrity and autonomy of political parties have been enhanced significantly. The overall result may still be some improvement on the situation in the 1990s, even considering the structural problems related to the rise of populist politics in Eastern Europe. Generally, Bulgaria should again be placed largely in model 1 (high risk; see table 7-4) with an indication of a tendency for improvement.

The conclusion drawn from the Bulgarian case is that when it comes to political financing, preserving the autonomy of parties depends on two variables. The first variable is political finance regulations. The second variable relates to the integrity of the political process and the role of parties therein. If there is an unstable party system with fragmented and weak parties and several newcomers to the political scene, it is very likely that occasional or more systemic links between these parties and organized crime groups will develop. If party weakness and fragmentation is accompanied by the demise of ideology more

---

30. For analysis of Bulgarian populism, see Meseznikov, Gyarfasova, and Smilov (2008); Smilov and Krastev (2008).

Table 7-4. *Impact Risk of Organized Crime in the Egalitarian-Parliamentary Model*

	Poor regulation of political finance: no working scheme of state subsidies; no control over the observance of restrictions of expenditure and the raising of private donations; no transparency rules	Well-regulated political finance: extensive state aid schemes; efficient control over expenditure limits and fund-raising restrictions; sufficient levels of transparency
Party system and ideology		
Weak and fragmented party system; political process void of ideology[a]	High risk	Medium risk
Strong and stable party system with programmatic ideology	Medium risk	Low risk

a. Della Porta and Vannucci (1999, p. 121): "The use of corrupt practices would seem to be negatively correlated to the . . . ability of parties to elaborate long-term programs, mobilize ideological resources, distribute participatory incentives, and gain the support of the electorate of opinion."

generally, the chance of organized crime meddling in politics is even higher.[31] This risk exists because ideology is an instrument to secure loyalty and mobilize voters, and in its absence, it is substituted for by increased expenditure during elections—vote buying, pressure on voters, and so on.

As mentioned, Bulgaria fits types 2 and 3 of the descriptions noted in table 7-1. In the 1990s the country leaned toward type 3, but it has somewhat shifted to type 2 since the beginning of the new century. Bulgaria is definitely not to be positioned in type 4. Despite popular perceptions to the contrary, the evidence that it is a high-risk country is rather weak. Thus we come back again to one of the central questions we started with: the mismatch between the popular perception and the reality of organized crime, an issue taken up in the conclusion.

Conclusion: When Perception Becomes Reality

The analysis thus far establishes several points regarding the link between organized crime and political finance in Bulgaria. First, it is argued that Bulgarian organized crime is a top-down phenomenon, which has filled the

---

31. For the link between the lack of ideology in political parties and their corruption, see della Porta and Vannucci (1999, pp. 118–22). Bulgaria seems to parallel the Italian development: parties become more vulnerable to corruption in general when the ideological connection is missing.

vacuum created by the deconstruction of the communist state and its secret and police services.

Second, it is suggested that, judging on the basis of hard data and analysis of the political process in the country, the phenomenon of organized crime is less systemic and embedded than it is perceived. Distinguishing between the narrow and broad definitions of organized crime, it becomes clear that organized crime in Bulgaria falls into the narrow concept (as criminal groups operating narrowly in such areas as prostitution, smuggling, and drugs), while the perception of the population is that it falls into the broad concept (as having a deep symbiosis with the political world, denying it any meaningful autonomy).

Consider data from sociological surveys illustrating these perceptions.[32] It is a common belief among Bulgarians that the only winners in the transition are the following social groups: political parties, their leaders, and their close circles (36 percent); criminal power and economic groups (29 percent); and the establishment and former communists (12 percent). These data illustrate the level of criminalization of the political sphere in the popular imagination—both politicians and criminals are placed as opposition to the honest, common people, who are the greatest losers in the transition, according to 47 percent of the respondents. People's criminalization of the political elite seems to be the means through which they vent their deep frustrations with the transition.

Third, the Bulgarian model of political finance is categorized as egalitarian-parliamentary, and it is argued that there is a medium risk of serious impact of organized crime on the financing of political actors due to both structural and political finance regulation considerations.

The mismatch between perception and reality raises concerns, given that in politics perceptions tend to become or generate realities of their own. The widespread perception that Bulgaria is affected by organized crime in the broader sense—namely, that the country is a state of the mafia, as the Misha Glenny dicta would have it—delegitimizes and weakens political parties and provides fertile grounds for populist newcomers. As discussed, such novices have been especially successful since 2001. The weakening and fragmenting of the party system has an impact of its own: weak and fragmented party systems are more susceptible to organized crime. Thus inflated perceptions of a phenomenon may create real opportunities for its expansion. Delegitimizing and weakening political parties and the democratic fabric have brought on this very effect. Especially instructive in this regard is the deleterious effect that the case of Michael Chorney had on the political career of Ivan Kostov (see box 7-1).

---

32. The data are from April 2006. See Open Society Institute (2008).

Box 7-1. *The Effect of Perception on Politics: The Case of Michael Chorny*

In October 2003 the notorious Russian businessman Michael Chorny announced that he had been blackmailed for political donations by former prime minister Ivan Kostov and that, as a result, one of his companies had funded the Union of Democratic Forces' party foundation, Democracy, in the amount of $200,000. Democracy declared that it had received the money from a company based in Cyprus that had no connection with Michael Chorny.

In 2000, upon Bulgaria's entrance to NATO, Chorny, together with a number of other Russian businessmen residing in Bulgaria, had been expelled from the country by the UDF government of Ivan Kostov, which was under pressure from NATO. A 2000 report by the head of the National Security Service, Atanas Atanasov, accused senior members of the UDF government, and especially the minister of interior, Bogomil Bonev, of illegal lobbying for the financial interests of Chorny. This report became the reason for the dismissal of Bonev as minister. In the 2001 presidential race, UDF candidate Petar Stoyanov used the report during a presidential TV debate with Bonev, who was also running for the presidency. Bonev started judicial proceedings against Atanasov, accusing the latter of abuse of powers in the production of the report. A court found Atanasov guilty of abuse of powers, but an appellate court judgment acquitted him.

In 2004 a Sofia court quashed Chorny's expulsion order. However, the new chief of the NSS, Ivan Chobanov, reissued the order, rectifying some of the procedural flaws mentioned by the court. In the meantime, Chorny started civil proceedings for libel against some of the members of the UDF government and the executive director of Democracy, Grozdan Karadzhov. The court fined Karadzhov for libel against Chorny, and in 2006 the court fined former finance minister Muravey Radev for the same reason. Both of them had accused Chorny of being part of international criminal networks and of meddling illegally in Bulgarian politics.

Ultimately, the whole scandal turned on a succession of legal nonissues: an alleged criminal accusing a former prime minister of accepting illegitimate donations. Most of the allegations of organized crime connections were successfully fought in court. No legal consequences have fallen on the parties involved on the substance of the problems. Yet these legal nonissues had one substantial tangible effect: the lasting delegitimation in the eyes of the public of Ivan Kostov and his legacy as a reformist. The destruction of the legitimacy of the SDS, the proreform, center-right party of the 1990s, no doubt opened the gate to new populist players in Bulgarian politics and began an extended period of instability of the party system.

The details of the Michael Chorny case illustrate a specific feature of Bulgarian public discourse on organized crime. On the one hand, it seems that it is public knowledge that businessmen such as Chorny are part of organized crime and the underworld. After all, most of the media (apart from his own newspaper, *Standart*) treat Chorny either openly as a criminal or at least as a person whose wealth is of illegitimate origin. Further, official decisions, such as the order expelling Chorny from the country, are motivated by the threat he is thought to present to Bulgarian national security. People see this order as an acknowledgment of the connection between Chorny and the mafia.

On the other hand, no independent Bulgarian judicial body has ever established that Chorny is guilty of any crime, let alone organized crime. On the contrary, Bulgarian courts have pronounced such allegations libelous. This state of affairs creates a degree of public confusion: people know who the criminals are, but they do not know exactly why they are criminals and what the character of their crimes is. This situation is fertile ground for the creation of myths as to the nature and scale of crime and corruption in the country and explains the mismatch between the realities and the public perceptions of the effect of organized crime on political finance.

The point is not that Bulgarian authorities should be complacent and should not take organized crime seriously. Of course it is a problem, one that calls for a responsible and decisive response. However, any action should take the complexity of the situation into account. In terms of political finance, the impact of organized criminal groups should be countered not only by specific finance rules, money-laundering restrictions, and party-funding regulations but also by structural considerations. These include the stability of the party system, the programmatic character of the parties, and the quality of the process of representation. If these factors are not considered, public discontent and frustration could continue unhindered, and politicians will keep being associated with organized criminal networks undermining the interests of people.

In cicumstances of deep distrust among politicians and political elites in general, which specific party finance policies could have a positive effect? The Bulgarian case demonstrates that transparency rules and public funding are essential to alleviate the most immediate pressures on the political process from criminal interests. These measures, however, do not automatically restore trust: indeed, the Bulgarian case study shows that if the people believe in the broader concept of organized crime, party finance rules per se are insufficient to create confidence that political elites act in the public good.

Appendix A: TIM

Many believe that a powerful economic group has emerged as an organized criminal group and probably still has certain activities linked to the underworld. According to leaked diplomatic cables, TIM, founded in Varna in 1993, is thought to have been organized by about ten former marines who had been part of an elite military unit before it was disbanded in the early 1990s.[33] TIM filled the vacuum created by Multigroup's decline, following Iliya Pavlov's killing in 2003. The name of the group presumably derives from the first initials of its three main figures: Tihomir Ivanov Mitev (Bulgarian citizen, born October 10, 1958), Ivo Kamenov Georgiev (Bulgarian citizen, born September 22, 1969), and Marin Velikov Mitev (Bulgarian citizen, born October 5, 1957).

It is believed that twelve people control all of TIM's companies—which in 2003 were estimated to number over 150 and include over 10,000 employees—with each of the twelve holding fixed shares in the assets and running separate sectors of the group's business empire. Despite trying to portray itself as a purely legitimate business group, TIM remains very secretive about its corporate structure and ownership, and its companies and divisions are entangled in a complex set of relationships. It is allegedly involved in extortion and racketeering, intimidation, prostitution, gambling, narcotics trafficking, car theft, and trafficking in stolen automobiles.

TIM's home base of Varna has a large Russian population, and TIM is thought to have connections to Russian organized crime, including the notorious Russian crime figure Michael Chorney. Tihomir Mitev oversees TIM's industrial operations. His older brother, Marin, controls TIM's core business interests in Varna and the surrounding region, while Ivo Georgiev oversees TIM's Sofia operations and the group's financial interests. Other notable members of the group include Miroslav Petrov Nestorov (Bulgarian citizen, born March 12, 1964), who is in charge of the group's strategic planning and also is director of TIM's large service sector subsidiary, Mustang Holdings; Yordan Dimitrov Yordanov (Bulgarian citizen, born November 24, 1974), who oversees most of TIM's media interests and also sits on Mustang's board; and Nikolai Bozhidarov Nikolov (Bulgarian citizen, born August 28, 1949), Mustang's CEO and husband of Varna's chief architect and city planner.

TIM's initial activities involved collecting bad debts (a line of business that has contributed to the group's negative public image but that still remains one of its main activities) and providing security services in the Varna region. In the

---

33. See www.balkanleaks.eu/bgoc.html.

mid-1990s the group branched out to agriculture and foodstuffs. Its current interests include grain storage and poultry farming as well as the Suhindol winery (through the Severco-Gamza company), which predominantly produces red wines for both domestic consumption and export. In Varna TIM's presence is seen and felt everywhere. Its media interests include M-SAT television (a Varna-based broadcaster available nationally by cable and satellite), five other cable television stations, two cable television operators, Alpha Radio (also available nationally), *Cherno More* newspaper (the largest circulation newspaper in Varna and its surrounding region), and the advertising agency servicing these media interests. TIM also owns a chain of restaurants, cinemas, video rental shops, sports clubs, Internet gaming clubs, and bingo halls. The recently launched, large-scale Alley One project plans to build seven hotels, 500 eating and entertainment facilities, and 300 shops on a 250-acre tract on the Black Sea coast near Varna. This project became the focus of huge controversy in the city of Varna, as many citizens and organizations protested against it.

TIM controls some of the largest quarries of inert materials in Bulgaria, and through its trading company, Chimimport, it also has a significant share of the production and trade in fertilizers, petroleum products, and chemicals. TIM's takeover of the Central Cooperative Bank (CCB), the group's largest acquisition to date, was facilitated through Chimimport. After acquiring CCB, TIM continued to expand its financial sector operations by acquiring specialized financial service companies, including the insurance company Armeets. Again going through Chimimport, in 2002 TIM acquired a majority stake in Newton Financial Management BG, owner of the Bulgarian pension insurance company Sila. Newton Financial Management BG has since been renamed CCB Group Assets Management. TIM has used its substantial financial sector presence to offer one-stop shopping for combined banking, insurance, and pension services. In 2003 Chimimport bought 49 percent of Bulgaria's second-largest air carrier, Hemus Air, later taking over 100 percent ownership. In 2004 Chimimport also acquired 100 percent of a smaller airline, Viaggio; the takeover was approved by Viaggio's largest shareholder, Todor Batkov, Michael Chorny's lawyer and personal representative. With its combined interests in Hemus and Viaggio, TIM also has privatized the Bulgarian flag carrier, Bulgaria Air.

References

Beare, Margaret, ed. 2003. *Critical Reflections on Transnational Organized Crime, Money Laundering, and Corruption.* University of Toronto Press.

Coulloudon, Virginie. 1997. "The Criminalization of Russia's Political Elite." *East European Constitutional Review* 6, no. 4.

Della Porta, Donatella, and Alberto Vannucci. 1999. *Corrupt Exchanges: Actors, Resources, and Mechanisms of Political Corruption.* New York: Aldine de Gruyter.
EUMAP. 2001. *Judicial Independence in the EU Accession Process.* Budapest: Open Society Institute.
———. 2002. *Judicial Capacity.* Budapest: Open Society Institute.
Glenny, Misha. 2008. *McMafia: Crime without Frontiers.* London: Bodley Head.
Holmes, Stephen. 1997. "Crime and Corruption after Communism." *East European Constitutional Review* 6, no. 4.
Meseznikov, Grigorij, Olga Gyarfasova, and Daniel Smilov, eds. 2008. "Populist Politics and Liberal Democracy in Central and Eastern Europe." Working paper. Bratislava: IVO (IPA).
Nikolov, Yovo. 1997. "Organized Crime in Bulgaria." *East European Constitutional Review* 6, no. 4: 80–85.
———. 2000. "Who Killed Lukanov and Why" (in Bulgarian). *Capital Weekly,* April 14.
Open Society Institute. 2008. *Civil Society in Bulgaria: Citizen Actions without Engagement.* Civil Society Index. Sofia: Centre for Liberal Strategies (http://osi.bg/downloads/File/State%20of%20Society%202008.pdf).
Petrunov, Georgi. 2010a. *Money Laundering in Bulgaria: The Policy Response.* Sofia: RiskMonitor Foundation.
———. 2010b. *Sex Trafficking and Money Laundering: The Case of Bulgaria.* Sofia: RiskMonitor Foundation.
Petrunov, Georgi. 2010c. *Report of SGOC* (Standing Group on Organized Crime) *Newsletter* 9, no. 1.
Prosecutorial Office. 2005. "Organized Crime and Terrorism" (http://prb.bg/main/bg/Documents/386/).
Smedovska, Rada. 2010. *Specialized Institutions for the Combat of Organized Crime, Comparative Legal Study.* Sofia: RiskMonitor Foundation.
Smilov, Daniel. 2006. "EU Enlargement and the Constitutional Principle of Judicial Independence." In *Spreading Democracy and the Rule of Law? Implications of EU Enlargement for the Rule of Law, Democracy and Constitutionalism in Post-Communist Legal Orders,* edited by Wojciech Sadurski, Adam Czarnota, and Martin Krygier. New York: Springer Verlag.
———. 2008. "Dilemmas for a Democratic Society: Comparative Regulation of Money and Politics." DISC Working Paper 4/2008. Central European University (www.disc-ceu.org/wp-content/uploads/2008/10/discwp-2008-04.pdf).
———. 2010. "Bulgaria: Discontents and Frustrations of a Newly-Consolidated Democracy." In *Democratization and the European Union: Comparing Central and Eastern European Post-Communist Countries,* edited by Leonardo Morlino and Woljciech Sadurski. London: Routledge.
Smilov, Daniel, and Ivan Krastev. 2008. "The Rise of Populism in Eastern Europe: Policy Paper." In *Populist Politics and Liberal Democracy in Central and Eastern Europe,* edited by Grigorij Meseznikov, Olga Gyarfasova, and Daniel Smilov. Bratislava: Institute for Public Affairs.

Smilov, Daniel, and Jurij Toplak, eds. 2007. *Political Finance and Corruption in Eastern Europe: The Transition Period.* Farnham, Surrey: Ashgate.

Volkov, Vadim. 2002. *Violent Entrepreneurs: The Use of Force in the Making of Russian Capitalism.* Cornell University Press.

Woodiwiss, Michael. 2003. "Transnational Organized Crime: The Strange Career of an American Concept." In *Critical Reflections on Transnational Organized Crime, Money Laundering, and Corruption*, edited by Margaret Beare. University of Toronto Press.

DONATELLA DELLA PORTA *and* ALBERTO VANNUCCI

8
Italy: The Godfather's Party

Political finance in liberal-democratic countries is often by its nature a domain of unresolved ambiguities and embarrassment. The organization of any political activity—especially during electoral campaigns, when political financing is more intense—has an economic cost. But the rhetoric of popular participation, politics as vocation, and mobilization in the pursuit of high values conflicts logically and symbolically with this material and monetary dimension of "politics as a business." When the friction between ideological appeals to long-term collective purposes, on the one hand, and everyday political needs and practice, on the other, is too forceful and becomes manifest to the public, some scandal or "purification ritual" is practically inevitable.

The consequences of the *mani pulite* (clean hands) investigations in Italy during the early 1990s—with the collapse of the party system and the dramatic eclipse or transformation of all major parties—may be considered a paradigmatic case of this potential short circuit between two distinct spheres of political activity: the public sphere and the hidden sphere.[1] In the public sphere politicians operate overtly, their acts aimed at being recognized—and judged—by the public. The hidden sphere, however, is often the most relevant: "It's the

1. *Mani pulite* investigations started on February 17, 1992, in Milan, when Mario Chiesa, Socialist city councilor and president of a municipal old people's home, was arrested while accepting a bribe. Chiesa began to collaborate with the magistrates, setting off a chain of confessions by businessmen, bureaucrats, and politicians. In its development, the *mani pulite* investigation brought about the most serious political crisis in the history of the Italian Republic, quickly extending to the uppermost levels of the political and economic system. In a matter of months, the magistracy opened a breach on a scene of corruption and political illegality without precedent in the history of the Western democracies: more than 500 parliamentarians were implicated, dozens of former ministers, five former premiers, thousands of local administrators and public functionaries, the army, the customs service (responsible for investigating financial crimes in general), the main publicly owned companies, and even sectors of the magistracy itself.

daily practice of individuals, politicians and their clients, entering in exchanges, agreements, [and] transactions. In this activity favours are offered, which are repaid with other favours, or votes, or money, destined to the politicians, to their group, faction, party, movement."[2] Obviously, these practices are kept secret, as their going beyond restricted circles would involve loss of consent, political defeat, or legal prosecution; nevertheless, they are often tolerated by common political morality. The diffusion of irregular financing amplifies the friction between purposes officially pursued in the political arena and the concrete motives and interests that come into play.

Two vicious cycles reinforce the demand for irregular political financing. Transparent and voluntary donations and the mobilization of supporters in the maintenance of party machines are substitutes for the search for underground funding sources. Such internal contributions (from political party membership fees, voluntary work, and other donations) are however discouraged precisely by the delegitimization of political actors, which derives from their current practice of irregular financing as well as their possible involvement in scandals.[3] The recourse to irregular contributions may then feed upon itself, making incentives to search for them stronger—ceteris paribus—while the potential of other traditional sources evaporates. The second vicious cycle is associated with the prisoner's-dilemma logic of irregular financing, which may induce inflationary dynamics in political competition. As soon as a political party or candidate gets periodic access to irregular sources and contributions, he or she obtains a surplus of resources and therefore a competitive advantage against his or her rivals. Political competitors, therefore, have an incentive to collect hidden financing as well. This dynamic emerges either when opponents lack evidence to denounce the transgressor or when opponents have something to fear in case of mutual defection from an implicit conspiracy of silence, which often includes the implicit agreement among cartel parties.

We can see these vicious cycles developing in the Italian case. Illegal financing to parties rooted in Italy since the end of World War II, when the country was contested territory between the United States and the Soviet Union, and conspicuous flows of money came from abroad to Christian Democrats and other pro-Western parties, on the one side, and to the Communist and Socialist Parties, on the other. When in the 1960s and 1970s external financing was reduced, those parties—obliged to maintain oversized apparatuses—started systematically accessing public resources, allocated through the operation of public

---

2. Pizzorno (1993, pp. 286–87).

3. External factors, such as the diminishing impact of ideological appeals and political identities, produced the same effect, especially after the fall of the Berlin wall.

bodies and enterprises, as well as institutionalizing bribery in public contracting. Precise rules set the percentages of bribe payments and their redistribution among the parties.[4] Both vicious cycles generated the apparent paradox of leaving political parties and leaders able to gather and maintain electoral consensus but with a very low level of trust and general legitimacy.

When systemic corruption emerged, thanks to *mani pulite* inquiries, irregular party financing was in fact one of the most frequent charges against politicians and their parties. Bettino Craxi, former prime minister and leader of the Socialist Party, in a famous speech in the Chamber of Deputies on July 3, 1992, expressed the generalized "two-faced moral" that lies behind irregular financing:

> Under the cover of irregular funding to the parties, cases of corruption and extortion have flourished and become intertwined. . . . What has to be said, and in any case everyone knows, is that the greater part of political funding is irregular or illegal. The parties and those who rely on a party machine (large, medium, or small); on newspapers, propaganda, promotional and associational activities . . . have had, or have, recourse to irregular or illegal additional resources. If the greater part of this is to be considered criminal behavior, pure and simple, then the greater part of the political system is a criminal system. I do not believe there is anybody in this hall who has had responsibility for a large organization who can stand up and deny what I have just said. Sooner or later the facts would make a liar of him.[5]

Irregular political financing is a very broad category, however, which may include several types of corruption-related behavior and is clearly dependent upon the characteristics of the public regulation of the matter.[6] We can distinguish between different types of illegal party financing based on the kind of resources demanded by the political actors (votes and political support or money and economic support) and their partners in the corresponding informal exchange (electors or party supporters, entrepreneurs or interest groups, bureaucrats, and criminal organizations; table 8-1). As the content of the exchange influences the severity of possible formal punishment in case of the disclosure of irregular or illegal financing, the sequence of would-be counterparts of political actors, offering them political or economic resources (and asking for other "commodities" in exchange) reflects to a certain extent the potential for scandal.

---

4. Della Porta and Vannucci (1999, 2005a, 2005b, 2007, 2012).
5. TNM (1993, pp. 87–88).
6. Pinto-Duschinsky (2002).

Table 8-1. *A Typology of Irregular/Illegal Contributions to Political Actors*

		Resources demanded by or offered to political actors in informal or illegal exchanges	
Potential for scandal	Partners in informal or illegal exchanges	Votes or political support	Money or other economic support
small	Electors/militants	Vote buying/clientelism	Illegal/irregular donations and contributions
	Entrepreneurs/firms/ interest groups	Organized support/ lobbying	Illegal/irregular political financing, bribes
	Public servants/ bureaucrats	Patronage	Bribes sharing/purchase and sale of public office
large	Mafiosi/organized crime	Organized crime protection in market for votes/electoral support of organized crime	Criminal political financing, bribes

Low-profile political transactions involving electors and party activists are routine. These transactions are justified as responsive to particularistic demands and in keeping with the democratic process. Similarly, the logic of exchange in the lobbying relationship between politicians and entrepreneurs may be condoned by the public, since it is indirectly associated with the profit-maximization dynamic of economic entrepreneurship, especially when, in the competitive interplay of several interests, the pressure of the latter is not directly reducible to plainly illegal acts. Less acceptable is the hidden relationship between bureaucrats or public servants and their political appointers or sponsors, due to the role's official commitment to the public interest. This unacceptability is especially true when bribes or purchase of public office is involved.

At the darkest level of irregular/illegal financing, the partner of political actors is organized crime. Here, the political risks and legal sanctions for the political actors are maximized, as any connection is actually unjustifiable to the public and severely punished by the law. Circulation of information is extremely dangerous, while the blackmailing power of counterparts is maximized.[7] Nevertheless, where criminal organizations are using force in a territory, as is the case in at least four southern regions of Italy (the Cosa Nostra in Sicily, the

---

7. Casas-Zamora (2010).

Ndrangheta in Calabria, the Camorra in Campania, and the Sacra Corona Unita in Apulia), political actors have in fact entered into mutually profitable relationships with godfathers, relationships that sometimes are intense, multifaceted, and stable over a long period of time.

In the Italian case, however, the criminal influence over the political sphere adapts to changes in the official regulation of political financing. Within the norms of public financing of political parties, introduced in Italy in 1974 and repeatedly modified, we may observe a constant rise in the generosity of electoral reimbursements, in the amount of funds provided to party central offices, in a lack of public legitimization (expressed in a popular referendum in 1993), and in the ineffectiveness of controls on the sources of private financing as well as on parties' and candidates' electoral expenses.[8] As strict regulations made *legal* private contributions difficult, parties had no incentive to reveal their real revenues and expenditures, at either the center or the periphery, leading to a massive underreporting of private contributions, encouraged by missing or ineffective formal controls. Further, even when in existence, sanctions were rarely applied.[9] The 1993 law introduced a system of automatic *reimbursements, calculated as a fixed quota of the votes* obtained in elections, instead of general *subventions* (canceled by the referendum). It also regulated access to the media, limited the use of opinion polls in electoral periods, fixed a maximum amount of political funding and spending, and backed the new rules with formally tough sanctions (which nevertheless remained largely unapplied). Further regulation did not alter this framework but set a higher limit on the tax deductibility of private contributions and increased per-vote reimbursement quotas, distributing these over the entire legislature.[10]

As a consequence of the substantial underreporting of private financing, irregularities in official party budgets were widespread and controls and enforcement were ineffective. In addition, criminal contributions became more easily disguised within the financial operations of the candidates' political machines. Irregular financial support to politicians and party structures was eventually easily concealed, since verifications were traditionally almost nonexistent. Circumvention of political finance norms is a common practice in Italy, especially at the local level, where organized crime is more influential, politicians' demand for money more intense (because public contributions are limited to central structures), and inspections and sanctions are absent. During the 1990s, in fact, when new laws instituting direct election of local administrators induced a

---

8. Della Porta and Vannucci (2000).
9. Pujas and Rhodes (1998).
10. Laws 157/1999 and 61/2006.

strong personalization of political competition, in some contexts criminal organizations became a decisive ally for contending candidates.

Money, as we have seen, is often not the first and foremost resource at stake in well-oiled electoral transactions between criminal and political actors. Often politicians pay mafiosi to "buy," or gather to their lists, votes controlled by criminal groups embedded in local society. In a similar context, the reimbursement-per-vote mechanism created by the Italian statute on electoral financing in 1993 may have amplified such a demand for votes in the market regulated by Mafia families, since what was paid by politicians to gather support organized by criminal groups could be considered an economic investment later refunded by the state.

There is also a weak point in Italy's laws pertaining to criminal organizations. Approved in September 1982, after a series of murders of high-ranking officials, article 416/bis of the Penal Code specifies Mafia-type criminal organizations, transforming a sociological (that is, a metajuridical) concept into a judicial category and restricting the previous flexibility and arbitrariness that had characterized law enforcement.[11]

> [A Mafia-type organization] consists of three or more persons ... [making] use of the power of intimidation afforded by the associative bond and the state of subjugation and conspiracy of silence (*omertà*), which derives from it, to commit crimes, to acquire directly or indirectly the management or control of economic activities, concessions, authorizations or public contracts and services, either to gain unjust profits or advantages for themselves and others, or to prevent or obstruct the exercise of the vote, or to procure votes for themselves or for others at a time of electoral consultation.[12]

However, the last clause about the influence on the electoral process, which was added in 1992, appears rather vague in the specification of the nature of the exchange and has remained virtually unapplied. The vote procurement activity of Mafia-like groups may assume diverse and subtle forms due to the (often) intangible nature of the resources (judicial or administrative protection, guarantees, promises or expectation of electoral mobilization) involved in the deal. It is therefore very difficult, often impossible, for prosecutors to demonstrate vote procurement (or vote obstruction) by criminal organizations. A more detailed specification of the contexts, resources, and actors that can be involved in such transactions would probably be useful.

11. Paoli (2004, p. 266).
12. Italian Penal Code, article 416/bis.

Moreover, even when disclosure, denunciation, and application of legal sanctions against politicians for their collusion with criminal organizations happen, only mild repercussions follow: the electoral effects are few and the reaction of the political class is one of indifference or de facto absolution. A similar outcome is consistent with our previous analysis: the network of bipartisan connections between organized crime and politics nourishes a general blackmailing power within the political elite, while connivance consolidates in the economic and political spheres. In addition, the acceptance of Italian criminal groups as organizers of consent and as regulators in vote-exchange activities renders the electoral market relatively impervious to scandals, while organized crime's sponsorship and mobilization effort can hardly be distinguished (except for their superior efficacy) from the ordinary clientelistic networking of local *capobastone*.[13] As a consequence, we observe deterioration in public morality accompanied by a higher threshold of public tolerance for scandals involving politics and organized crime.[14]

In the complex exchanges between organized crime and corrupt politicians, money is often at stake. In Italy, in spite of the evidence of an extensive and long-lasting network of hidden exchanges between political actors and several criminal organizations in southern Italy, one of the most striking features of these relationships is the remarkable absence or exceptionality of direct financial contributions to party political activity and campaigns by organized crime. Also, in the Italian case, the flows of money—especially from bribes and extra profits on public contracts–were shared among corrupt politicians and mafiosi as well as pseudocriminal firms, politicians, and administrators. In addition, other valuable political and economic resources were often at stake, ranging from a general and wide-ranging political or criminal protection to more context-specific favors.

In the following paragraphs we present a model for the analysis of these kinds of dangerous liaisons, trying to explain in a more general framework the peculiarities of the Italian case and providing empirical cases to illustrate it. The information derives from a data set built of judicial acts related to about sixty procedures for Mafia crimes; interviews; parliamentary acts (the Parliamentary

---

13. A *capobastone* is the local boss of a Mafia family within Calabria's criminal organization, Ndrangheta.

14. An example may suffice: in 2004 Giulio Andreotti, former prime minister, was judged by the Supreme Court responsible for the crime of association with the Mafia until 1980, even if not sanctioned due to expiration of the statute of limitation. In spite of this, in 2006 he was named by the center-right coalition as president of the Senate (the second most important institutional position in the state); even if not elected, he nevertheless obtained 156 senatorial votes, defeated by only 9 votes by Franco Marini, the center-left candidate.

Anti Mafia Commission's debates and hearings); decrees of dissolution of municipal councils due to mafiosi penetration; and newspaper stories.

Organized Crime and Political Finance in Italy: A Typology

Exchanges between political actors (individuals, factions, and parties) and criminal organizations are a natural consequence of their control of valuable exchangeable resources. There is the search for consent and power by political actors and the protection of businesses by organized crime. In Italy, with some exceptions, mafiosi and politicians have maintained specific roles, with political actors controlling the electorate and the Mafia providing protection. In some areas of southern Italy, the two factions have developed some cooperative interactions crucial to their success in either political activity or criminal activity.[15] As judge Giovanni Falcone observes:

> The Mafia doesn't enjoy getting involved in politics. Political matters aren't of much interest unless it feels that its power or means of income have been directly threatened. It's enough to elect directors or politician "friends" and sometimes even members of the [Mafia] organization. And this would be to direct the flow of public spending so that laws that favor their chances of making money pass and others that could have adverse effects on their business get vetoed.[16]

Tommaso Buscetta confirms: "It is not by way of politics that the Mafia exists. The Mafia exploits politics."[17] The intersection where politicians and criminals meet is a subterranean market. The goods exchanged in this market are, on the one hand, public decisions (ranging from single administrative acts to general laws and regulations, favorable sentences and judicial acts, omission of controls, information, and political protection) and, on the other hand, protection from violence and intimidation, electoral support and votes, bribes, and financial contributions.

We propose a very general framework for the analysis of four models of interaction between criminal and political organizations, stressing their relation with prevalent practices of irregular political financing (table 8-2).[18] It is

---

15. Della Porta and Vannucci (1999, 2012).
16. Falcone (1991, p. 165).
17. Buscetta (1992, p. 23).
18. See Morlino (1991) for a typology on the relationship between interest groups and political parties, partly adapted in modeling the exchange of political actors and organized crime. A similar typology, taking into consideration the degree of institutionalization of organized crime and the dynamics of electoral competition, has been proposed by Sberna (2011, pp. 61–62).

Table 8-2. *Four Models of Exchange Interaction between Political Actors and Organized Crime*

	Organized crime	
Political actors	Criminal protection firm (centralized monopolistic organizations)	Gang/group operating in illegal markets (competitive criminal networks)
Political guarantors (structured parties/strong candidates)	**Symbiosis** Criminal organization as stable, long-lasting consent organizers, support collectors, guarantors in the market for votes; money sharing in a wider bribes-collection activity regulated by mafiosi (public contracting procedures; public licensing). Examples are the relationships between the Cosa Nostra, the Christian Democrats, and some of its leading figures (Ciancimino, Lima, Gioia, Andreotti's faction) in Sicily until 1992 after 1987.	**Gatekeeping** Political parties/actors as gatekeepers for various criminal actors seeking immunity and protection; money and other exchange resources are used in medium- and short-term relationships to influence political/administrative decisionmaking. Examples are relationships between political leaders and criminal organizations during destabilizing conflicts in a fragmented and competitive criminal environment (as in Campania and Apulia).
Political actors not capable or willing to provide durable protection (destructured parties/weak political candidates)	**Replacement/colonization** Criminal organization as founder/organizer of parties; mafiosi entering directly into political competition through their influence on party selection of candidates; criminal organizations as guarantors in the market for votes or enforcers of political alliances; criminal colonization of local governments and party structures. Examples are autonomist parties after World War II and after 1992 in Sicily, political careers of mafiosi, and criminal organizations' control of local administrations in southern Italy.	**Neutrality/occasional exchanges** Mafiosi as occasional partners in short-term corrupt exchanges of different resources (contingent protection, favors) with political actors. Examples are interactions with public administrators in northern and central Italy, generally mediated by accomplished entrepreneurs, following the expansion of organized crime's illegal activity and economic interests outside its area of territorial control.

important to distinguish between criminal organizations that are relatively centralized, hierarchical, and monopolistic in structure and the more dispersed and competitive kind.[19] There are also different types of political actor: a party or faction rooted in the territory, with its locally prominent and influential candidates, is to be distinguished from weak and unstructured political subjects.

For different reasons, both the Mafia and the political actors are subject to severe uncertainty when it comes to their capability to remain in business. Political uncertainty is a logical consequence of competitive democratic politics, where the right to occupy certain elective public roles, by its nature precarious, derives from the variable outcomes of electoral and political processes.[20] The life expectancy of criminals, as well as of the organizational structures within which they operate, is even more insecure and unpredictable, due to the illegal and often violent nature of their interactions: The "mafiosi time horizon is in turn influenced by the struggle against the state and by the competition among mafiosi: both factors, when they become more intense, provoke the disappearance of protectors, generating instability."[21] A demand for protection in this context clearly emerges, especially when there is a broader guarantee of a favorable resolution of disputes in which their expectations are challenged.

Our hypothesis is that the degree of institutionalization and organizational strength is associated with the time horizon under which the political and criminal actors operate. These are also associated with the influence of the discount rate they apply to their payoffs to come. Their actions and prospects affect their bargaining power and the nature and content of their resulting relationships. As their time horizon expands, so does their credibility as guarantors: they become more trustworthy potential providers of a reliable protection. On the other hand, "if the future looks uncertain, protectors will maximize present over future income. They will more likely either sell bogus protection or charge extortionary prices, or both. . . . Finally, if customers know that the mafioso's 'life expectancy' is short, they will be more reluctant to buy protection."[22] The same holds true for customers—criminals, for instance—seeking political protection but discouraged by the perception that their would-be political guarantors do not appear to be destined for a long and brilliant career. Generally

---

19. This is a radical simplification: structural features of organized crime could be better analyzed as a continuous variable ranging from a more hierarchical to a polycentric network (Williams, 2001).

20. Moe (1990, p. 227).

21. Gambetta (1992, pp. 267–68).

22. Gambetta (1993, p. 33). Also see Reuter (1983). For an analysis of Italian political parties as supplier of private protection in the market for corrupt exchanges, see Vannucci (1997); della Porta and Vannucci (1999, 2007, 2012).

speaking, criminal organizations' influence over political decisionmaking may be obtained voluntarily by political actors using several means: political resources, such as organizing votes and consent or regulating the market for votes; economic resources, such as providing money and financial support to political actors or simply bribing them; and violent resources, such as intimidation or elimination of political rivals.[23] We concentrate here on political and economic resources. If organizational features, reputation, and historical legacies of collective actors create expectations of profitable long-term relationships, then predatory strategies (choices maximizing short-term profits) as well as defection are discouraged, monitoring and enforcing costs are lowered, and trustworthiness assets come into play. This facilitates the evaluation of those qualitative attributes, otherwise difficult to assess, of intangible resources at stake in the exchange: political authority, which can be bought with financial support or is used to provide consent; pressure over electoral campaigns; policymaking; and particular acts or omissions.

When long-lasting relationships are expected on both sides, political resources (which require time to be organized and mobilized) can be profitably used in transactions between politicians and criminal organizations, substituting for (or complementing) direct financial support. What emerges is a symbiotic relationship of reciprocal protection between political and criminal actors.[24] No specific exchange commodity is intended to reciprocate the deal, but a wider and durable protection contract can be flexibly applied to unforeseeable circumstances to guarantee both sides' interests. Take, for instance, this statement of the mafioso collaborator Tommaso Buscetta:

> Every family head in the Mafia selects a man whose characteristics already make him look approachable. Forget the idea that some pact is reached first. On the contrary, one goes to that candidate and says, "Onorevole, I can do this and that for you now, and we hope that when you are elected you will remember us." That candidate wins, and he has to pay something back. You tell him, "We need this, will you do it or not?" The politician understands immediately and acts always.[25]

---

23. Obviously, violence and threats could also be used by mafiosi to directly intimidate public decisionmakers. In this case, however, we enter into the realm of extortion, which we do not take into consideration here, concentrating our analysis on voluntary exchanges between politicians and organized crime that influence the political process.

24. Symbiosis is the outcome of a cooperative exchange relationship between strong criminal and political actors, which we analyze here. Obviously, this is not the unique possible ending of the story: open contrast and conflict is the opposite result, when interactions are punctuated by homicides and intimidations on the one side and strict regulation and prosecution on the other.

25. CPATB, 374.

The mobilization of political resources by criminal organizations requires a previous long-term investment on the part of criminals in the acquisition of social connections, information, intelligence, and territorial control. Analogous resources are necessary for criminal organizations, also, in order to operate convincingly as guarantors in the cumbersome market for votes, where the politicians, as vote seekers, are confronted with issues of scale (to negotiate each vote individually would enormously increase transaction costs), trust (it is difficult to verify the fulfilment of an agreement), enforcement, and payment.[26]

Moreover, the authority of criminal organizations over the local expression of affiliate votes, families, and supporters—which in certain contexts may be a significant portion of the total electorate—is in itself a valuable resource that would otherwise be wasted. In a tape-recorded conversation, a boss of the Calabrese Ndrangheta family explicitly expresses his intention to avoid this regrettable outcome in regional elections: "The other ten *locali* where we can obtain votes," the mafioso boss said, "—lets see who the hell we can put in place to keep watch in the region, to have someone who could guarantee us something, at the very least some public work."[27] As a consequence, a general demand emerges for politicians willing to be the target of electoral support gathered by local families (*ndrine*) in the same geographical area (*locali*), naturally balanced by the expectation to get "something" in exchange in the future.

We may expect that electoral support, ceteris paribus, will substitute financial support as a means of exchange, reflecting quite pragmatic considerations. As expressed by the Parliamentary Anti Mafia Commission: "It is natural for the Cosa Nostra to influence votes. Its influence results not from an ideological choice but instead from a search for advantage, and from exploiting fully its roots in the society and territory."[28] Using votes as a commodity in implicit or explicit contractual agreements with politicians, the mobilization of votes can have for a criminal organization the same effects as financial contributions—and at a lower economic cost: circulation of the Mafia's vote targets may be enough.[29] Moreover, it guarantees a long-term influence over the political counterpart, as criminal groups have at their disposal intimidation resources to self-enforce the deal, minimizing risks of cheating. The "boss of all bosses," Salvatore

26. Gambetta (1993, p. 184).
27. TRCOS, I, 5.
28. CPMF, 16.
29. The simple reputation that a politician enjoys the protection of organized crime may be enough to guarantee him a competitive advantage in electoral terms. As reported by the Parliamentary Anti Mafia Committee: "Support from the Cosa Nostra can also involve supplying a constant 'supervision' of the candidate, who, as he makes his rounds in his electoral constituency together with members of the [Mafia] family, is not only protected in terms of personal safety, but shows voters that he is backed by 'men who count'" (CPMF, p. 16).

Riina, according to the mafioso Baldassare Di Maggio, stressed this point: "We, obviously, give our votes to the politicians we prefer and by prior agreement with them, but they must do what we say, 'otherwise we ruin them.'"[30] Finally, it may be preferred also by political actors, since it is less dangerous: while money flows may leave an indelible trace, a politician supported by a criminal organization may always affirm—as always happens in Italy—that they were not aware of that criminal sponsorship.[31]

Being reliable partners in political exchanges or guarantors in the market for votes requires the level of resources that are at the disposal of socially rooted and long-established criminal organizations. Such organizations have, with relatively centralized internal apparatuses, dominance over territorial spheres of licit and illicit activities. Their provision of private security is akin to the power syndicate described by A. Block.[32] Moreover, the ability of criminal organizations to guarantee the functioning of some troublesome markets may generate flows of money in unexpected directions. In the market for votes, for instance, kingpins usually collect from politicians the price for their guarantee of the fulfilment of pacts with electors. In corruption, the rent deriving from public contracts is shared among several actors, while criminal actors regulate the whole business.

When symbiotic and cooperative relationships prevail, political and criminal actors operate as reciprocal protectors in their respective spheres of interest and activity. Therefore, they may strengthen each other through increasing returns, reducing uncertainty about their future prospects in political and illegal markets.[33] The resulting equilibrium may be quite robust, as the decades of fairly peaceful and mutually fruitful exchanges between Cosa Nostra and Christian

---

30. TPMP, 130. "Unlike interactions between private donors and politicians, where quid pro quos are seldom articulated explicitly and elected politicians always retain the possibility not fulfilling the donor's expectations, the normal codes of etiquette—and uncertainty in the case of drug traffickers—do not apply" (Casas-Zamora, 2010). As the collaborator Nino Calderone explains: "When I was in Sicily there were so many politicians involved with the mafia. Members of parliament, city councilmen, regional councelors who were helped by the mafia, who asked what would be binding, heavy favors of the mafiosi (*uomini d'onore*). Normally, they did these favors, but they could also say no without anything happening. But when the mafia were to ask a favor of the politicians they had no choice: they had to do what was asked. They could not say no, or make excuses" (Arlacchi, 1992, p. 210).

31. Electoral exchange may be preferred by criminal organizations and political actors simply due to its relative efficiency. Politicians, in fact, do not have to "produce" electoral consent using as an input irregular funds flowing into their political structures—a costly, risky, and uncertain process. In this case, in fact, the desired output—electoral success—is guaranteed directly by their criminal partners. Organized crime, on the other hand, takes profit from otherwise undervalued political resources under its control, and in the meantime it shows its rootedness on the territory, increasing its prestige and bargaining power.

32. Block (1983).
33. Pierson (2004).

Democratic factions attest. Actors seem to be aware of this potential virtuous cycle, as confirmed by a Camorra repentant, the white collar *consigliori* of the clan Bidognetti, who describes the reasons underlying his political campaign supporting a candidate:

> The fact that it had to do with one of our candidates meant that it had to do with a candidate of the Bidognetti clan: the message had come through an embassy or rather through illegal channels (lawyers or family members) that Bidognetti was being held at that time and yet continued to manage the clan's affairs. I organized a meeting near my warehouse. ... Given the candidate, I reassured those present that, in the future, we would be rewarded for our support in that "if he grew, we grew." For example, among other things, I would've had other contracts with neighboring communities in the province and I would have thus been able to hire the children of my employees who would have needed work. As I've stated elsewhere, after a brief talk, Cosentino left me election materials.[34]

The scenario changes when there is a higher level of doubt about whether political actors will remain in charge and the extent to which they have authority over the decisionmaking process, due to the weak institutionalization of parties or the weakness of their candidates. The reason may be an exogenous shock, such as in Italy, where the party system collapsed in the 1990s due to corruption inquiries. Different strategies are available for relatively strong and stable criminal actors lacking trustworthy political protectors. First, they may try to replace parties by promoting new political organizations or by taking over and replacing unstructured parties. Second, mafiosi can continue to operate as guarantors in unsteady markets where political actors are purchasers of votes or providers of corrupt services or they demand some kind of enforcement to increase the stability of their precarious political exchanges. Finally, criminal actors can simply acquire specific services when they could be used to bribe politicians or party administrators.

The symbiotic and replacement models are closer to the criminal traditions of two Italian criminal organizations, the Mafia and the Ndrangheta, and in certain phases also to those of the Camorra and the Sacra Corona Unita. Moreover, when criminal groups operate as protection agencies, they may also enforce exchanges in the market for votes: as a *camorrista* told the judges "I do not solicit politicians. They solicit me during election time. They need me, I don't need them."[35] The selling of votes to politicians, which is forbidden by Italian law, has

---

34. TRNOC, 23.
35. APN, 8.

assumed especially noteworthy proportions in southern regions of Italy, where they are regulated by criminal organizations.

When criminal structures are more unstable, competitive, and decentralized, the mafiosi are less credible in their ability to mobilize electoral support, which requires enduring commitments and roots at the local level. Their political partners cannot fully rely on them as effective guarantors in the market for votes, as their more ephemeral existence fosters incentives toward both cheating and predatory strategies, nourishing more instability. Moreover, they can less effectively safeguard their partners against uncertainty in the electoral and political processes. Nevertheless, like enterprise syndicates, criminal organizations can reinvest a quote of their illicit profits in bribing and political financing in order to obtain specific privileges, administrative and judiciary acts, and favors as well as more general political protection against their "professional risks." The results delivered in these cases depend on the characteristics of the political counterparts.

As long as their political counterparts are expected to be long-lasting and reliable partners, criminal actors have a stronger incentive to buy from them all-purpose and stable political protection, for instance to reduce the uncertainty and the severity of legal enforcement, to expand the longevity of their criminal careers, to obtain competitive advantages against competitors, and to influence the allocation of benefits in public decisionmaking. Money flows here can be quite frequent and intense. Financing is not necessarily bound to specific favors, as in corrupt deals, since political actors reciprocate with a sort of insurance against potential troubles and inconveniences in their criminal activity. Politicians serve as a sort of gatekeeper of criminal organizations, and through this relationship the latter gain access over wide-ranging political decisions, reciprocated mainly with economic resources and occasionally by other rewards.

Finally, when both political and criminal actors suffer a lack of solidity and organizational strength, they can hardly supply each other more durable safeguards against uncertainty. They may coexist with limited interactions; even so, they can enter into occasional mutually advantageous exchanges. In this case, as the time horizon shrinks, transactions will likely involve more limited, contingent, and well-defined resources. Money will normally be preferred to a doubtful recruitment of voters in the political exchange, whose reciprocation would require trust over the counterpart's lasting authority. This is the ideal setting for a corrupt exchange. Bribes are more frequent, as quid pro quo for precise political favors, not as a general financial support for unspecified future rewards. Actually, corruption is a sort of natural substratum in every arena where criminal and political actors interact. To pay politicians, officials, and magistrates, or to corrupt police agents so that they turn a blind eye to illegal trafficking, is often a necessary condition for criminals to reduce the risks of those activities and to crush competition: "Organized crime almost always involves corruption."[36] If bribery is observable in all four models presented in table 8-2, only in this context does it tend to become the prevailing, if not the exclusive, mode of interaction between them.

In the following paragraphs we examine more closely these four models, providing empirical evidence from the Italian case. A methodological caveat is in order. Real-world situations are not so easily adaptable to these conceptual maps. In the ever-changing underworld where political actors and criminal organizations are entangled, as they manage their subtle and invisible arrangements, there is a wide constellation of contingencies and dimensions that may affect the resulting outcomes. Long-lasting, crystallized equilibrium between politics and organized crime may be suddenly disrupted by endogenous and imperceptible rifts. Violent conflicts and seemingly irreducible contrasts may likewise quickly settle down without any apparent reason, turning into an orderly environment where corrupt politicians and criminal actors peacefully do business together. As Italian history illustrates, examples of similar dynamics abound.

The Symbiotic Relationship between Organized Crime and Political Actors

When both criminal and political actors' expectations converge toward stable, long-term, reciprocal protection, the symbiotic dimension prevails. Besides their direct support during elections, the mafiosi can offer protection in other areas, reducing the instability in political exchanges, which sustains nomination within public bodies and the formation of coalitions in local governments but also corrupts clientelistic deals. In short, their services avert the uncertainty that would otherwise worry unprotected political subjects.

---

36. Maltz (1985, p. 24). Since the costs that public agents can impose on illegal operators are particularly high "corruption has a centrality for illegal markets that it does not have for legal markets generally" (Reuter, 1983, p. 123). The profits coming from illicit activities can be reinvested in corruption in order to be exempted from the application of the law or to acquire more rigorous enforcement against competing criminal organizations (Benson, 1988, p. 75). Corruption can then contribute to the creation of a dominant position in the illegal markets. Organized crime demands long-term corrupt relationships with the public agents who have the power to sanction them; these efforts "can be undertaken only by a fairly large firm that has reason to expect that it can enjoy most of the market and get a satisfactory return on the investment" (Schelling, 1967, p. 66). In fact, "this expectation of mutually profitable contracts between repetitive violators and enforcers . . . explains the development of organized crime: an organization is engaged more continually in violations than its individual members are and can, therefore, make arrangements with judges or police that would not be feasible for these members" (Becker and Stigler, 1974, p. 4).

In the 1950s there was a turning point in the relationship between the Mafia and politics in Sicily when the rural Mafia turned into the urban Mafia, and exchanges with politicians changed. Particularly from 1958 to 1963, the years of the so-called sack of Palermo (uncontrolled urban expansion), with Salvo Lima as mayor and Vito Ciancimino as chief of public works, according to the judges "a pact was stipulated between the Mafia, the municipal administration, and construction companies that became a model for crime in many areas of the South."[37] Ciancimino, later mayor himself, "did not stop acting in a general way to promote the interests of private speculators, but in a more specific way was successful in favouring Mafia figures close to him."[38]

Criminal influence over political participation is also at stake in the exchange. Criminal groups can organize the votes and control the support of their affiliates, relatives, and friends. According to the Mafia repentant Tommaso Buscetta, the terms of this political exchange are quite simple: "Each candidate sold his electoral availability in exchange for money. That's it."[39] In this electoral market, according to Buscetta, an ex-post approximate calculation on the "political value" of the criminal organization's support is difficult but possible:

> The politician usually knows which votes he'll have; he's already got a percentage. He already has his outlook, but when this percentage increases he knows full well. . . . If his share in that village is of one hundred votes and suddenly, when he has peacefully reached an agreement with me—no negotiations, there are no negotiations, at least not in the Mafia—he'll see three hundred votes; he'll know that two hundred came from me, from my involvement. So, he knows better than anyone else that he must respect me because those votes will always belong to him.[40]

The competitive advantage guaranteed by a criminal organization's support, especially in contestable political markets, is a strong incentive for politicians to demand of the mafiosi a safeguard against the uncertainty of electoral results or an input to bolster their likelihood of success. As Buscetta states, "The politician looked for the mafiosi because he knew that he could get much more than the one who had candidated on his own."[41] The long-term prospects wrapping

---

37. APN, p. 15. Sicilian political life was consequently conditioned by the "men of honour." This was the case, for example, in the political ascent of Salvo Lima, "decided by Cosa Nostra, with public meetings of politicians and 'men of honour' in Monreale. . . . Already mayor of Palermo, Salvo Lima was personally accompanied to these meetings by the most noted and authoritative members of the Mafia" (TPMP, p. 829).
38. TRP, 86.
39. CPATB, 353–54.
40. CPATB, 375.
41. CPATB, 374.

electoral exchanges in this symbiotic context are plainly stated by the repentant mafioso Leonardo Messina. In his description, the politicians seeking the Cosa Nostra's support—and reciprocally, the mafiosi who trust them—are expecting to set up a perennial investment in order to build lasting political capital, a durable asset, which they can use later without a direct mafiosi involvement:

> Cosa Nostra guides a candidate for many years, until he's able to take off. The first years it gets to know the candidate, then it guides him and introduces him. After this, the candidate no longer needs the district because he's created his own circle, his own friendships, etc. In any case, many politicians have contact with the upper echelon of Cosa Nostra. During elections, orders come down to vote for this or that guy, but we don't know what agreements they've made and what they gave. Sometimes, at the regional, local, or national level, we otherwise vote as a family. If orders to support a guy arrived from the top [meaning it's an order from the regional level of Cosa Nostra], that's fine, but if you had to vote for two or three people, one was the guy from the top, the others we looked for ourselves.[42]

Camorra bosses also seem to prefer similar long-lasting protection contracts with politicians, to consolidate positive expectations and trust. The repentant *camorrista* Pasquale Galasso states: "In most cases, these politicians are voted where there is, for years, a durable relationship."[43]

The blocks of voters that criminal organizations are able to mobilize in some southern regions are considered impressive in both size and discipline. For example, according to the former Mafia affiliate Antonino Calderone:

> The family of Santa Maria del Gesù is the most numerous and has about 200 members.... We are talking about a terrifying, massive force, if you keep in mind that every man of honour [Mafia member], between friends and relatives, can count on at least forty to fifty people who will blindly follow his directives.... If we think that in Palermo, in my time, there were at least eighteen administrative districts, and that each of these areas included not less than two or three [Mafia] families, we can readily understand the significance of Mafia support in electoral competition.[44]

The arithmetic of Cosa Nostra's electoral membership base is straightforward.

---

42. CPALM, 550–51.
43. CPAPG, 2279.
44. DAP, 39.

[The mafiosi] can really play around with the votes. Just consider that there are fourteen or fifteen *mandamenti* [districts], each of which consists of two or three families; each of which consists of forty or fifty men, each of whom has a wife, children, son-in-law, father-in-law, etc. It's easy to understand how many votes they can carry. When this large block of votes gets to where it needs to go, it represents an enormous influence.[45]

In Apulia, according to the repentant Salvatore Annacondia, the Sacra Corona Unita can similarly organize a wide electoral support:

Those people are always connected to us in one way or another. Of 50,000 inhabitants, I could control 30–40 percent.... Because in that area I had a thousand people that swore to give me their votes. These people knew that we'd find them at the polling station ... because we knew the exact voting booth, the courtroom where they went to vote. We had people stationed in each place. Then when one signs the cross or his name, he gives us a clear sign.[46]

Similarly, in Campania the criminal organization Camorra used its influence over blocks of votes to address internal relationships among politicians and to reach the desired equilibrium, causing some trouble when irreconcilable demands were to be satisfied:

During election time, the special relationships between a politician's electoral network and the criminal syndicate were translated into electoral support.... The notably consistent blocks of votes that the Mafia was able to manage were divided at the table among the most trusted representatives of the organization. In the final elections a conflict emerged, ... because Alfieri had to divide his votes throughout all of Campania between the Democratic and the Socialist parties.[47]

The electoral strategy of the Camorra clan of Casalesi has been calibrated on the social characteristics of potential voters, reproducing traditional schemes of southern Italy's clientelistic political machines. According to a Camorra repentant:

On the management of the electorate by the Casalesi clan, specifically there was a means of influencing the votes of the poor electorate, which was totally different from that used to target the more affluent voters. In

---

45. CPAAC, 319–20.
46. CPASA, 2508–09.
47. APN, 9.

reference to the former, in fact, the Casalesi clan ... would gather and store large quantities of food staples (pasta, tinned tomatoes, sugar, milk, or bulk products, but at low cost).... Walter Schiavone would go, then, from house to house to point out the name of the candidate to vote for and on that occasion stated, "If you don't take offense, drop by my house as there are groceries for you." The poor voters would go, then, to Walter Schiavone's house to take the gift boxes guaranteeing their votes.... Certainly for the wealthier voters (such as the businessmen, professionals, etc.) this system wasn't used, but there was a general effort from all clan members to channel votes to the candidate chosen by the clan.[48]

Criminal organizations rooted in the social environment, moreover, do not need an overt—and costly—material engagement in electoral campaigns. They can use informal communication, oblique signals, and an understanding of social norms to convey their intention to support certain candidates. For instance, as the repentant mafioso Tommaso Buscetta explains, traditionally the public exposure of contiguity between local mafia bosses and political candidates is enough:

I remember that when help was offered to the candidate, or the candidate required the help of a specific district, we would go to that particular district in the company of the candidate and always would meet the village representative of Cosa Nostra to have a coffee, nothing else, because people could see that the representative of that district had received a visit from the mayor or the next candidate, and so the votes went to the candidate the we wanted.[49]

Buscetta vividly describes that in this context electors always "know it, know it. You have no idea how many bells ring in Sicily, faster than phone calls, these things are known, there is *u zu Peppino* who wants you to vote for [a certain person], and you do not have to know what this politician is going to do, either. The Mafia does not intimidate, it is not necessary."[50] Similar mechanisms of social control operate in Campania, as explained by the repentant *camorrista* Pasquale Galasso:

During the elections, all friends of businessmen, of all types, debate at that time, but in certain small towns the people are overwhelmed. It's enough that, as a representative of the Camorra, I tell a person to vote for this guy, he votes for him with his family, and he shows me this in the piazza....

48. TRNOC, 188.
49. TPAN, 672–73.
50. CPATB, 384.

You can see firsthand if that person and all of his family have voted for that name.... You give the head of the family a name, you check to see if another head of family has given the same name to a different relative. And in the end those are the seats.[51]

The repentant mafioso Gaspare Mutolo confirms:

We had strict orders to vote for the Democrats [Democrazia Cristiana], because it was the only good party; they were the only people that at least in Palermo you felt could do you a favor.... They gave me the copy with the numbers and I, for what I could do among my family and my village, I did it in a peaceful way.... You didn't need to check if he gave it or not. There was trust.[52]

Criminal organizations maintain that the votes they control are both useful (in resources controlled and expected permanence in power) and reliable (in respecting illegal agreements). As a repentant mafioso reveals, "It is important to know which political figures receive electoral support from Cosa Nostra because, if that is the case, it is possible to turn to them for favors in compensation for the electoral backing already given."[53] This reflects the informal norms of behavior that regulate the relationship. According to the repentant mafioso Vincenzo Marsala: "The basic rule was that only political propaganda in favor of the Democrazia Cristiana was accepted.... It was conceded, however, that sometimes you could vote for members of other political parties, but in a purely personal capacity, in return for personal favors received, and still with a ban on propaganda."[54] Each mafiosi group's support was directed toward specific Christian Democratic candidates:

I therefore believe that, when vote orders such as the aforementioned were given, they concerned politicians that the Mafia had interest in positioning in certain places. In the other cases the votes were given to the men of the Democrazia Cristiana that, by their power, could ensure the fulfillment of certain benefits.... In reality, contact with politicians can't be sustained by just any affiliate but only by those members of the "family" that, like the district bosses, have an elevated status in the hierarchy of the organization.[55]

---

51. CPAPG, 2279.
52. CPAGM, 1284–85.
53. DAP, 39.
54. TPAN, 713.
55. TPAN, 713.

The functioning of this unofficial rule minimizes dangerous contacts and the dissemination of information, as the repentant mafioso Gaspare Mutolo confirms:

> There was, let's say, a rule that was more than anything else a rule of respect and of confidentiality, namely, not everyone could speak with these important people. At that time, those who could speak with, let's say, the Honorable Salvo Lima were Stefano Bontate, Gaetano Badalamenti, Mimmo Teresi, Vitale.... We all had to follow the standard procedure, because there were men specifically meant to be in contact with these people, otherwise anyone felt authorized to disturb a person of this rank. But anyone who had the need could make contact through the designated people.[56]

While the preference toward Andreotti's faction was stated at a regional level and often also in municipalities where the same political equilibria prevailed, at a local level the criminal organization had necessarily to adapt to specific contingencies, eventually multiplying transactions with a plurality of political candidates. The repentant Antonino Giuffrè explains this aspect:

> Where I come from, lets say that the top politicians and mafiosi have always gone hand in hand and have always brought forward men of the ring of Salvo Lima, who depended on Senator Andreotti.... [But] it's not exclusively the Lima ring that is entitled to Cosa Nostra at the regional level, no, because there are others ... other differences, other reference points that are always useful.[57]

The repentant mafioso Marino Mannoia illustrates how the Mafia boss Stefano Bontate stressed the electoral influence of Cosa Nostra in a presumed meeting with the Christian Democratic leader Giulio Andreotti, asking for a clarification after the assassination of the regional president Piersanti Mattarella in 1980. "In Sicily, we're in command, and if you don't want to completely obliterate the Democrazia Cristiana you must do as we say. Otherwise we'll not only take your votes in Sicily but also in Reggio Calabria and throughout southern Italy."[58] The power to allocate packages of votes becomes then a resource to enforce agreements, sanctioning the breach of informal contracts. According to the state's witness Di Maggio, during a meeting of the Cosa Nostra committee,

> Riina [the Mafia boss] complained that the DC [Democrazia Cristiana] did not help the organization during the maxi-trial. The meeting ended

56. TPAN, 760–61.
57. CPAM IVX-II, 762.
58. TPMP, 107.

with the decision to vote for the PSI [Partito Socialista Italiano] ... to slap the DC. It was allowed, however ... to continue to vote for single DC candidates, provided that they were "friends" and were ready to continue to help those families with whom they were in contact.[59]

However, the Mafia's electoral basis, while significant, may in this estimate be biased by a sort of cognitive dissonance. Other sources, in fact, are testament to the fact that the impact of criminal consent is often not decisive. A repentant mafioso, Antonino Giuffrè, remembers that in 1987, when the Cosa Nostra godfather Salvatore Riina decided to support the Socialist Party instead of the Christian Democrats, the mafiosi themselves were disappointed by their limited impact. "We felt as though we were the masters of the vote. ... It was a bit of an ugly situation. ... Let's just say that errors were made. ... Alas, I always said that they were, specifically, Riina, number one militarily, but politically, sad to say, we couldn't say this, between quotation marks: 'unn'era arrivato' [he was obtuse]."

The Socialist Party in the province of Palermo had in fact a relatively small increase of only 30,000 votes, from 11.2 percent in 1983 to 15.4 percent in 1987.[60] Moreover, the long-term nature of mutual protection, which also assumes ideological and identifying characteristics, defused the potential menace of voter withdrawal. It was just a bluff, actually, while the unilateral and unnegotiated support of the Socialist Party was not reciprocated. The repentant mafioso Marino Mannoia states: "The idea of shifting votes from the Democrats to the Socialist Party was revealed to be a failure because the socialists hadn't come together. Moreover, this shift was a bluff in practice, because many men of honor (*uomini d'onore*) had said yes, but they didn't make an effort to get votes for the PSI, beginning with me."[61]

More recently, in the 2001 regional elections campaign, the indirect sponsorship by the "Boss of all bosses," Bernardo Provenzano, of a local candidate was not enough to guarantee him the seat. The mafioso Antonino Giuffrè received from Provenzano a poster of a UDC (post-DC party) candidate, with a message: "The Bagheria subordinates (*picciotti*) have the pleasure of supporting this gentleman." Giuffrè said: "It has a very important significance when Provenzano says to me, *the Bagheria picciotti*. It means that there are people in our circle who take responsibility for the trustworthiness of the doctor in question." The mafiosi's electoral campaign was conducted discreetly, to avoid overexposure

---

59. DAP, 50.
60. CPAM-IVX-II, 931–32. A similar delusion emerged among mafiosi after the regional elections of 1991, when in spite of the full support of the Cosa Nostra families in Enna, the Christian Democrat candidate Raffaele Bevilaqua, himself "organically integrated in the criminal organization," was not elected (CPAM-IVX-II, 932).
61. TPMP, 108.

of the candidate: "Discussion family by family, in a private way, expressly to try not to ruin it." The outcome was disappointing, however: 5,713 votes were not enough for D'Amico to win the seat.[62]

When electoral sanctions are not effective, mafiosi can nevertheless use their traditional weapons, violence and intimidation, to sanction violated pacts. This is the reason that, according to the repentant mafioso Giovanni Brusca, the shooting of Salvo Lima was a consequence of the ineffectiveness of electoral pressure: "Because if we'd only taken his votes, thus not voting for the DC, we wouldn't have been able to take away the strength he had, because the votes weren't only . . . Mafia votes, there were votes from many others who were involved in politics. . . . So if we had taken away only the Mafia votes, we wouldn't have obtained the result we wanted."[63]

Logically distinct from the previous case, even if in practice it often overlaps, is the operation of organized crime as a protection agency in the market for votes. Electoral exchanges between politicians and the Mafia, forbidden by Italian law, seem to have assumed especially noteworthy proportions in Campania, Calabria, and Sicily. In general, from illegal transactions involving electoral support emerges a demand for guarantees of reciprocation between sellers (voters) and buyers (politicians). Mafia groups are well equipped to supply such protection: "A more ideal setting for the Mafia can scarcely be imagined. Although the market for votes exists in areas of Italy where there is no Mafia, in Sicily it appears to be larger and more efficient."[64]

In this context, money flows from politicians to mafiosi, who become middlemen and enforcers in the exchanges of money for voters, exchanges that otherwise could be thwarted by mistrust. Examples abound in southern Italy. One of the candidates in the 1991 Sicilian elections paid the local Mafia family 25 million liras for its "control and protection. . . . Even if no violence was deployed, it was understood that those who did not respect the vote suggestion of the family could suffer consequences."[65] In Calabria, EUR 15,000 was the price, in the 2005 regional election, for a Udeur (a small post–Christian Democratic Party) candidate who was suspected of "reaching an agreement with YYY, boss of the Ndrangheta, through the intermediation of XXX, whereby money was pledged in exchange for votes."[66] In Campania, according to several

---

62. Palazzolo (2003b, p. 6).
63. CPAM-IVX-II, 932.
64. Gambetta (1993, p. 184).
65. TPMP, 897.
66. Foschini and Sannino (2010). The authors prefer not to mention names to maintain anonymity; instead the authors use YYY and XXX to represent the individuals involved in this particular case.

judicial inquiries, the rates in the sale of votes were quite stable: politicians paid between EUR 30 and EUR 70 per vote to Camorra bosses, with blocks of 100 to 150 votes on sale for EUR 1,500.[67]

In spite of the huge amount of information made available by judicial inquiries on the relationship between mafia and politics, there is a striking lack of empirical evidence of money flows from Italian criminal organizations to political actors. A major case of political financing involving criminal actors in Sicily represents in fact a paradoxical case of conflict of interests. The Salvo cousins, Antonino ("Nino") and Ignazio, have been charged with playing three roles simultaneously. First they were the private holders of an economic empire grounded in tax collection contracts in Sicily. Second, they were boss and vice-boss, respectively, of the Mafia family of Salemi.[68] Third, they were grand electors and leading exponents in the Christian Democratic Party. Nino Salvo himself admitted (although minimizing its duration and significance) that he channeled political financing to Sicilian parties as a strategy to influence and reward those decisionmakers from whom he had derived his fortune. By his account, the Salvos bought an all-encompassing protection from several parties.

> Until 1962 both my father-in-law and I, during election campaigns, have contributed to the costs of these campaigns in favor of all of the parties, without favoring any one party. In other words, since, as a result of a real legal battle, we were able to obtain the concession of numerous tax collections offices, we felt it our duty, in the years immediately following the favorable outcome of this dispute, to contribute to the electoral campaigns, in a way proportionate with the strength of each of the various parties.[69]

The motivation for this financial and material support seems ambiguous, because apparently criminal, economic, and political roles overlapped. At first glance money does not seem related so much to their role as Mafia bosses as to their role as tax collectors benefiting from a very advantageous calculation of their commission, which was almost 10 percent, compared with a national average of 3 percent.

The Salvos' influence on the Christian Democrats' political equilibrium, according to Mario Fasino, derived essentially from the "relationships they had weaved throughout with several DC factions. . . . But there was the possibility for them to offer work and then also election support during the campaigns. . . .

---

67. Lucarelli (2006).
68. According to TPMP, 112–14, this family was "used by leading members of Cosa Nostra for political contacts in Rome."
69. TPIS.

Finances, petrol, faxes; in short, financial support."[70] Their financial contribution, however, was also aimed at offering a competitive advantage to the Christian Democratic faction, which was organically associated with the Cosa Nostra. The Salvos' support, both financial and political, to Andreotti's faction was in fact decisive for its success in Sicily: the Salvos, Fasino explains, were "an economic and political presence with the power to influence between half and two-thirds of the entire Christian Democratic representation on the regional council.... For a long time they provided crucial support for the electoral success and expansion of Andreotti's group in Sicily."[71]

Financial flows from criminal organizations to candidates do exist, naturally, but they assume the traits of ordinary bribes paid for specific services. When politicians seem to forget their promises, the mafioso has the authority to enforce the deal. That is precisely what occurred to a Sicilian regional councilor, according to mafiosi repentant Sebastiano Messina: "I slapped him ... because I had given him money and he had not kept his commitments. He'd been busy doing other things, and then when we went to his house he didn't want to bring the country representative. He could no longer come into our territory."[72]

On their side, political actors may reciprocate with a general concern for a criminal organization's interests. A demand for protection of rights and expectations tends to emerge in every context characterized by high levels of illegality and corruption. When property rights are uncertain—since relationships between citizens and the state are regulated by arbitrary and inefficient procedures—conflicts and mistrust boil up. Political organizations can respond to such demands by supplying protection. As Pizzorno observes:

> We could say that the party system in Italy was not a participation system anymore, having become a protection system.... A good politician, especially at the local level, was mainly a good protection supplier. A firm could find it profitable to belong to a political area, which does not mean necessarily a party's area but even a faction's area, or even an area close to a certain political actor.... It could then obtain public contracts, privileged information, absence of controls, and so on. Sometimes there was no specific benefit, but the firm could simply be admitted to the "inner circle" to acquire privileged and protected citizenship.[73]

70. TPUS 1996.
71. TPMP, 163.
72. CPALM, 553.
73. Pizzorno (1996, p. 269).

In Italy, in fact, until their fading in the 1990s, the major political parties supplied protection to guarantee reciprocal fulfillment of corrupt exchanges. Authority within parties became a resource for the strengthening of trust: expectations that the actors involved would honor their promises in corrupt deals or would safeguard their rights in other uncertain relationships with the state.[74]

For criminal organizations, political protection translates into influence on public decisionmaking and political responsiveness to the organizations' interests and needs. Given this political protection, any uncertainty regarding criminal operations is reduced. The first and foremost resource needed by mafiosi who are fugitives or already in jail is impunity. According to several judicial documents, Mafia and Camorra members primarily wanted protection in investigations and acquittals in trials. As a state's witness, Gaspare Mutolo says, "The unanimous belief was that one could usefully influence the action of the courts through politicians and that, further, the function of Sicilian politicians was critical for 'Roman politics' [or national-level political decisions] with regard to Sicilian matters involving the Cosa Nostra."[75]

The cases range from a politician who sees that house arrest is arranged to another one (Salvo Lima) who negotiates the transfer of particularly uncooperative public officials.[76] According to the state's witness, Carmine Schiavone, the nonintervention of the police during several summits of the Camorra clan Nuvoletta, which involved "tens and tens of armed fugitives," followed from "the political protection that the Nuvolettas had thanks to the support they offered to Gava [Christian Democrat and former minister of budget, justice, and home affairs] and other politicians."[77]

A paradigmatic case of a symbiotic relationship is shown in the trial of Giulio Andreotti, leader of a major faction of the Christian Democratic Party. Since 1946 Andreotti had been one of the most powerful politicians in Italy, a member of almost every postwar government, holding a variety of ministerial posts (foreign affairs, finance, the budget), and prime minister on seven occasions, the first in 1972 and the last between 1989 and 1992. In 1991 he was nominated a senator for life. According to the judges, Andreotti had "participated in the maintenance, reinforcement, and expansion of the Mafia, putting at its disposal the influence and power derived from his position as the leader of a political current as well as

---

74. Della Porta and Vannucci (1994, 1999, 2007, 2012); Vannucci (1997).
75. DAP, 24.
76. TPMP, 38.
77. Barbagallo (1997, p. 37).

the relations he had fostered in the course of his activities."[78] The ultimate judgment confirmed the validity of this accusation for his activity until 1980, without condemning him for expiration of the statute of limitation.[79]

Before being murdered by the Mafia in 1992, the leader of Andreotti's faction within the Christian Democratic Party in Sicily, Salvo Lima, had been mayor of Palermo and a member of the Italian and European parliaments. He and his followers joined Andreotti's faction in 1968, and he brought with him "his existing, organic relations with some of the most important figures in the Mafia—Stefano Bontate, Gaetano Badalamenti, and Antonio and Ignazio Salvo (men of honour of Salemi) among them."[80] According to a member of the mafiosi collaborating with the authorities, "Andreotti was precisely the person to whom Lima constantly turned concerning decisions to be made in Rome involving the interests of Cosa Nostra."[81] The Mafia boss Giovanni Brusca recalls:

> During the "Mafia wars" Nino Salvo told me to tell Totò Riina [another leading Mafia boss] that Andreotti wanted us to stay calm and not to kill too many people, otherwise he would be forced to intervene with special laws.... Riina replied that Andreotti should be advised that we had been at his disposal for votes and other matters, now he should let us work in peace. We voted DC on the advice of Lima and Andreotti.[82]

With the most powerful party faction in the Christian Democratic stronghold of Sicily behind him, an alliance with Andreotti was decisive for whoever wanted to be elected national secretary of the party. Thus Andreotti gained significant bargaining power in national and regional agreements for the allocation of political and institutional roles. In this symbiotic alliance, the Mafia obtained a twofold benefit: on the one hand, as we have seen, an authoritative and all-embracing political protection; on the other, access to decisionmaking processes influenced by an articulated political structure, that is, the Andreottan faction of the Christian Democrats, which could "satisfy the many-sided interests of the Mafia in political and administrative life."[83] The overlap between politics and organized crime was such that, as Tommaso Buscetta comments, "there were internal wrangles within the DC and each boss of a district [the intermedium territorial subdivision of the Cosa Nostra] participated in the commission on behalf of his political 'vassal,' saying, 'Let's kill one of those and spare one of

78. TPMP, 100.
79. CCSA.
80. TPMP, 884.
81. TPMP, 13.
82. Bolzoni (1997).
83. TPMP, 884.

these.' The conflicts within the commission of the Cosa Nostra mirrored exactly the political divisions within the DC."[84]

The leadership of the Cosa Nostra counted on Andreotti's relationship with the president of the First Section of the Court of Cassation, who had annulled sentences against Mafia bosses involved in the so-called supertrial against the Mafia that had been promoted by Judge Giovanni Falcone. According to fellow collaborator Gaspare Mutolo, "everything was quiet because the Cosa Nostra had a mathematical certainty that the supertrial would end favorably. But this favorable prospect suddenly reversed, the first inklings of it coming in November 1991." The guilty sentences passed on the Mafia bosses were confirmed in January 1992, after a College of the Court of Cassation was unexpectedly nominated to hear the case. The Mafia boss Totò Riina is supposed to have commented, "Even that sod Lima has double-crossed us."[85] The murder of Salvo Lima on March 12, 1992, and the later killing of Ignazio Salvo marked the beginnings of the Mafia's reprisals, striking at "the symbol of the political grouping which had used the Cosa Nostra and failed to deliver on its promises. . . . The murder was both a punishment for Andreotti (since it was politically very damaging) and a warning concerning his future actions."[86] Claudio Martelli, a minister in Andreotti's government at the time, states that following Lima's murder, Andreotti "was scared, either because he did not understand or because he did."[87]

As the Andreotti case shows, Italian criminal organization activities are intertwined with political processes not only at the local level but also at the national level. The Parliamentary Anti Mafia Commission argues that "consideration of Mafia connections should not focus only on the 'lower branches' of politics. . . . This collusion tends to spread beyond local circles because Mafia heads, who control votes and direct them towards local politicians, are also willing to support regional and national candidates, who in turn are linked to local politicians by party loyalties or, more often, faction or group loyalties."[88]

Political protection extends to settle disputes, assign contested rights, and dispose "kindnesses" favoring their criminal counterparts. The collaborator Giovanni Brusca, in a trial testimony, presents a wide sample of situations when the mafiosi benefited under the protection of influential Christian Democrat politicians— Salvo Lima and the Salvo cousins, expressly:

---

84. TPMP, 115.
85. TPUS 1998, 336–39.
86. DAP, 32.
87. TPMP, 786–87.
88. CPMF, 2.

For example, we needed funding for the Cooperativa Kaggio and, through politicians, we got the funds . . . thanks to the . . . Salvo cousins and the Salvo cousins through Lima, through their political power. So when you spoke of favors, which were not necessarily about . . . trials or laws, these kinds of favors they provided. For example, in Palermo there were economic interests, both of Riina and of many other politicians, in the building land in the city, which wasn't a small thing. . . . They allocated the plots of land, that is to say, they gave instructions to the various mayors or representatives, namely the regional bosses. . . . However, the strong one was always Lima, the one who gave instructions. . . . There were jobs, USL [Unita Sanitaria Locale] jobs, there were many things. . . . For example, we went to get loans, and through Salvo, we got them. Like . . . when we acquired the territory in Contrada Don Tommaso, we got a loan through Salvo from the [Banca] Commerciale, if I remember correctly, thanks to the Salvo cousins and their political strength. For example, jobs at the collection's office to employ people. They were a whole series of activities, not just . . . they weren't just jobs.[89]

The mafiosi may simply demand nondecision—that is, abstention from interference with an equilibrium that is satisfactory to the criminal interests. The collaborator Salvatore Cucuzza describes this strategy as prevailing between the Sicilian Cosa Nostra and the Christian Democrats until the early 1990s:

Up until that time, I voted for that party because it didn't do anything. . . . In fact, from the . . . early years of the 1970s up until the giant trial, one cannot say that the Democrats had done anything very noteworthy. . . . [We voted Democrazia Cristiana] because it didn't do anything, this is why. . . . Not even a favor. Because what we had was enough, namely, there was the freedom to do whatever we wanted, at that time. If you think about all of the murders and that there wasn't a single disciplinary action.[90]

The mafioso, in other words, felt secure and guaranteed against future difficulties by this collaborative relationship with the Andreotti faction of the Christian Democrats in Sicily. "I said to myself, Mizzica, I'm good here," remembers Salvatore Cucuzza. "If anything happens there's the chance for people of a certain level—those at the level of Mr. Andreotti—to intervene—and to eventually fix any problem."[91] The repentant *camorrista* Pasquale Galasso similarly

89. TPAA.
90. CPAM-IVX-II, 934.
91. CPAM-IVX-II, 933.

describes national-level politicians, who "during the elections, would ask these people for votes, promising any simple favor."[92]

Replacement or Colonization: When Organized Crime Enters the Political Arena

When structured criminal organizations, operating as local monopolies in the supply of protection in more or less muddled markets, face political actors having uncertain prospects of duration and success, short time horizons, and fragile roots in society, there will be a different outcome from that discussed above. In this case there is a difference in the nature of resources demanded, in the expected duration of the relationship, in the bargaining power of counterparts, and in the costs and opportunities for criminal and political actors.

Protection is highly desired by the political actors, but their unstable future discourages criminal organizations from undertaking an agreement. Nonetheless, criminal organizations are often required to stabilize their alliances with political actors, since fixing the roles and the allocation of resources contributes to the peaceful and orderly development of illicit markets. In fact, under certain conditions, powerful criminal "protection agencies" may try to replace political actors, occupy their structures, and colonize the whole administrative structure.

Extreme cases are the collapse of the party system or an institutional crisis. Even the ordinary dynamics of electoral competition may induce analogous results. If elections are truly competitive, criminal actors can hardly stipulate long-term contracts (stating the allocation of future public contracts, zoning, licenses, guarantees of immunity, and so on) with such unstable political partners. This is the case when a competitive party or party coalition not supported by the Mafia contests elections. In this case the mafiosi can adopt at least two strategies.

First, they can enter into an exchange relationship with all the main competing parties, thereby assuming the role of informal regulators and enforcers of hidden consociational pacts. There are some drawbacks to this strategy: criminals could be victims of collusive pacts among politicians. Further, criminal actors may be weakened precisely by their involvement in political affairs, with increased risks of visibility and exposure without any reliable shield against inquiries.

Second, the mafiosi may use their reputation and coercive resources to ensure a steady competitive advantage in local elections to one of the political actors. This process would render elections less and less competitive. From a dynamic perspective, we may expect that if a strategy of colonization/occupation—implying

---

92. CPAPG, 2310.

supply of mafiosi protection to specific political careers—is successful, the political actor may obtain from it additional resources of authority and consent in the political market, therefore increasing his or her bargaining power and eventually emancipating himself or herself from his or her criminal counterparts.

Cosa Nostra bosses sought the establishment of a mafioso political party as a component of a wider plan of regional independence or stronger autonomy in Sicily. This plan coincided with a deconstruction of the existing party system and, more generally, a dramatic crisis of political equilibrium. In these critical junctures of Italian history—immediately after the end of World War II and in the mid-1990s, when *mani pulite* investigations sanctioned the end of the so-called First Republic—the mafiosi reaction to a maximum of uncertainty in the political realm was a vague aspiration for complete self-sufficiency in political representation and competition in Sicily. The replacement of traditional parties with a Godfather's Party never materialized. However, since then, new political actors have emerged as partners for possible cooperative interactions with the Cosa Nostra.

The first phase of this scenario came true in the autumn of 1944, when a new political party, the Movimento Indipendentista Siciliano (Sicilian Independence Movement), held its first congress.[93] A political platform was approved, promoting violent insurrection against the Italian provisional authorities and stating an alliance with the local bandit Salvatore Giuliano. The promulgation of a special statute of autonomy for Sicily in 1946 induced a rapid withdrawal from the extremist program. The Sicilian Independence Movement entered into the electoral process, winning 8.7 percent of the votes in 1946 and 8.8 percent in 1947. The party disappeared from the political scene after it was defeated in the regional elections of 1951. In the meantime, Mafia bosses abandoned the project to support other consolidating parties, particularly the Christian Democratic Party, which was destined to hegemonize the political scene for decades to come.

A second, even less realistic, program for the replacement of long-established parties materialized in the mid-1990s, coinciding with the sudden collapse of the party system and the disappearance of Cosa Nostra's traditional political counterparts, primarily Christian Democrats. A free space in the political market was thus opened, and consequently some Mafia bosses considered the feasibility of a new party's entering into the scene, promoting an independence project. According to Tullio Cannella, an exponent of the Christian Democrats, the Cosa Nostra boss Leoluca Bagarella, whom he helped while he was in hiding, was doing the following:

---

93. CPAM-IVX-II, 517.

He began to ask very clearly for favors. He'd learned that, good or bad, I knew some people that were actively involved in politics. . . . That is to say, people who believed in "Sicilianity" extolled the values of "Sicilianity," so from this, I had a Sicilian movement. . . . Then Bagarella told me, "You need to begin to get involved, you have to start moving, you see that you can join these people, go talk to them, because there are even projects in other places, in Catania, in the Calabrias, where we have movements that have already been born, already organized, already operating, and they're all our friends." I began to move because I actually liked to engage myself in these things, but I still didn't know where he could lead, so I took it upon myself. Sicilia Libera was established in October of 1993.[94]

The newborn party, Sicilia Libera, was in fact conceived as a piece of a wider scheme of deconstruction of the state's authority in the southern regions, following also Cosa Nostra's terrorist campaign in 1993, when the criminal organization was attempting to shape a new political elite according to its needs. After an initial minimal financing of just 10 million liras (about EUR 5,000), the new party was soon abandoned to its destiny by Leoluca Bagarella. According to Tullio Cannella,

Bagarella was already well aware of the rise of Silvio Berlusconi at the head of a new political movement that would ensure, by virtue of preexisting commitments, to resolve the issues that were at the heart of Cosa Nostra, being: serving hard time and the crime of association with the Mafia. Let me clarify that these were, so to speak, the priorities that the agreement with Berlusconi would have allowed us to address and solve in the short term. This strategy, it did not exclude; rather, it walked hand in hand with the separatist of whom I've already spoken, and was mainly supported by Bagarella and by Nitto Santapaola in Catania through Alfio Fichera, but for which completion was not anticipated anytime soon.[95]

The emergence of new, trustworthy political partners determined a sudden abandonment of the autonomist project, which in fact required a long-term risky investment in an uncertain political market, while the mafiosi's interests could not wait. As explained by Bagarella to Cannella, the Cosa Nostra tried to apply the traditional terms of an implicit electoral pact to Forza Italia, the party founded a few months later, going on to win the 1994 elections—along with media tycoon Silvio Berlusconi:

94. TPDC, 1448–49.
95. TCBD, 42.

We are moving in another direction that is more concrete, which is easier to implement, while a nationalist project goes through years and years of work, we have the connections. In essence, Bagarella told me that they were aligning with, I say this honestly, with Forza Italia, thus they had several candidates, some friends of members of Cosa Nostra, and each candidate had created a sort of electoral compact with their stakeholders, a sort of commitment, and so they voted for them, so much so that even Calvaruso said to me, "You know Giovanni Brusca takes me ... to these places, meetings, flyers go out all day long for Forza Italia." So this was the thing I learned, after which we had nothing else.[96]

The repentant mafioso Antonino Giuffrè confirms the shift of Cosa Nostra's electoral support toward Forza Italia: "It was in 1994 that a change of direction occurred. There was a moment in which Forza Italia took the field, and then Cosa Nostra began to look for connections and guarantees from people who were brought into this party. Provenzano gave us his blessing, even though he was skeptical by nature of the political field, he always had his own way of expressing himself to the politicians."[97] According to Giuffrè, within the Cosa Nostra a general protection (that is, noninterference in criminal affairs and a loosening of judicial pressure) was expected from the new political party and its leader, akin to that which had been obtained by some Christian Democrats in the previous decades.

Toward the end of 1993... you began to hear talk of the rise of an important person like Berlusconi. This news came to Cosa Nostra, and for a period was a matter of debate and careful evaluation. All of the news came to Cosa Nostra. They even made inquiries to see whether it was a subject that might be of interest to Cosa Nostra and if it might possibly cure those ills that had plagued Cosa Nostra for years.... We needed to relieve the pressure being exerted on Cosa Nostra by judges and law enforcement and, in particular, the harsh sentences that began to rain down on our heads, as well as confiscation of goods and solitary confinement of mafiosi bosses.[98]

According to Giuffrè, Cosa Nostra's support of Berlusconi's party was then allowed, "because it gave excellent guarantees.... Cosa Nostra's concern was that the top rank of the political movement assume well-specified responsibilities in

96. TPDC, 1541–42.
97. Oliva and Palazzolo (2006, p. 144).
98. Palazzolo (2003a).

order to deal with all of our problems and to provide 'clean' men, who would do the bidding of Cosa Nostra in Sicily."[99]

Similarly, according to a repentant *camorrista*, the support of his criminal clan to a Forza Italia local politician was not reciprocated by a specific return but by a general availability to provide personal favors as well as by a shared belief that that party was more inclined to satisfy the general interests of the criminal group:

> I myself have asked several people to do me the courtesy of voting XY.[100] Of course, when I asked this courtesy from my friends in Trentola, no one refused me. Almost the entire organization is occupied with the elections of XY.... Even after the elections of XY and up until the time of my arrest I would always meet up with him.... We'd also talk about the political situation in reference to our court case. XY told me, among other things, that the victory of the Forza Italia coalition would have resulted in an easing of the pressure on us, and in particular referred to the provisions of the law on cooperative justice (*collaboranti di giustizia*).... We concluded that the rise of Forza Italia could change the situation in the sense that the judges of the left would be resized by the Office of the Prosecutor of Naples.... I've never received personal favors from Mr. XY. I don't know if others may have received favors, or if we've asked for them. It's clear, however, that Mr. XY, who expressly received our help for his election, was available to us for anything we could ask for. If we'd asked him for some kind of public job, there was no way that he could refuse. He himself had explicitly told us that he was at our disposal.[101]

When the political environment appears less stable and orderly, protective services of organized crime are even more valuable. The mafiosi's authoritative arbitration can in fact provide a degree of certainty in these murky electoral and political markets. According to the repentant mafioso Antonino Calderone, the criminal organization may prefer a more "chaotic" and unpredictable political process, as in ill-functioning democratic procedures, precisely in order to increase its bargaining power and expectations of impunity:

> Why does Cosa Nostra try to give the votes not to the parties on the left, but to parties like the Democrazia Cristiana, the liberal party, the republicans,

---

99. TCBD, 43. Ideological as well as pragmatic motives lay behind the electoral choice, according to repentant mafioso Giovanni Brusca: "There are many collaborators that say I voted for Forza Italia, and it's true, but I did it solely and exclusively to go against the left, for my own ideological cause."
100. Authors prefer to maintain the anonymity of candidate XY.
101. TRNOC, 178.

or the social democrats? Because, according to them, it's about democratic parties, and when there is democracy, the politicians disagree: the more chaotic the politics, the more they take advantage, because they then face fewer obstacles. They try to create as much disarray as possible in order to stay afloat.[102]

We may add that the mafiosi may prefer, may even deliberately promote, some uncertainty in political interactions because it increases demand for the protection and enforcement services they sell. In Campania, for instance, until the mid-1990s the political scenario was characterized by competitive pressure from different actors to renew a medium-term agreement with the local bosses, who could monopolistically decide whom to trust according to previous experiences. As explained by the repentant *camorrista* Pasquale Galasso:

> Regarding politicians at the national and honorable level . . . when the elections are announced they introduce themselves to the Camorra and to Carmine Alfieri [the *camorrista* boss], and pass on word that they'd be willing to make an agreement in order to ask to be voted for. Then the elections are a totally different thing. When there are about five or six months before the election, first there's the bustle of all the politicians that have been in touch with the Camorra, and they come forward to get our votes. So yet again they express their willingness, and at that moment a market is created. . . . In the end, Alfieri and those of us in the organization quantify what we can offer. In exchange, the official serves as political power; he could be useful to us in various friendships with institutional relations, mainly with judges and many other things. In the end you need to take stock of whether the Honorable so-and-so has considerable political force.[103]

The assessment of the *camorrista* boss is straightforward, aimed to establish the partner's trustworthiness in future uncertain contingencies:

> In the end, Alfieri had come to decide possibly to dump someone and to support another official after having considered them and reasoned in these terms: "This one gives me something; what does he give me? If he's elected, which committee will he join? If he goes, for example, to the Judiciary Committee, that's fine, but I want the promise of a mafioso (*uomo d'onore*) that he will attend to my judicial problems."[104]

102. CPAAC, 284.
103. CPAPG, 2277–88.
104. CPAPG, 2310.

While the potential for mutually profitable exchanges between criminal and political actors remains, in this scenario mistrust and suspects arise, since both politicians' determination and capability to maintain their promises are difficult to ascertain, as previous experiences are missing, reputation is ill defined, and future opportunities are unclear. Essentially, why should in this case the mafiosi trust politicians?[105] The implicit menace of violent retaliation could suffice here, but the application of violent sanctions has a cost and should be avoided whenever possible. In a tape-recorded dialogue, the Mafia boss Giuseppe Guttadauro expresses his worries about the conduct of the future regional president Totò Cuffaro, whom he will finally accord his doubtful confidence:

> What interests me is that you make a commitment to solving a problem. When, for example, he says with a life sentence: "I want to take on all of the responsibilities in the world." But whether they let him go or not, what do we have to lose? However, I give Toto my unconditional support as president of the region. This is beyond question. Have I explained myself? So go, now, and find the best way to have less damage and better output.[106]

Facilitating and enforcing political agreements, organized crime contributes to settling disputes and stabilizing local governments, making for an orderly allocation of budgetary resources and the distribution of appointments to key public posts. For instance, the Camorra repentant Pasquale Galasso states that after the election of the town's council in Poggiomarina (near Naples), he "was asked to intervene with a reluctant councillor to tell him, with all the weight of [his] Camorra fame, to ally himself with Antonio Gava [a Christian Democratic political boss], who had promised him the position of mayor." An agreement therefore emerged between the two main Christian Democratic representatives in the local government. According to this account, this agreement became stable only thanks to the presence of the *camorrista*: "For the duration of that government," Galasso continues, "I was the tongue, convincing the one, who didn't want to renounce to his position as mayor, and the other, who wanted to occupy it, to remain united."[107] Criminal groups were obviously paid in exchange for their services, with cash or with open access to the decisionmaking processes, whose stability they had helped build.

---

105. Generally speaking, in fact, they seldom do trust them, as evidenced by Nino Calderone with involuntary irony: "It is difficult for a politician to become a 'man of honor.' There is a strong sense of mistrust in Cosa Nostra toward politicians because they are treacherous, they do not keep promises, and they are sly. They are people who break their words and are without principles" (Arlacchi, 1992, p. 208).

106. Bianchi and Nerazzini (2005, p. 27).

107. Barbagallo (1997, pp. 149–50).

In extreme cases, criminal enforcement requires the application of physical intimidation or assassination of those who disturb the fragile harmony among political actors. This is the case of the assassination of the powerful Christian Democratic exponent Ludovico Ligato in Reggio Calabria. According to a state witness, his elimination "should be framed as a moment of the conflict inside the Reggio's business committee," given the fact that Ligato, with his political power and his contacts with a rival Mafia band, "interfered in the political life of Reggio."[108] The murder had the effect of consolidating the nascent political coalition in Reggio: "After the assassination—or better, because of it—the game was made and the new agreements were implemented thanks to a series of very important decisions, which in previous time would have been discussed for months in the city council."[109] Any element that might have disrupted the coalition and its plans for doling out public resources was thus eliminated. Thanks to this violent pacification, the market for corruption could expand undisturbed and benefit Reggio's business committee, which was composed of "prominent figures in the dominant political class, who were able to influence the choices of local and central public agencies," of "'favored' national companies that routinely received public contracts," and of "local entrepreneurs who acted in symbiosis with local organized crime and were thus the actual executors of the work."[110]

The repentant mafioso Gaspare Mutolo describes the ambiguity surrounding Cosa Nostra's pacification role within political disputes: "Mafiosi's protection is both demanded and feared by political actors, but in any case it does not have to be confused with violence. On the contrary, it is aimed at guaranteeing precarious 'rights' and expectations in otherwise fluid political agreements." The recourse to Mafia boss arbitration in quarrels was usual also for leading political figures: "When he wanted to go, he went; it was normal, also because these people weren't viewed as criminals, but as people who in the end were good.... There were issues, a mafioso had one, the other another, and a peaceful agreement needed to be reached. Through the eyes of these people, they were peacekeepers, not assassins."[111] Besides, dispute settlement was usually sanctioned spontaneously, relegating physical coercion as *extrema ratio*: "Any politician could have a person that can dodge a conflict. In the end, if these people work hard, they're doing it for good, not for bad: in fact, the issue was that, if they couldn't find a way to agree, to be more flexible, surely they'd kill everyone, as someone had been killed."[112]

108. Ciconte (1994, p. 168).
109. Ciconte (1994, p. 168).
110. CD, n. 256, 1993, 2.
111. CPAGM, 1276.
112. CPAGM, 1283.

Among the methods reported in table 8-2 we do not consider the center-periphery variable. The local dimension of interaction may nevertheless be relevant, especially when we consider the relative weakness of small political subjects and administrative structures confronted with the almost military enforcement apparatus of a criminal organization. Local administration and party structures, as well as candidates for municipal and provincial office, in other words, are especially vulnerable to a complete colonization by organized crime. Different variables have to be considered.

Locally, we may expect a different incidence in relative cost of electoral campaigns and, consequently, an increase in the need for money, depending on variables operating on both sides of the political markets.[113] A stronger demand for protection and support in electoral competition emerges when local political arenas are contestable. This demand could be fulfilled by criminal organizations capable of reinvesting in the political arena as part of their illicit profits. Moreover, the presence of organized crime in a territory creates a distortive and inflationary input in electoral campaigns and, more generally, in political activity: "Decentralization processes open up new arenas of political competition that add to the cost of politics."[114] Candidates not benefiting from mafiosi protection suffer a competitive disadvantage, which implies higher costs in economic and other material terms (such as increased risks for their personal safety). The candidates' expected security cost increases, as well as their incentive to seek an alternative criminal sponsorship, if one is available.

The backing of political actors by criminal organizations may be decisive at the local level. A distorted principle of criminal subsidiarity seems to apply in some cases, where the criminal organization defines the codes of behavior handled by the lowest administrative and political authorities. Even without direct intimidation or violent interference in the political process, local politics may be captured by Mafia-like organizations in three ways. One is through the direct involvement of politicians and candidates. This way, being less noticeable, has a lower risk of public exposure and denunciation. Another way is through political actors who are either neutral to or hostile to criminal organizations abstaining from participation in the political competition, which in this situation is much harder and riskier (even if immeasurably more rewarding in symbolic terms). Third, capture of the local political process can happen thanks to the limited scale of political and administrative activity at the local level, which permits criminal organizations to more closely control the process.

---

113. We are grateful to Salvatore Sberna, with whom we discussed the following points related to the effects of criminal financing of political activity at a local level.

114. Casas-Zamora (2010).

A concomitant variable is represented by the electoral system. In Italy, after the majoritarian reform in 1993, electoral victories can be determined even by very small differences in votes, often making the value added of criminal support a decisive factor. Even with a slight majority, in fact, the mayor or the provincial president may be guaranteed a strong majority in elected assemblies and, therefore, relatively secure control over decisionmaking. Corresponding to this centralization of political authority, the supporting local criminal organization does not have to compete, negotiate, or conflict with other criminal groups.

To sum up, the linkages between organized crime and politicians seem to be frequent at the local level, which in the Italian case is often characterized by a high, but personalized and clientelistic, competition.[115] In this situation, criminal organizations can easily resort to their powers of intimidation as well as to their control over electoral participation and financial support. There is, in these cases, a colonization of municipalities or local public structures. Italian law sanctions colonization by dissolving the elections and substituting a state commissar to that function. Between 1991 and 2008 there were 181 cases of dissolution of local administrations, almost all in the four Italian southern regions where the Mafia, the Ndrangheta, the Camorra, and the Sacra Corona Unita operate.[116]

The monopolization of the local political markets and the occupation of administrative structures by criminal organization may also imply financial assistance to supported candidates, which tends to be concealed in a large organizational contribution to the campaign. In a Calabrian municipality, for instance, the intervention of the local *ndrina* (subunit of the Ndrangheta criminal organization) was decisive in the settlement of a dispute between two conflicting political factions. The criminal organization in fact imposed on local parties a second nomination for the former mayor, firmly dissuading a potential challenger and thereby stabilizing the preexisting political equilibrium. During the electoral campaign the *ndrina* actively promoted support of candidates on the mayor's list, which included the nephew of the local boss, who was elected and became councilor. Besides persuasion, other forms of pressure were also applied. In one instance, a member of the criminal gang seized people's electoral certificates and then gave them back in the proximity of the ballot box. The reason was to symbolically assert the gang's control over the whole electoral process by use of threats. In another Calabrian municipality, the local *ndrina*, led by the Fiarè family, was represented by the mayor, who was affiliated with the criminal organization. He was elected in 1993 and 1997, when no alternative candidate

---

115. Della Porta (2006).
116. Mete (2009).

dared to challenge him. During his mandate, the criminal organization deeply influenced administrative activity in public contracting, licensing, and hiring.[117]

When criminal organizations can enforce unstable coalitional pacts, settle political disputes, and colonize the local administration, the resulting decision-making may be profitable for several actors. Entrepreneurs, in addition to politicians and criminal organizations, are included in the consequent allocation of public resources and privileges. As the Camorra repentant Pasquale Galasso describes, every Camorra clan had a "prime political sponsor," and together they planned which works should be financed, which firms should stipulate public contracts, and which sites should be earmarked for construction:

> The politician who directs the financing of the contract, and thus its assignment or concession, acts as a mediator between the company (which is almost always from the north or the center and is quite large) and the Camorra. This mediation occurs by forcing the company to pay a kickback to the politician or his direct representatives and to accept that subcontracts be assigned to [local] companies, directly controlled by the Camorra. The relationship becomes more complicated, since the local companies flank the principal company as equal partners in the job. In this case, an overall management of the operation emerges that involves politicians, businessmen, and *camorristi*.[118]

According to Neapolitan judges, each participant could obtain significant benefits from this triangle:

> The entrepreneur obtains from the politician work and the possibility to make a profit from the *camorrista* ... social peace and credit in the relationships with the local administration. The *camorrista* obtains money from the entrepreneur, judicial "protection" from the politician, and social legitimation from both. ... The politician receives electoral force and the capacity of an illicit influence on the public functions, added to relevant economical resources.[119]

Entrepreneurial intermediation by organized crime has a double advantage: the money flow is less compromising in case of disclosure, even when it is irregular, as there is no evidence of the direct involvement of criminal organizations; entrepreneurs can apply their professional skills and budgetary expertise to conceal, or "launder," these financial flows, while identification and transaction

---

117. Sberna (2011).
118. APN, 9.
119. Barbagallo (1997, p. 163).

costs are lower, since the politician's counterpart can more easily bargain and gather and transmit information. For instance, in a Sicilian municipality, according to the decree of dissolution,

> The mayor, already elected to the same office in June of 1999, has been bound for some time to the aforementioned businessman, identified as a member with high-level responsibilities and strong Mafia ties in the area as well as the administrator of residential and commercial properties on behalf of the same clan. The administrator has obtained support for the campaign with respect to the spring 2000 consultations with the businessman, capable, by virtue of the considerable fortune and number of employees, to influence the electoral consensus by directing it in a way favorable to the interests of the Mafia clan of which he is a top representative.[120]

Money, as a circumstantial bribe or a less goal-oriented payment, can become the preferred means of exchange in these cases. In local arenas pragmatic considerations prevail, while political actors are approached on the basis of their presumed availability and receptiveness. The mafioso collaborator Giuseppe Pulvirenti illuminates this point: "Because it's not that we only approached the Democrats [Democrazia Cristiana]! For our own interests in the administration, we approached anyone, perhaps even a communist. This doesn't matter, as long as they took the money."[121] The interests of criminal and political actors then converge in the cartelized control of local decisionmaking, where relevant profits—particularly in the public contracting sector—may be shared. In this context criminal organizations regulate the functioning of the whole market, ensuring a constant flow of bribes in the overall distribution of politicians. Angelo Siino, the mafioso responsible for public contracts, has quantified the amount of bribes paid: "In general Mafia contracts [worth] 30 billion . . . [are] distributed. Lima at a certain point was in a position to hide parts of this because, naturally, they were mafiosi who did the lion's share. . . . The percentage was divided as such: 2 percent to the Mafia, 2 percent to the Andreotti group. The 0.5 percent was for the provincial control commission."[122]

Bribes are then paid to political actors, who find themselves in a weaker bargaining position, as a sort of "offer they cannot refuse" within the context of specific transactions: what is given to and what is expected from them, and when, has to be more clearly stated here, as trust is a scarce resource, and clouds of uncertainty surround the future permanence in charge of political partners.

120. Sberna (2011).
121. CPAM-IVX-II, 933.
122. CPAM-IVX-II, 934.

Money becomes the precise and quantifiable *numerarie* in these exchanges, which permit criminal actors to ask for immediate reciprocation of valuable resources allocated by politicians. Bribes could be (and sometimes actually are) demanded by mafiosi groups and also by more stable political actors as a component of a symbiotic relationship. However, as soon as the time horizon of their interaction widens, there is a common interest of political and criminal actors—who may in the meantime develop good reasons to trust each other— in avoiding risky transmission of assets (such as bribes), which can be quite easily detected by control agencies. Their common long-term expectation allows for more elusive, but very important, resources (such as the mobilization of electoral support and political pressure to be shielded against police action and judicial inquiries) to become crucial.

Political Gatekeeping and Occasional Exchanges with Criminal Networks

A criminal group that operates as a protection firm, supplier of guarantees, and enforcer of fragile rights in social, political, and economic interactions is usually monopolistic.[123] In some contexts, however, the criminal group may resemble a more dispersed and competitive network of criminal actors. This is the case, for instance, when several criminal gangs manage the production, distribution, and selling of illegal commodities or the exercise of illegal activities in a disordered environment, without any authority capable of regulating these activities and resolving quarrels. This is also true when protection firms become paralyzed or ineffective due to state prosecution or to a defeat in a criminal war. In this case, the time perspective of the criminal organization also shrinks, and therefore its credibility suffers.

Relationships with political actors, in this case, reflect the different nature of the services supplied by criminal actors: cheating becomes more profitable, and reputational assets lose their value. While political protection may be more desirable to criminal actors, few political actors are willing to supply it; political actors are presumably less interested in entering long-lasting relationships with criminal gangs that promise to be only ephemeral partners.

Economic resources are still available, however, to criminal actors who typically need them to launder their illicit profits. If all-purpose political financing is less probable, due to doubt about reciprocation, more circumscribed deals

---

123. According to Schelling (1984), organized crime can be distinguished from other forms of criminality precisely by its tendency to monopolize, regulate, and enforce exchanges in illegal markets.

are possible. A sort of informal gatekeeping— to the advantage of competing criminal groups, each offering economic resources—is possible when the political actors have long-term authority over public structures. In the most critical phases, politicians may simply wait until a winning criminal organization emerges. As stressed by repentant *camorrista* Pasquale Galasso: "Over the years I realized that the entire sequence of murders that destroyed me and my family, like many others in Campania, ultimately makes the game really just that of these politicians, who are quick to distance themselves and wait for the winner, to then align themselves for management of business and votes."[124]

In such a competitive criminal environment, the sponsored politician can even retreat—without being punished—from promises made to a losing clan, sanctioning, with his privileged gatekeeping to public resources, the new equilibria of the underworld. According to a repentant *camorrista*, this was the case of an elected member of Parliament after the defeat of the Bidognetti clan:

> I also had supported Mr. XY during the elections of 2001, and during this time I'd had other meetings with him.[125] On these occasions he reassured me of the chance of being rewarded for my support in different ways, including through my integration into the framework of the CE4 consortium.... Immediately after the elections I personally called the honorable Mr. XY on his cell phone, and I said to him, "Your honor, I need to ask you a favor!"... He said because of my criminal record, and because "certain situations had changed," he couldn't help me. I specified that I was, therefore, displeased that he'd said no because I was one of his "good voters."... I insisted upon my request because I wanted to remain a part of the waste management business, and because my exclusion meant a loss of prestige at both the network and entrepreneurial levels. By network, I mean the Camorra. The honorable Mr. XY explained to me ... that by now the economic interests of the Casalesi clan had been focused ... on the geographical region controlled by the Schiavone ... and furthermore, the Bidognetti had been bumped off because it didn't have any power over Santa Maria La Fossa. This resulted in my exclusion. In short, the honorable Mr. XY told me that he'd adapted to the choice that had been made up-stream by the Casalesi clan, who had decided that the waste-to-energy plant should be made in Santa Maria La Fossa.... He therefore had to follow these lines and to favor only the Schiavone clan in the management of the deal and, as a consequence, keep the Bidognetti out, and thus me as well.[126]

124. APN, 13.
125. XY is the same candidate mentioned before, whom the authors intend to keep anonymous.
126. TRNOC, 28.

To sum up, when in extremely competitive criminal environments weaker criminal gangs—without the organizational capacity to credibly propose and enforce vote buying—encounter stable political protectors, there is an incentive for the latter to adopt more opportunistic strategies. On the other hand, criminals' demands for protection by political actors in administrative affairs or judicial procedures might be paid through bribes (or other valuable resources). Politicians have in this case the power to choose which among competing criminal groups should benefit from the allocation of public resources. If such gatekeeping operates effectively, the criminal group may in fact derive from it a monopolistic advantage over its competitors.

A different model emerges when both political and criminal actors are unable to offer each other guarantees of protection. Political and criminal spheres may then coexist with only limited interactions. Pessimistic expectations concerning future roles and strength, however, do not prevent other kinds of arrangement. In such cases, since neither partner trusts the other's ability to meet its obligations, they will tend to limit their transactions to relatively well-defined resources, possibly with tit-for-tat exchange of rewards. Corruption is the most natural (and frequent) mode of interaction in this context: through bribes, criminal actors acquire specific favors, influence decisions, or gain access to privileged information from political (as well as administrative) agents. Corrupt exchanges between several criminal gangs and political actors might be the outcome. The benefits are mainly confined to the economic dimension, with limited direct impact on the electoral and political sphere.

Bribe payments connote more or less sporadic deals between political agents and the corrupting criminal organization, as in the case of the northern and central regions of Italy, where criminal organizations export some of their financial assets and economic interests. Since criminal organizations have to move in a hostile and unfamiliar environment, they may trust entrepreneurs to recycle their money in real estate or to mediate their relationships with political actors. For instance, an entrepreneur whose firms reinvested Ndrangheta's capital in real estate in Milan is accused of having paid bipartisan bribes to at least two center-left and center-right political administrators in a nearby municipality to obtain permits and influence urban planning. Corruption was an ordinary practice, which the entrepreneur applied with professional expertise. In a tape-recorded conversion, he boasts about his ability "to teach the politician to take bribes, but with grace," as a more sophisticated form of retribution.[127] The entrepreneur apparently also had contacts with a regional councilor: "We know each other, I helped him get to know the other politicians in the area, and we've

---

127. Carlucci (2010b).

been in contact a lot over the last year. He wanted me to introduce him to more people in the area in order to win the electoral campaign of 2010."[128]

According to a report of the Parliamentary Anti Mafia Commission, the economic crisis eased the infiltration of organized crime in Lombardia.[129] Electronic gambling was instead the business of sixty-two societies where the Camorra reinvested its profits all over Italy. Again, the investment was mediated by an entrepreneur, who was sentenced in the 1990s for abetting Camorra. According to the judges, the entrepreneur was "the only economic topic of reference" of different clans. "It was the Mafia that was in need of him," because he had the expertise, the arrangements, and "the institutional connections."[130]

Conclusions

In southern Italy deep-rooted criminal organizations, with interests ranging from traditional illicit trafficking to public contracts, licenses, and real estate deals, have created a wide range of opportunities to establish cooperative interactions with political actors. A complex system of exchange has developed, involving frequent interchanges between the Mafia and politicians, where the Mafia offers votes and protection for public contracts and impunity, with money also used to buy specific resources. A relevant resource at stake here is protection, services that both criminal and political actors may supply to the other. As the time horizon of their expected relationships expands, the resources exchanged expand to votes, electoral support, and political participation.

Money and financial support are not the only—often not even the most advantageous—means of exchange in this longer-term contractual perspective. Using this theoretical lens we uncover eight features of the interaction between politics and organized crime in Italy:

—Evidence of financial contributions to electoral campaigns from criminal groups is lacking, despite the huge amount of data that emerged from judicial inquiries.

—On the contrary, often money flows in the opposite direction, from politicians to mafiosi, as a reward for the "orderly functioning" and protection they secure in the market for votes.

—Political resources are more regularly used as a means of exchange; criminal organizations have in fact used their assets to guarantee electoral consent to politicians or to mediate clientelistic-electoral exchanges.

128. Carlucci (2010c).
129. Carlucci (2010a).
130. Del Porto (2009, p. 7).

—Symbiotic relationships exist at a national and regional level when both criminal and political actors are credible and long-lasting partners.

—Criminal organizations foster the ex-novo establishment of their own political structures only during very limited intervals of profound institutional crisis, abandoning them as soon as new, trustworthy counterparts appear on the political scene.

—An inclusive colonization of political structures is realized quite often at a local level, especially in medium-size and small municipalities in southern Italy, where the pressure of organized crime may result in a complete realignment of the administrative activities and the electoral process.

—Money flows toward political actors from less structured gangs usually through the intermediation of entrepreneurs trusted by the criminal syndicate.

—In these cases, however, the attributes of the money transfer resembles a circumscribed return in a corruption deal, not the wider-ranging transactions that occur when the counterparts are more authoritative criminal protectors.

The theoretical scheme presented in table 8-2 would require a wider amount of empirical evidence to be corroborated. We base our analysis on the Italian case, where criminal organizations are closer to the ideal type of protection firm. As a result, the data accommodate the symbiotic and replacement/colonization models. In several situations, especially in the south, criminal organizations control territory, which allows them to directly provide votes rather than the money to buy votes. In some cases a reciprocal relationship of protection develops between a centralized criminal organization and a party in power. In other cases, however, the criminal organization intervenes in elections, where competition is personalized rather than ideological, and Mafia support does not scandalize the public. Neither investigators nor regulatory electoral authorities have enough resources to intervene in these illegal exchanges.

We can assume that the symbiosis between politicians and organized crime is influenced by the type of market the organized criminal group is interested in. In the Italian case the involvement of organized crime in public contracts strengthens the relationship between the various Mafias (the Ndrangeta and the Camorra) and the politicians who control public contracts. The territorial dualism—that is, the historically rooted cleavages between the "modern" north and the "backward" south—allows the national parties to mask their political deals in the south as a necessary adaptation to southern culture and mentality.

References

Books and Articles

Arlacchi, P. 1992. *Gli uomini del disonore*. Milan: Mondadori.

Barbagallo, F. 1997. *Napoli fine novecento*. Torino: Einaudi.

Becker, G. S., and G. J. Stigler. 1974. "Law Enforcement, Malfeasance, and the Compensation of Enforcers." *Journal of Legal Studies* 3, no. 1: 1–18.

Benson, B. L. 1988. "Corruption in Law Enforcement: One Consequence of 'Tragedy of Commons' Arising with Public Allocation Processes." *International Review of Law and Economics* 8 (June): 73–84.

Bianchi, A. M., and A. Nerazzini. 2005. *La mafia è bianca*. Milan: Bur.

Block, A. 1983. *East Side, West Side: Organizing Crime in New York, 1930–1950*. New Brunswick, N.J.: Transaction.

Bolzoni, A. 1997. "Brusca all' attacco di Andreotti." *La Repubblica*, April 15, p. 19.

Buscetta, T. 1992. "Questione di rispetto." Interview by Enzo Biagi. *Mafia* (supplement of *Panorama*), October.

Carlucci, D. 2010a. "Milano, le inchieste triplicate in un anno. Così le cosche controllano l'hinterland." *La Repubblica*, sez. Milan, January 22 (http://milano.repubblica.it/dettaglio/milano-inchieste-triplicate-in-un-anno-cosi-le-cosche-controllano-lhinterland/1836600).

———. 2010b. "Ndrangheta e corruzione, arrestati politici di Pd e Pdl a Trezzano sul Naviglio." *La Repubblica*, sez. Milan, February 22 (http://milano.repubblica.it/cronaca/2010/02/22/news/_ndrangheta_e_corruzione_arrestati_politici_di_pd_e_pdl_a_trezzano_sul_naviglio-2613579/).

———. 2010c. "Il lobbista della ndrangheta e i politici: 'Le mie cene pagate agli assessori Pdl.'" *La Repubblica*, sez. Milan, March 10 (http://milano.repubblica.it/cronaca/2010/03/10/news/il_lobbista_della_ndrangheta_e_i_politici_le_mie_cene_pagate_agli_assessori_pdl_-2613516/).

Casas-Zamora, K. 2010. "Dirty Money. How to Break the Link between Organized Crime and Politics." *Americas Quarterly* (Spring) (www.americasquarterly.org/casas-zamora).

Ciconte, E. 1994. "Ludovico Ligato." In *Cirillo, Ligato e Lima. Tre storie di mafia e politica*, edited by N. Tranfaglia. Bari-Roma: Liguori.

Del Porto, D. 2009. "Le mani dei casalesi su bingo e scommesse." *La Repubblica*, sez. Naples, April 28, p. 7.

Della Porta, D., and A. Vannucci. 1994. *Corruzione politica e amministrazione pubblica*. Bologne: Il Mulino.

———. 1999. *Corrupt Exchanges*. New York: Aldine de Gruyter.

———. 2000. "Corruption and Political Financing in Italy." Paper prepared for Transparency International workshop, Prohibiting Bribe Payments to Foreign Political Parties. Florence, October.

———. 2005a. "The Governance Mechanisms of Corrupt Transactions." In *The New Institutional Economics of Corruption*, edited by J. Lambsdorff, M. Taube, and M. Schramm. London: Routledge.

———. 2005b. "The Moral (and Immoral) Costs of Corruption." In *Dimensionen politischer Korruption*, edited by U. von Alemann. Wiesbaden: Vs.

———. 2006. *La politica locale*. Bologne: Il Mulino.

———. 2007. *Mani impunite*. Roma-Bari: Laterza.

———. 2012. *The Hidden Order of Corruption. An Institutional Approach*. Farnham, UK: Ashgate.

Falcone, G., with M. Padovani. 1991. *Cose di Cosa Nostra*. Milan: Rizzoli.

Foschini, G., and C. Sannino. 2010. "Sud e liste 'inquinate.' Le mafie si preparano al voto." *La Repubblica*, March 19 (www.repubblica.it/politica/2010/03/19/news/mafia_regionali-2753846/).

Gambetta, D. 1992. *La mafia siciliana*. Turin: Einaudi.

———. 1993. *The Sicilian Mafia*. Harvard University Press.

Lucarelli, O. 2006. "Allarme di Bassolino sul voto." *La Repubblica*, sez. Naples, May 14, p. 2.

Maltz, D. M. 1985. "Toward Defining Organized Crime." In *The Politics and Economics of Organized Crime*, edited by H. E. Alexander and G. E. Caiden. Lexington, Mass.: Lexington Books.

Mete, V. 2009. *Fuori dal comune. Lo scioglimento delle amministrazioni locali per infiltrazioni mafiose*. Acireale: Bonanno.

Moe, T. M. 1990. "Political Institutions: The Neglected Side of the Story." *Journal of Law, Economics, and Organization* 6 (special issue): 213–53.

Morlino, L., ed. 1991. *Costruire la democrazia. Gruppi e partiti in Italia*. Bologne: Il Mulino.

Oliva, E., and S. Palazzolo. 2006. *Bernardo Provenzano. Il ragioniere di Cosa nostra*. Rubbettino: Soveria Mannelli.

Palazzolo, S. 2003a. "Il pentito Antonino Giuffré: 'Dell'Utri vicino a Cosa nostra.'" *La Repubblica*, January 7 (www.repubblica.it/online/cronaca/giuffretre/dellutri/dellutri.html?ref=search).

———. 2003b. "Provenzano aveva il suo candidato." *La Repubblica*, sez. Palermo, November 20, p. 6.

Paoli, L. 2004. "Organised Crime in Italy: Mafia and Illegal Markets—Exceptions and Normality." In *Organised Crime in Europe*, edited by C. Fijnaut and L. Paoli. Dordrecht: Springer.

Pierson, P. 2004. *Politics in Time*. Princeton University Press.

Pizzorno, A. 1993. *Le radici della politica assoluta*. Milan: Feltrinelli.

———. 1996. "Vecchio e nuovo nella transizione italiana." In *Il paese dei paradossi*, edited by N. Negri and L. Sciolla. Rome: La Nuova Italia Scientifica.

Pinto-Duschinsky, M. 2002. "Financing Politics: A Global View." *Journal of Democracy* 13, no. 4: 69–86.

Pujas, V., and M. Rhodes. 1998. "Party Finance and Political Scandal in Latin Europe." Working Paper RSC 98/10. European University Institute.
Reuter, P. 1983. *Disorganized Crime: The Economics of the Visible Hand*. MIT Press.
Sberna, S. 2011. "La criminalità organizzata e la politica locale. Attori, risorse e interazioni." Ph.D. dissertation, Istituto Italiano di Scienze Umane.
Schelling, T. 1967. "Economics and Criminal Enterprise." *Public Interest* 7: 61–78.
———. 1984. "What Is the Business of Organized Crime? In *Choice and Consequence*, edited by T. Schelling. Harvard University Press.
Vannucci, A. 1997. *Il mercato della corruzione*. Milan: Società aperta.
Williams P. 2001. "Organizing Transnational Crime: Networks, Markets and Hierarchies." In *Combating Transnational Crime: Concepts, Activities, and Responses*, edited by P. Williams and D. Vlassis. London: Frank Cass.

Judiciary and Parliamentary Sources

APN. Richiesta di autorizzazione a procedere. April 7, 1993. Supplement, *La Repubblica*, April 15, 1993.
CCSA. Suprema Corte di Cassazione. Sezione Seconda Penale, sentenza n. 49691/2004, December 28, 2004.
CD. Chamber of Deputies. "Domanda di autorizzazione a procedere in giudizio." XI legislatura, doc. IV.
CPAAC. Commissione parlamentare antimafia. Audizione del collaboratore di giustizia Antonino Calderone, Presidente Luciano Violante, seduta 11, XI legislatura.
CPAGM. Commissione parlamentare antimafia. Audizione del collaboratore di giustizia Gaspare Mutolo, Presidente Luciano Violante, seduta 25, XI legislatura.
CPALM. Commissione parlamentare antimafia. Audizione del collaboratore di giustizia Leonardo Messina, Presidente Luciano Violante, seduta 15, XI legislatura.
CPAM-IVX-II. Commissione parlamentare d'inchiesta sul fenomeno della criminalità mafiosa o similare (2006). *Relazione conclusiva*, doc XIII, n. 16, tomo II. Communicated to president on January 19.
CPAPG. Commissione parlamentare antimafia. Audizioni del collaboratore di giustizia Pasquale Galasso, Presidente Luciano Violante, sedute 51 e 61, XI legislatura.
CPASA. Commissione parlamentare antimafia. Audizione del collaboratore di giustizia Salvatore Annacondia, Presidente Luciano Violante, seduta 56, XI legislatura.
CPATB. Commissione parlamentare antimafia. Audizione del collaboratore di giustizia Tommaso Buscetta, Presidente Luciano Violante, seduta 12, XI legislatura.
CPMF. Commissione parlamentare d'inchiesta sul fenomeno del la mafia. *Relazione finale su mafia e politica*, approved April 6, 1993. Supplement, *La Repubblica*, April 10, 1993.
DAP. Public prosecutor at the Court of Palermo. Domanda di autorizzazione a procedere contro il senatore Giulio Andreotti, March 27, 1993. *Panorama*, April 11, 1993.
TCBD. Tribunale di Caltanissetta. Decreto di archiviazione nei confronti di Berlusconi Silvio e Dell'Utri Marcello, n. 1370/98 R.G.N.R., n. 908/99 R.G.I.P., 3 maggio 2002.

TNM. *Tangentopoli. Le carte che scottano.* Supplement, *Panorama*, February 1993.

TPAA. Tribunale di Palermo. Sentence in the trial against Andreotti Giulio. Appeals Court, May 2, 2003.

TPAN. Tribunale di Palermo. Sentence in the trial against Andreotti Giulio, October 23, 1999.

TPDC. Tribunale di Palermo. Sentenza di primo grado contro Dell'Utri Marcello e Cinà Gaetano, December 11, 2004.

TPIS. Doc. nr 7 / Atti irripetibili / Interrogatory of Antonino Salvo, July 3, 1984 (www.ecorav.it/arci/approfondimenti/scheda6/scheda6.htm).

TPMP. Note of the public prosecutor in the judicial proceeding, n. 3538/94 R.G.N.R. against Andreotti Giulio. *La vera storia d'Italia*. Naples: Tullio Pironti, 1995.

TPUS 1996. Tribunale di Palermo. Udienza, June 20 (www.ecorav.it/arci/approfondimenti/scheda6/scheda6.htm).

TPUS 1998. Sentenza di primo grado contro Riina Salvatore et alii, n. 12/98, July 15.

TRCOS. Tribunale di Reggio Calabria, 2008. Excerpts from Ordinanza "Onorata Società," gennaio, I-V (www.repubblica.it/2008/01/sezioni/cronaca/arresti-ndrangheta/indice-intercettazioni/ indice-intercettazioni.html).

TRNOC. Tribunale di Napoli. Ordinanza cautelare contro Casentino Nicola, November 7, 2009, n. 36856/01 R.G.N.R., n. 74678/02 R.G.GIP.

TRP. Court of Palermo, SC n. 411/90/R.G., January 17, 1992.

Contributors

KEVIN CASAS-ZAMORA
Secretary for political affairs, Organization of American States

LEONARDO CURZIO
Senior researcher, Centro de Investigaciones Sobre América del Norte, Universidad Nacional Autónoma de México (CISAN UNAM)
Visiting professor, Centro de Investigación y Docencia Económicas (CIDE)

DONATELLA DELLA PORTA
Professor of sociology, Department of Political and Social Sciences, European University Institute

DELIA M. FERREIRA RUBIO
Independent consultant
Board of directors member, Transparency International

MAURICIO RUBIO PARDO
Professor, Universidad Externado de Colombia

DANIEL SMILOV
Associate professor, Political Science Department, University of Sofia
Program director, Centre for Liberal Strategies

BRUNO WILHELM SPECK
Professor of political science, Universidade Estadual de Campinas (UNICAMP)

ALBERTO VANNUCCI
Associate professor, Political Science Department, Università di Pisa

Index

Accountability: Brazil, 70, 72–73; and state capture, 24. *See also* Auditing; Disclosure requirements
Acuerdos de la Uribe (Colombia), 92
Alem, Ricardo, 118–19, 127
Alianza Democrática M-19 (Colombia), 77–78
Almaraz, Miguel Ángel, 152
Alternativa Popular (Colombia), 76
Alves Filho, Garibaldi, 64
Amphetamines, 34–35
Andrade, Castor de, 61
Andreotti, Giulio, 216, 220, 221–22, 223
Angelov, Slavi, 171
Annacondia, Salvatore, 213
Anonymous donations: Argentina, 25, 26, 32, 33; Brazil, 52; Bulgaria, 182, 186; Costa Rica, 112, 125
Anti Mafia Commission (Italy), 206, 240
Araya, Rolando, 117, 122
Arbitrariness in decisionmaking process, 37–38, 200
ARENA (National Renewal Alliance Party, Brazil), 47
Argentina, 12, 14–15, 22–41; campaign finance rules in, 5–6; political finance regulations in, 25–31; presidential campaign (1999), 31–33, 36–37; presidential campaign (2007), 33–37; recommendations, 37–39; state capture and organized crime in, 24

Arias, Oscar, 118, 119, 121
Astorga, Luis, 144, 154
Ataka Party (Bulgaria), 169
Atanasov, Atanas, 189
Auditing: Argentina, 25–26, 27, 33, 38; Brazil, 68, 70; Bulgaria, 184–85; Costa Rica, 110, 131; Mexico, 143, 144, 155, 158
Auxilios parlamentarios (Colombia), 78

Badalamenti, Gaetano, 216, 222
Bagarella, Leoluca, 226, 227
Banco de los Trabajadores, 84
Bank secrecy, 39, 122, 143
Barco, Virgilio, 93
Basic Statute of Political Parties and Movements of 1994 (Colombia), 78
Batkov, Todor, 192
Bavaria (company), 100
Beltrán Leyva cartel, 151
Beltrones, Manlio Fabio, 141
Bergonzoli, Nicolas, 97
Berlusconi, Silvio, 227–28
Bernal, Alejandro, 96
Betancur, Belisario, 77, 82–83, 89, 91–92
Bicheiros (Brazil), 62
Bingo, legalization of, 63, 64
Biscaia, Antonio, 61–62
Blizt Committee (Colombia), 97
Block, A., 207
Bloque de Búsqueda (Colombia), 94
Bolivia, drug trafficking in, 46–47

250 Index

Bond issuance for campaign finance, 112
Bonev, Bogomil, 189
Bontate, Stefano, 216, 222
Borissov, Boiko, 169, 176
Botero, Catalina, 158
Bozhkov, Vasil, 173, 174
Brazil, 12, 15, 42–75; accountability of political institutions, 72–73; benefits to candidates and elected officials from organized crime, 52–53; campaign costs, 5; campaign finance rules, 49–52, 70–71; cocaine trafficking in, 46–47; damage control for organized crime by elected officials, 58–60; deal brokering by elected officials, 60–61; elected officials' benefits to organized crime, 53–61; influence peddling by elected officials, 54–55; *jogo do bicho*, 45–46; law enforcement, 54–55, 71; lawmaking influence of organized crime, 55–56, 61–65; moral decay of politicians in, 67–68; policymaking influence of organized crime, 55–56, 61–65; political candidates from organized crime, 68–70; political financing in, 47–52; politicians' immunity to investigation, 55, 57, 72; protection of illicit businesses by elected officials, 57–61; recommendations, 70–73; state capture, 57, 65–70
Brazilian Bar Association, 67
Brazilian Democratic Movement (MDB), 47
Bribery: Argentina, 24; Brazil, 44, 52, 53, 60–61, 66; Bulgaria, 174; Colombia, 78, 90, 93, 102; Italy, 197, 209–10, 220, 237; of local officials, 6; Mexico, 139, 148; as organized crime, 1–2
Broad Progressive Front (FAP, Mexico), 150
Brusca, Giovanni, 218, 222, 223
Bulgaria, 12, 16–17, 165–94; campaign finance rules, 179–85; causes and origins of organized crime in, 174–76; political context for, 168–74; political finance and organized crime, 176–79, 185–87; public funding, 183–84; recommendations, 187–90; transparency in, 184–85
Bulgaria Air, 192
Bulgarian Socialist Party (BSP), 168, 169, 182, 186
Buratti, Rogério, 64
Buscaglia, Edgardo, 146
Buscaglia-González scale, 147
Buscetta, Tommaso, 202, 205, 211, 214, 222

Cachoeira, Carlinhos, 64
Caicedo Velandia, Agustin, 86
Caixa Economica Federal (Brazil), 64
Calderón, Felipe, 136, 154
Calderone, Antonino, 212, 229
Calderón-Fournier, Rafael Angel, 117, 119, 121, 128
Cali cartel, 84–85, 88, 89–90, 94, 95
Camarena, Enrique, 144
Camorra (Italy), 199, 208, 212, 234, 235
Campaign contributions: anonymous, 25, 26, 32, 33, 52, 112, 125, 182, 186; foreign, 39, 110, 115, 116, 119–21, 128, 132, 140, 182; private, 6–7, 16, 24–27, 34, 49–52, 77, 79–80, 102, 109, 110–15, 120–21, 123–26, 140, 156, 181–82, 185, 199. *See also* Public funding
Campaign duration limits, 27, 28, 38–39
Campaign finance rules: Argentina, 25–31; Brazil, 49–52, 70–71; Bulgaria, 179–85; Colombia, 76–80; Costa Rica, 108–15, 122–30; enforcement of, 5–6; Italy, 197–201; Mexico, 137–44; research needs for, 9. *See also* Campaign contributions; Regulatory framework
Candido, Rachel, 69
Cannella, Tullio, 226
Capaccioli, Héctor, 34, 35
Capobastone (Italy), 201
Carrillo Fuentes, Amado, 31, 153

Index   251

Cartel de los sapos (Colombia), 87
Casas-Zamora, Kevin, 1, 15, 107
Casey, Lionel James, 118
Castaño, Carlos, 96, 97–98
Castrillón Henao, José, 7
CCB Group Assets Management, 192
Center for Liberal Strategies, 171
Center for the Study of Democracy, 171
Central Cooperative Bank, 192
Central Intelligence Agency (CIA, U.S.), 94, 96
César Farias, Paulo, 49
César Godoy, Julio, 151
Chimimport, 192
Chinchilla, Laura, 128
Chobanov, Ivan, 189
Chorney, Michael, 188–90
Christian Democratic Party (Italy), 207–08, 215, 219, 220, 224, 226
CIA (Central Intelligence Agency, U.S.), 94, 96
Ciancimino, Vito, 211
Cigarette smuggling, 88
CISEN (National security agency, Mexico), 156
Citizen Action Party (PAC, Costa Rica), 114, 122, 124–25, 129
Citizens for European Development of Bulgaria (GERB), 169
Ciudad Juárez cartel, 153
Civil society: Brazil, 51, 69–70; Bulgaria, 171; Costa Rica, 130; Mexico, 138; oversight role of, 11–12
Claudio de Oliveira, Luiz, 69
Clientelism, 88–89, 141, 201
Cocaine trafficking: Argentina, 34; Brazil, 46–47; Latin America, 4
Collective incentives, 139
Collor de Mello, Fernando, 49
Colombia, 12, 15, 76–106; Cali cartel, 84–85; campaign finance rules, 76–80; decentralization in, 6; drug trafficking in, 46–47; lessons from, 99–102;

Medellin cartel, 81–84; Millennium Operation (1999), 96; narco-traffickers' distrust of politicians, 89–90; *neocapos*, 85–87; organized crime history in, 90–99; Pacto de Ralito, 98–99; Pacto de Recoletos, 95–96; Panama Summit (1984), 93–94; Panama Summit (1999), 96–98; party system in, 6; *pepes* attacks (1993), 94–95; political finance and organized crime in, 3, 10; politicians in, 87–90; recommendations, 102–05; smuggling and clientelism in, 88–89; Tranquilandia raid (1984), 92–93
Committee for the Re-Election of the President (CREEP, U.S.), 9
Competitiveness of elections: Colombia, 91; Italy, 198, 204, 211–12; Mexico, 139–40, 152; and political finance, 4–5
Constitution (Brazil), 57, 63
Constitution (Costa Rica), 109
Constitution (Mexico), 143
Constitutional Court (Costa Rica), 122
Constitutional Reform Convention (Argentina), 25
Contract killings, 172–73
Corporatism, 68, 138, 140
Corral, Canicoba, 31
Correa, Rafael, 6
Corruption: Argentina, 23; Brazil, 43, 56; Bulgaria, 171, 176; Costa Rica, 128; Italy, 201, 207, 209–10, 239; social tolerance for, 24, 137, 177
Cosa Nostra (Italy): and Christian Democratic Party, 216, 223, 224; electoral influence of, 206, 207–08, 212–13; and Forza Italia, 227–29; local government influence of, 234; and Movimento Indipendentista Siciliano, 226; territorial control by, 198–99
Costa Rica, 12, 15–16, 107–35; campaign finance rules in, 108–15, 122–30; political finance and organized crime in, 3, 115–23; recommendations, 131–33

Council of the Judiciary (Argentina), 38
Counterfeiting, 173
Craxi, Bettino, 197
Creel, Santiago, 141
CREEP (Committee for the Re-Election of the President, U.S.), 9
Cronyism, 142
Cuba, Colombian drug trafficking connections in, 104
Cucuzza, Salvatore, 224
Cuffaro, Totò, 231
Curzio, Leonardo, 16, 136
CV (Comando Vermelho, Brazil), 42, 47
Cybercrime, 23

Damage control for organized crime by elected officials, 58–60
DEA. *See* Drug Enforcement Agency (U.S.)
Deal brokering by elected officials, 60–61
Decentralization: Costa Rica, 129; Italy, 233; Mexico, 138, 142; and political finance, 6; and state capture, 24
Della Porta, Donatella, 17, 195
Del Valle Alonso, Boris, 150
Democratic Revolutionary Party (PRD, Panama), 119
Democrazia Cristiana (Italy), 17
Devolution of powers, 6
Di Maggio, Baldassare, 207, 216
Diniz, Waldomiro, 64
Direct elections, 47
Disclosure requirements: Argentina, 25–26, 27, 32–33, 37, 38–39; Brazil, 50–51, 70; Italy, 197, 201, 235
Dogan, Ahmed, 173
Don Berna (Adolfo Paz), 94
Donchev, Sasho, 174
Double bookkeeping, 138, 139
DPS (Movement for Rights and Freedoms, Bulgaria), 169
Dreyfus, P., 23
Drogas La Rebaja (drugstore chain), 84, 85
Drug Enforcement Agency (DEA, U.S.), 86, 92, 94, 97, 116, 126

Drug trafficking: Argentina, 34; Brazil, 46–47; Bulgaria, 173; Colombia, 76; Costa Rica, 108; distrust of politicians, 89–90; Latin America, 2–3, 4; Mexico, 146–47; transnational nature of, 104. *See also specific drugs*
Ducler, Aldo, 31, 32
Duhalde, Eduardo, 26, 32, 33, 138
Duncan, Gustavo, 102

Ecuador, party system in, 6
Egalitarian political finance model, 181
EHG Enterprises, 115
Elections: Argentina's 1999 presidential campaign, 31–33, 36–37; Argentina's 2007 presidential campaign, 33–37; Brazil, 47–48; competitiveness of, 4–5; Costa Rica, 110; direct vs. indirect, 47–48; Italy, 210–25
Electoral Court (Brazil), 70
Electoral Court (Colombia), 77
El Greg (Gregorio Sánchez Martínez), 150, 162
Elizalde, Manuel, 116–17, 125
Embezzlement, 66–67, 68
Ephedrine trafficking, 33–37
Escobar, Pablo, 3, 7, 76, 78, 81–84, 88, 89, 94–95, 104
Escuderie LeCoque (organization), 67
Espírito Santo (Brazil), 65, 66
Estrada, Federico, 89
European Union, 165, 167, 168, 170, 179
Extortion, 23, 42, 52
Extradition, 89, 98, 101, 116, 120, 150

Failed States Index, 147
Falcone, Giovanni, 202, 223
FAP (Broad Progressive Front, Mexico), 150
FARC (Fuerzas Armadas Revolucionarias de Colombia, Colombia), 92, 100
Fasino, Mario, 219, 220
Federal Code of Electoral Institutions and Procedures (Mexico), 140
Federal Institute of Elections (IFE, Mexico), 141

Ferreira Rubio, Delia M., 14, 22
Ficha limpa requirement (Brazil), 72
Figueres, José, 115–16
Fionna, Roberto, 117–18
Forbes on wealth of drug kingpins in Mexico, 137
Foreign campaign contributions: Argentina, 39; Bulgaria, 182; Costa Rica, 110, 115–16, 119–21, 128, 132; Mexico, 140
Forero Fetecua, Rafael, 84
Foro privilegiado (Brazil), 57, 72
Fortunati, José, 63
Forza, Sebastian, 35
Forza Italia (Italy), 227–28, 229
Fox, Vicente, 143
Franco, Moreira, 62
Frente para la Victoria (FPV, Argentina), 33, 34, 37
Friends of Fox (Mexico), 143
Fuerzas Armadas Revolucionarias de Colombia (FARC, Colombia), 92, 100
Fundación Prensa y Democracia (Mexico), 160
Fundación Sudamericana, 32
Fund for Peace, 147

Gacha, Rodriguez, 96
Galan, Luis Carlos, 83, 90, 92, 93
Galasso, Pasquale, 212, 214–15, 224–25, 230, 231, 235, 238
Gambling, 45–46, 62–63, 64
Garotinho, Antony, 64
Gava, Antonio, 231
Gaviria, Cesar, 93, 94
Gaviria, Gustavo, 81, 91
Gaviria, Hernando, 91
Gaviria, Roberto, 81–82
Georgiev, Ivo Kamenov, 191
GERB (Citizens for European Development of Bulgaria), 169
Germany, political finance in, 181
Giuffrè, Antonino, 216, 217, 228
Giuliano, Salvatore, 226
Gleny, Misha, 166, 171, 188

Global coordination to combat organized crime, 104–05
Gomez, Alfredo, 81
Gómez, Hernando, 97
Gómez, Servando (La Tuta), 151
Gonzalez, Felipe, 83
González Ruiz, Samuel, 146
Gratz, José Carlos, 65, 66–67
Guajardo, Mario, 152
Guardia, Fernán, 127
Guerrilleros (Colombia), 76, 77
Gulf cartel, 152
Gutiérrez Rebollo, José de Jesús, 153, 154
Guttadauro, Giuseppe, 231
Guzmán, Joaquín "El Chapo," 137, 145

Habeas corpus, 60
Haiti, Colombian drug trafficking connections in, 104
Hancock, John, 2
Hancock, Thomas, 2
Hank-González, Carlos, 121–22
Hartung, Paulo, 67
Heard, Alexander, 2
Hemus Air, 192
Hendrix, Joaquín, 149
Hermilda, Doña, 82
Hermoso, Valle, 152

IFE (Federal Institute of Elections, Mexico), 141
Ignacio Ferreira, José, 68
Indirect elections, 47
Instituto de Estudios Liberales (Colombia), 92
International Overseas Services, Ltd., 116
Italy, 12, 17, 195–245; campaign finance rules, 197–201; political candidates from organized crime, 225–37; political finance and organized crime in, 8, 202–10; political gatekeeping in, 237–40; recommendations, 240–41; symbiotic relationship between organized crime and political actors, 210–25

Index

Jamaica, territorial control by organized crime in, 8
Jimenez, Alvaro, 89
Jiménez Gomez, Carlos, 93
Jogo do bicho (Brazil), 45–46, 62
Juarez cartel, 25, 31–33, 36–37, 138, 153
Judicial independence, 38
Justicialist Party (Argentina), 32

Karadzhov, Grozdan, 189
Kaulitz, Alfredo Cristalinas, 162–63
Kidnapping, 89, 100
Kirchner, Cristina Fernández de, 27, 33, 37
Kirchner, Néstor Carlos, 27
Kostov, Ivan, 183, 188–89
Krastev, Ivan, 167–68
Kyulev, Emil, 173, 174

Labastida, Francisco, 143
Landim, Francisco Pinheiro, 60, 61
Lara Bonilla, Rodrigo, 76–77, 83, 92, 93, 99
La Rue, Frank, 158
Latvia, corruption in, 171
Law and Justice Party (RZS, Bulgaria), 169
Law enforcement: Argentina, 24; Brazil, 42–43, 46, 52, 54–55, 71; Bulgaria, 171, 174–75; Colombia, 103; decentralization's impact on, 6; Italy, 200; Mexico, 146, 153; and state capture, 24; weakness in, 4
Lawmaking influence of organized crime: and arbitrariness in decisionmaking process, 37–38, 200; Brazil, 54, 55–56, 61–65; Italy, 205, 231
Law on Political Parties of 1990 (Bulgaria), 184
Law on Political Parties of 2005 (Bulgaria), 181–82
Lehder, Carlos, 82–83
Libertarian Movement Party (PML, Costa Rica), 124, 128
Libertarian political finance model, 181
Lider Party (Bulgaria), 169
Ligato, Ludovico, 232

Lima, Salvo, 211, 218, 221, 222, 223
Lineart printing house, 66
Lleras Camargo, Alberto, 76
Local governments and politicians: Brazil, 69–70; campaign costs in, 5; Costa Rica, 110, 130, 132–33; Italy, 225–26, 234; Mexico, 157–59, 162
López Michelsen, Alfonso, 83, 91, 93
López Obrador, Andrés Manuel, 150
Los Chamizos (Colombia), 87
Los Chemas (Colombia), 84
Los Cíclopes (Colombia), 86
Lujambio, Alonso, 143
Lukanov, Andrei, 172
Lukoil, 174
Lula da Silva, Luiz Inácio, 64, 158
Lupsha, Peter, 1, 145, 146

M-19 guerrilla group, 83, 88
Madrazo, Roberto, 156
Mainardi, Ivo, 63
Majoritarian representation systems, 179–80, 234
Maluf, Paulo, 49
Mancuso, Salvatore, 97–98
Mani pulite (clean hands) investigations, 195, 226
Mannoia, Marino, 216, 217
Manuel Castillo, Carlos, 118
"Marlboro war" (Colombia), 88
Marsala, Vincenzo, 215
Martelli, Claudio, 223
Martinelli, Ricardo, 5, 6
Mattarella, Piersanti, 216
Mauro, Max, 65
McAlpin, Clovis W., 115, 125
Medellin cartel, 81–84, 89, 94, 104
Medicine mafia, 33–37
Medina, Santiago, 95
Mejía, Marco Antonio, 150
Melo, Fernando, 117–18
Mendonça, Leonardo Dias, 60
Menem, Carlos Saúl, 27
Mercado Abierto (financial firm), 31

Mérida Initiative (Mexico), 157
Messina, Leonardo, 212
Messina, Sebastiano, 220
Mexico, 12, 16, 136–64; campaign costs in, 5; campaign finance rules, 137–44; Colombian drug trafficking connections in, 104; governmental response to organized crime, 154–57; local vs. federal political finance issues, 157–59; political finance and organized crime in, 3, 144–59; Quintana Roo and Tamaulipas situation, 149–54; recommendations, 159–63; regional context for, 137–44
Millennium Operation (Colombia, 1999), 96, 99
Mitev, Marin Velikov, 191
Mitev, Tihomir Ivanov, 191
Mollinedo, Nicolás, 150
Money laundering: Argentina, 37, 38; Brazil, 47, 64; Bulgaria, 173; Mexico, 146
Moura, Nobel, 69
Movement for Rights and Freedoms (DPS, Bulgaria), 169
Movimento Indipendentista Siciliano (Italy), 226
Multiparty systems, 48
Mutolo, Gaspare, 216, 221, 223, 232

Naím, Moisés, 138
Narcomicos, 102
Narco-terrorism, 157
National Drug Intelligence Center (U.S.), 121
National Electoral Council (NEC, Colombia), 77, 79, 80
National Institute to Fight Drug Trafficking, 153
National Liberation Party (PLN, Costa Rica), 107,112, 114, 115, 116, 117, 118, 119, 121, 122, 123, 124, 125, 126, 127–28, 129
National Movement for Stability and Progress (NDSV, Bulgaria), 169

National Registration for Chemical Precursors (Argentina), 37
National Renewal Alliance Party (ARENA, Brazil), 47
National Service for Combating Organized Crime (Bulgaria), 173
NATO. *See* North Atlantic Treaty Organization
Nava, César, 3
Navarrete, Carlos, 141
Ndrangheta (Italy), 199, 206, 208, 234, 239
NDSV (National Movement for Stability and Progress, Bulgaria), 169
NEC. *See* National Electoral Council (Colombia)
Neocapos (Colombia), 85–87, 98
Nestorov, Miroslav Petrov, 191
Newton Financial Management BG, 192
Nicaragua, Colombian drug trafficking connections in, 104
Nikolov, Mario, 177
Nikolov, Nikolai Bozhidarov, 191
Nikolov, Yovo, 171
Nixon, Richard, 9
NL (Nuevo Liberalismo, Colombia), 76, 83
Nogeira, André, 66
Nogeira, Cezar, 66
Nogeira, Flavio, 66
Noriega, Manuel Antonio, 16, 93, 119
North Atlantic Treaty Organization (NATO), 168, 179, 189
Nuevo Liberalismo (NL, Colombia), 76, 83

Ocampo, Santiago, 88
Ocean Hunter (company), 118
Ochoa, Fabio, 96
Ochoa, Jorge Luis, 85, 91
O'Donnell, María, 34
Oduber, Daniel, 116–17
Office for Electoral Offenses (Mexico), 158, 159
Oppenheimer, Andres, 32
Opposition candidates, 4–5

Order, Law, and Justice Party (Bulgaria), 176
Organization of American States, 158
Organized crime: benefits to candidates and elected officials, 52–53; defined, 22–23, 166–67; economics perspective of, 43; "industries" of, 23; Latin America, 2–7; law enforcement perspective of, 42–43; political candidates from, 68–70, 225–37; political finance connections of, 1–21; social science perspective of, 43. *See also specific countries*
Orlando, Leoluca, 160
Ortega, Jairo, 83
Ortega, Jesús, 151, 152
Ortega, Palito, 31, 32
Ortiz Group, 64
Overgas, 174

PAC. *See* Citizen Action Party (Costa Rica)
Pacheco, Abel, 122
Pacific Co. Ltd., 122
PAN (Partido de Acción Nacional, Mexico), 3, 140, 151, 152, 155
Panama: campaign costs in, 5; Colombian drug trafficking connections in, 104; party system in, 6
Panama Summit (Colombia, 1984), 93–94
Panama Summit (Colombia, 1999), 96–98
Panebianco, Angelo, 139
Parra, Guido, 82, 94
Partido de Acción Nacional (PAN, Mexico), 3, 138, 151, 152, 155
Partido de la Revolución Democrática (PRD, Mexico) 140, 149, 151, 152, 155, 156, 162
Partido Revolucionario Institucional (PRI, Mexico), 140, 149, 151, 152, 155, 156, 162
Parvanov, Georgi, 177
Pascoal, Hildebrando, 59
Patronage system, 162
Pau-Brasil scandal (Brazil), 49
Pavlov, Iliya, 172, 173, 174, 191
Paz, Adolfo (Don Berna), 94

PCC (Primeiro Comando da Capital, Brazil), 42, 47
Pepes (*perseguidos por Pablo Escobar*), 94–95
Perafan, Pastor, 90
Pérez Balladares, Ernesto, 3, 7
Perseguidos por Pablo Escobar (*pepes*), 94–95
Peru, drug trafficking in, 46–47
Petróleos Mexicanos (PEMEX), 143
Petrov, Alexey, 175, 176
Pires, Olavo, 68–69
Pizarro, Eduardo, 76
Pizzorno, A., 220
Plato o plomo (buck or bullet), 7
PLN (National Liberation Party, Costa Rica), 107, 112, 114, 115, 116, 117, 118, 119, 121, 122, 123, 124, 125, 126, 127–28, 129
PML (Libertarian Movement Party, Costa Rica), 124, 128
Poder Ciudadano (Argentina), 27, 32
Poland, corruption in, 171
Policymaking influence of organized crime: and arbitrariness in decision-making process, 37–38, 200; Brazil, 54, 55–56, 61–65; Italy, 205, 231
Political finance: Brazil, 47–52; and competitiveness of elections, 4–5; and decentralization, 6; enforcement of rules for, 5–6; Latin America, 2–7; organized crime's connection to, 1–21; and party systems, 6–7; research needs, 9–11
Political gatekeeping, 237–40
Political parties: Argentina, 31–37; Brazil, 47–51; Bulgaria, 167, 168–70, 181–82; Colombia, 76, 77, 79; Costa Rica, 109–15; Italy, 196–97; Mexico, 139; subsidies for, 110; weakness of systems, 6–7. *See also specific parties*
Ponce, Juan, 32
Populism, 87
Pork barrel projects, 78, 138
Porras, Evaristo, 83

Posados Ocampo, Juan Jesús, 145
PRD (Partido de la Revolución Democrática, Mexico), 140, 149, 151, 152, 155, 156, 162
PRD (Democratic Revolutionary Party, Panama), 119
Presidential elections: Brazil, 48; Colombia, 79–80; competitiveness of, 4–5; Costa Rica, 108, 110, 111
Press and Democracy Foundation (Mexico), 160
PRI (Partido Revolucionario Institucional, Mexico), 140, 149, 151, 152, 155, 156, 162
Mexico), 139–40, 149
PRI (Revolutionary Institutional Party, Costa Rica), 121
Prison system, 56
Private contributions: Argentina, 25, 26, 27, 34; Brazil, 49, 50, 51, 52; Bulgaria, 181, 182, 185; and campaign finance rules, 24; Colombia, 77, 79–80, 102; Costa Rica, 109, 110, 112, 114–15, 120–21, 123–26; Italy, 199; Mexico, 140, 156; Panama, 16; and party systems, 6–7
Proceso 8000 (Colombia), 95, 98–99, 100–01
Prohibition era (U.S.), 43
Proportional representation systems, 179–80, 181
Protection of illicit businesses by elected officials, 57–61
Provenzano, Bernardo, 217
PSD (Social Democratic Party, Mexico), 156
Public funding: Argentina, 25, 28; Brazil, 50; Bulgaria, 183–84; Colombia, 78, 79; Costa Rica, 108–09, 109, 110, 123, 130
Public opinion: Bulgaria, 165; Colombia, 103–04; Italy, 199; Mexico, 162
Pulvirenti, Giuseppe, 236
Purvanov, Georgi, 173
PUSC (Social Christian Unity Party, Costa Rica), 112, 122

Quintana Roo (Mexico), 148, 149–54

Rabelo, Abidiel, 58–59
Rabelo, Jabes, 58, 59, 69
Radio airtime, 50
Ralito Pact (Colombia), 97–99
Recoletos Pact (Colombia), 95–96
Recommendations: Argentina, 37–39; Brazil, 70–73; Bulgaria, 187–90; Colombia, 102–05; Costa Rica, 131–33; Italy, 240–41; Mexico, 159–63
Regional narcocracies, 147–48
Regulatory framework: Argentina, 25–31, 37; Brazil, 49–52, 70–71; Bulgaria, 179–85; Costa Rica, 108–15, 122–30; Mexico, 158; research needs for, 9. *See also* Campaign finance rules
Reno, Janet, 97
Resocialization program for drug traffickers, 97
Revolutionary Institutional Party (PRI, Costa Rica), 121
Riina, Salvatore, 206–07, 217
Riina, Totò, 223
RiskMonitor, 171
Rodríguez, Miguel Angel, 121–22, 128
Rodriguez Orejuela, Gilberto, 81, 84–85, 90, 95, 100–01
Rodriguez Orejuela, Miguel, 84, 85, 95, 100–01
Rodriguez Orejuela, William, 86
Romania, corruption in, 171
Rua, Fernando de la, 31
Rubin, Lloyd S., 117, 125
Rubio, Mauricio, 15, 76
Rule of law, 8

SABMiller, 100
Sacra Corona Unita (Italy), 199, 208, 213, 234
Salinas de Gortari, Carlos, 145
Salvo, Antonino "Nino," 219, 222
Salvo, Ignazio, 219, 222, 223
Samper Pizano, Ernesto, 3, 10, 79, 88, 90, 91, 92, 95

Sánchez Martínez, Gregorio (El Greg), 150, 162
SANS (State Agency for National Security, Bulgaria), 175
Santander, Steven, 150
Santo Domingo Group, 100
Santofimio Botero, Alberto, 82, 83, 91, 92, 93
SAO (State Audit Office, Bulgaria), 184–85
Sapio (foundation), 183
Saxe-Coburg Gotha, Simeon, 173
Schiavone, Carmine, 221
Selective incentives, 139
Self-funding of campaigns, 53, 61, 71
Servini de Cubria, Maria, 32, 35
Sicilia Libera Party (Italy), 227
Siino, Angelo, 236
60 Minutes report on Turbay's link to drug trafficking, 91
Smilov, Daniel, 16–17, 165
Smuggling, 88–89. *See also* Drug trafficking
Social Christian Unity Party (PUSC, Costa Rica), 112, 122
Social Democratic Party (PSD, Mexico), 156
Socialist Party (Italy), 217
Sociedad Agrícola Industrial San Cristóbal S.A., 116
Software piracy, 42
Sola, Morales, 34
Souza, Carlos, 69
Souza, Fausto, 69
Souza, Wallace, 69
Speck, Bruno Wilhelm, 5, 15, 42
Sport lotteries, 62
Standing Group on Organized Crime, 171
State Agency for National Security (SANS, Bulgaria), 175
State Audit Office (SAO, Bulgaria), 184–85
State capture: Argentina, 24; Brazil, 57, 65–70; Bulgaria, 167, 177; Italy, 233; threat from, 8
Stoyanov, Petar, 189
Stoykov, Ludmil, 177

Subnational governments. *See* Local governments and politicians
Sunshine Co. Ltd., 122
Supreme Elections Tribunal (TSE, Costa Rica), 110, 128
Symbiotic relationship between organized crime and political actors: Brazil, 44, 53; Colombia, 80; Italy, 205, 207, 208, 210–25, 221, 241; Mexico, 145–46, 158

Tamaulipas (Mexico), 3–4, 148, 149–54
Tarazá Without Hunger program (Colombia), 87
Tax secrecy provisions, 39
Television advertisements and airtime, 5, 50, 132
Tello Quiñones, General, 150
Teresi, Mimmo, 216
TIM (organized crime group), 174, 191–92
Timoteo, Agnaldo, 61
Tokatlián, Juan Gabriel, 147
Torre Cantú, Rodolfo, 152, 155
Torrijos, Omar, 88
Trademark violations, 42
Trafficking in persons, 23
Tranquilandia raid (Colombia, 1984), 92–93
Transparency: Argentina, 26, 28, 38; Brazil, 70; Bulgaria, 184–85; Costa Rica, 108, 125; Italy, 196; and state capture, 24
Transparency International, 32, 171
Trigos Perdomo, Carlos, 151
Triple crimen (Argentina), 35, 37
TSE (Supreme Elections Tribunal, Costa Rica), 110, 128, 130
Turbay, Julio Cesar, 91
Two-party systems, 48, 78

Unidad de Investigaciones Financieras (UIF, Argentina), 38
Union of Democratic Forces (UDF, Bulgaria), 169, 186, 189
United Kingdom, political finance in, 181

United Nations Development Program, 138
United Nations Office on Drugs and Crime (UNODC), 34, 158
United States: campaign finance rules in, 9; Colombian drug trafficking connections in, 104; drug trafficking market in, 146; extradition to, 89, 98, 101, 150; investigation into U.S. bank involvement with Juarez cartel, 31; organized crime in, 1–2; Prohibition era in, 43; and war on drugs in Mexico, 153, 157; Watergate scandal, 9, 10
Urban gangs, 42, 47
Uribe, Alvaro, 6
Usuga, Gabriel, 86

Valija-gate (Argentina), 33
Vallejo, Joaquín, 82
Vallejo, Virginia, 81
Vannucci, Alberto, 17, 195
Vanoy, Cuco, 87
Vargas, Getúlio, 45
Vega, Baruch, 96–97
Velasco Delgado, Francisco, 150

Venezuela, Colombian drug trafficking connections in, 104
Vera Salinas, Manuel, 150
Vesco, Robert Lee, 3, 115–17
Viaggio (airline), 192
Villanueva, Mario, 149, 150
Volkov, Vadim, 174
Voting age, 48

Watergate scandal (U.S.), 9, 10
Whistleblower protections, 38
Wikileaks, 173
Wilson, Antonini, 33
World-check screening system, 126

Xerox Company, 66

Yordanov, Yordan Dimitrov, 191
Youth gangs, 103

Zamora, Jaime Paz, 3
Zapata, Juan Ramon, 86
Zedillo, Ernesto, 153, 154, 156
Zetas, 137, 151, 152

BROOKINGS The Brookings Institution is a private nonprofit organization devoted to research, education, and publication on important issues of domestic and foreign policy. Its principal purpose is to bring the highest quality independent research and analysis to bear on current and emerging policy problems. The Institution was founded on December 8, 1927, to merge the activities of the Institute for Government Research, founded in 1916, the Institute of Economics, founded in 1922, and the Robert Brookings Graduate School of Economics and Government, founded in 1924. Interpretations or conclusions in Brookings publications should be understood to be solely those of the authors.

Board of Trustees

John L. Thornton
  Chair
Glenn Hutchins
  Vice Chair
Suzanne Nora Johnson
  Vice Chair
David M. Rubenstein
  Vice Chair
Strobe Talbott
  President
Robert J. Abernethy
Paul M. Achleitner
Liaquat Ahamed
Dominic Barton
Robert M. Bass
Alan R. Batkin
Crandall Bowles
Hanzade Doğan Boyner
Paul L. Cejas
Abby Joseph Cohen
Howard E. Cox

Arthur B. Culvahouse Jr.
Alan M. Dachs
Paul Desmarais Jr.
Kenneth M. Duberstein
Cheryl Cohen Effron
Alfonzo Fanjul
Ann M. Fudge
Ellen Futter
Jeffrey W. Greenberg
Brian L. Greenspun
Pete Higgins
Shirley Ann Jackson
Benjamin R. Jacobs
Kenneth M. Jacobs
Richard A. Kimball Jr.
Nemir Kirdar
Klaus Kleinfeld
Philip H. Knight
Rajan Bharti Mittal
Nigel Morris

James Murren
Thomas C. Ramey
Steven Rattner
Edgar Rios
James Rogers
Wilbur Ross
Haim Saban
Leonard D. Schaeffer
Amy W. Schulman
Lynn Thoman
Larry D. Thompson
Michael L. Tipsord
Andrew H. Tisch
Antoine W. van Agtmael
Beatrice W. Welters
John H. White Jr.
Tracy R. Wolstencroft
Daniel Yergin
Lei Zhang
Daniel B. Zwirn

Honorary Trustees

Elizabeth E. Bailey
Zoë Baird Budinger
Rex J. Bates
Richard C. Blum
Geoffrey T. Boisi
Louis W. Cabot
William T. Coleman Jr.
Kenneth W. Dam
Steven A. Denning
Vishakha N. Desai
Alfred B. Engelberg
Lawrence K. Fish

Cyrus F. Freidheim Jr.
Bart Friedman
David Friend
Lee H. Hamilton
William A. Haseltine
Teresa Heinz
Joel Z. Hyatt
James A. Johnson
Ann Dibble Jordan
Vernon E. Jordan Jr.
Herbert M. Kaplan
Donald F. McHenry

Mario M. Morino
Samuel Pisar
Charles W. Robinson
James D. Robinson III
Victoria P. Sant
B. Francis Saul II
Ralph S. Saul
Michael P. Schulhof
John C. Whitehead
Stephen M. Wolf
Ezra K. Zilkha

www.ingramcontent.com/pod-product-compliance
Lightning Source LLC
Chambersburg PA
CBHW030109010526
44116CB00005B/166